Sarita (my )

Not only are you hot, but you're also funny as hell and wise to boot.

Growing into MySelf

I think you're
MAGNIFICENT!
Such a great soul.

Much love &
oodles of kisses,

Thea

Growing into MySelf

Thea Euryphaessa

Matador
9 Priory Business Park
Kibworth Beauchamp
Leicestershire LE8 0RX, UK
Tel: (+44) 116 279 2299
Fax: (+44) 116 279 2277
Email: books@troubador.co.uk
Web: www.troubador.co.uk/matador

ISBN 978 1783062 690

British Library Cataloguing in Publication Data.
A catalogue record for this book is available from the British Library.

Typeset in Goudy Old Style by Troubador Publishing Ltd

Matador is an imprint of Troubador Publishing Ltd

For
Hilary Spenceley and **Marion Woodman**
whose teachings birthed a woman out of me

The way we imagine our lives is the way we are going to go on living our lives. For the manner in which we tell ourselves about what is going on is the genre through which events become experiences.

– James Hillman, *Healing Fiction*

CONTENTS

Prefaced: Glancing Backwords/Foreword Facing   xi

The Crack   1
A Chance Encounter   4
Waiting for the Sirens' Call   7
The Sacred Prostitute   10
The Prostitute and the Pearls of Wisdom   16
Waiting for a Pearl Like You   21
Are You Loathsome Tonight?   25
Spectre Remorse   29
A Bit Too Clean-Cut   36
No More Ms Nice Gal   43
The Goddess of Discord   58
The Invitation   83
Going Back to My Roots – An Odyssey   105
The Binding of Isaac   113
C is for Curiouser and...   128
... Corrupted   137
A Series of Unexpected Events   146
The Celebration   163
Watch the Throne   176
The Illustrated Man   190
Behaving Badly   196
The Fallout   206
Form and Substance   223
The Year Without a Summer   242
Ecstasis, Catharsis   260
Sankofa   272

Epilogue: The End Where I Begin   278
Selected Bibliography   279
Gratitude and Resources   282

PREFACED:
GLANCING BACKWORDS/
FOREWORD FACING

In November 2012 I dreamt I was explaining the opening of this book to my friend, Becky. On waking, I scribbled the details in my journal before marvelling over how clever the psyche is. In the dream I honoured the two-faced Roman god Janus who presides over beginnings and transitions and after whom the month of January is named. The gist of the dream was that the book's preface should have two faces: one looking back and the other facing forward.

While writing my first book, *Running into Myself: A Journey Through the Soul of the Feat* I knew there'd be an accompanying, follow-up book. I call such prescient intuitions, 'flash forwards': they're not based in concrete knowledge nor are they planned. Rather, they're a vague felt sense of something yet to unfold but which, with all the will in the world, I can't force or coerce into existence. On some level I just know and until such time as they're realised I have to get on with living my life.

At this point it may be tempting for you, the reader, to say: 'Well, you're a writer aren't you? It's your job to write articles, books, and such like. Surely it was inevitable you'd write another book?' To which I'd reply, 'Not necessarily.'

I mean, yes – I do write, but I don't seem to have much of a choice in the matter and I certainly don't make a living from it. In fact, there's something almost perverse about the demands writing makes on me – or, rather, *with* me. So it's not so much that I'm a writer; it's more I cannot *not* write. It's taken me several years to accept this but I've finally realised that, whether I'm paid to do it or not, writing is the one thing which reminds me, even in stony-broke moments (actually, less 'moments', more 'extended periods'), that I am indeed abundant and will always have something to offer the world.

So despite selling few copies of *Running into Myself* and making zero money from it, it still managed to change my life in ways I could never have imagined. In retrospect I'm deeply indebted to my younger, inexperienced self for writing that book.

In fact I'd like to take this opportunity to acknowledge that foolhardy aspect of myself and thank her for the courage she showed in stepping up to the challenge of a book, especially with so little writing experience. This book, quite literally, stands on the shoulders of its forerunner – apt, really, considering its main theme was running. Without her blind faith and fearlessness this book and many of the experiences documented throughout would never have happened. So, to my younger self I say this: 'You did good, girl. I'm proud of you.'

It's also made me realise that, sometimes, we need to look beyond instant gratification, beyond the money, beyond the yearning to be recognised and critically lauded and accept, with humility, the resources we have, right here, right now and make the most of them. The conditions will never be right, so the time to act is always *now*.

In my case I took a hundred thousand words or so and, based on the knowledge and experience I had at the time, arranged them the best way I knew how before finally sharing them with others. Because, what I now realise is, they were never just mine to keep to myself. The qualities, skills, and talents with which we're endowed are – whether we choose to acknowledge them or not – never ours alone.

I'll never know the far-reaching effects of my first book but I do know, from those individuals I have met, the effect it had on them and that alone has humbled and inspired me enough to keep writing. Thanks to that book I've made friends who have, in turn, shaped my life; generous friends who, when it all fell apart, held out hands and helped me back up. You can't put a price on that.

And so, here at the beginning, it's in the spirit of Janus that I bridge the gap from *Running into Myself* to *Growing into MySelf* – a book which, after the flighty, spirited direction of my earlier marathoning shenanigans, sees me slow down, put down roots, and descend into the dark netherworld of soul and sex and down, further still, into the realm of the ancestors.

This book assumes you've read *Running into Myself*. If you haven't you may wish to read it first as this one continues from where that left off and references events, stories, and individuals mentioned in that book (although this book, in many ways, stands alone). Whereas I used internet pseudonyms and nicknames throughout *Running into Myself* I revert to using proper names (albeit aliases) in this book. The only person whose nickname I continue to use is my close friend, Bing's – it just seems wrong to call her by any other name.

This book also jumps straight in and assumes you have a basic understanding of spiritual and psychological concepts such as chakras and archetypes. But if you don't, it doesn't matter. Most of this book is about my personal journey for which no specialist knowledge of anything is required other than an open mind and a willingness to be nosy.

Please do bear in mind that, as with my first book, I continue telling *myself* the story of my life. As such, there may well be dense and knotty sections in which I'm attempting to make sense of past events. Don't worry if you don't always get what I'm talking about either. I read books on depth psychology and mythology as casually as one might read a mass-market novel (in other words I'm a geek). My mind makes connections which may, at times, leave others wondering what the hell I'm on about. My advice is skim-read those sections and trust your unconscious is joining the dots even if it doesn't always make sense to you.

As I'll be discussing issues of an intimate and sexual nature (you have been warned) I wish to make clear, from the outset, that I speak only from my own personal experiences. I am not, neither do I profess to be, an expert in Tantra, a sex educator, a sex activist, or a theological scholar. Neither is this a sex manual. You'll find no illustrations of couples contorted into Houdini-like positions in a Nirvanic quest for sexual bliss nor are there any instructions on how to achieve mind-altering orgasms. Like many others I'm just trying to understand and get to grips with my body, preferably before I prune up and things disappear back from whence they came.

Neither am I a spokesperson for the Tantra organisation with whom I studied. They were happy, however, for me to use the real names of my teachers. I could have been all coy and cryptic about it but that would have been pointless seeing as I have numerous articles published online documenting snapshots from my journey. Googling my name and 'Tantra' would have revealed their names in 0.30 seconds. You may find several of my articles on their website but they were originally written under my own steam and posted to my own website before later being reposted to their website (to which I gladly consented).

Unlike the teachers, where occasionally mentioned I've changed the names of the women I met on the workshops I attended (except for Grace and Peej who are both unapologetically shameless). After all, just because they had an obsessive compulsive writer in their midsts doesn't mean they later wanted their private lives splayed across the pages of a book. So, from here on out all opinions and any errors are mine and mine alone.

Speaking of people's private lives being splayed across the pages of a book, I do share insights from my personal relationship. I felt *immensely* conflicted about doing this. But if I didn't discuss it there would be no story and no book. For the record I do not wish to demonise or wrong the man I discuss in these pages. I'm not encouraging anyone to side with me or feel sorry for me either. In our relationship no-one was wholly right or wholly wrong; rather, we were wholly human.

With this book I also wanted to honour my journey as a writer. I once heard that Anaïs Nin continued revising and re-editing all her diaries right up until her death. Whether or not this is true I'm not sure but when I heard this I felt cheated. I wanted to chart her journey through the written word, watch how it evolved as she did. It's for that reason I wanted my earlier work to remain as I originally wrote it so that, by the time I came to my next work, my progress would (hopefully) be self-evident.

One final thing: two days before I began writing this book I walked a labyrinth based on the same design as the one in Chartres Cathedral, France. Before entering I stood with trepidation at the threshold. My experience of labyrinths is that, much like a chrysalis, they swallow you up before, eventually, releasing you transformed in one way or another.

When I began writing I felt the same as I did at the threshold of the labyrinth – *afraid*. In *Facing the World with Soul*, Robert Sardello says 'the pattern of the consciousness soul is labyrinthine, a meandering, like a thread going through the convolutions of a shell, passing through the dark recesses of things...' In writing this book I was afraid of surrendering to the 'dark recesses of things,' afraid of what might be revealed, afraid I would never make it through and out again. This is why I warn you that in the spirit of the labyrinth the story will, at times, double back on itself and go over issues previously discussed, albeit from a different angle. When it does, please stay with it and trust there is a method in its meandering madness.

With this image of the labyrinth in mind I ask you, now, to surrender to the soul of the story as it takes you into its convoluted folds. My humble hope is it may transform some small corner of your consciousness as it had the good grace to transform mine.

Thea Euryphaessa
Manchester (UK), 2013

THE CRACK

Whenever I settle down to write I look for a way in, a crack through which I can squeeze my hand, grab a hold of the underlying thread, and tease out the mystery to which I then tend and transform, as best I can, into a coherent article – maybe a book. Once I'm in, I'm in. But as the opening informs the direction the piece will take it's crucial that I'm patient, set my ear to the ground, and await the vibrations emanating from the Great Below.

This opening sees me hurtling down the motorway from Manchester to Liverpool en route to a women-only Tantra workshop, in the dark and in a rush – the lattermost part of which summed up my relationship to sex at the time and largely explains why I'd signed up for said workshop in the first place.

The car's engine was screaming at my pedal to the metal insistence that it get a shift on, Coldplay's album, *Viva La Vida* was playing on loop, and I was in a state of disarray which, even now, causes me to stop typing, sigh, and drop my head into my hands.

Contemplating the warm darkness of my palms I'm reminded of those things of which my life was devoid at the time and which I'd pretended didn't matter but, deep down, did – very much indeed: pleasure, lust, affection, tenderness, intimacy, warmth, sensuousness, desire, romance, passion. Well, it's not that I didn't *think* they mattered; rather, I'd pretended I was immune from – what I perceived to be – the great disease that is vulnerability. From vulnerability it was only a hop, skip, and a jump to weakness and its close cousin, neediness. Consequently, I was afraid of fully opening myself up to another, of completely surrendering, of losing control.

In an attempt to protect myself I'd walled myself off and retreated up into the lofty realm of my head where I'd decided it was safe. 'Up there' everything can be ordered, rationalised, and compartmentalised. But feelings, emotions, intuitions, and such like are messy, chaotic, and for the most part, unpredictable.

In fact, have you ever noticed how all the trouble goes on 'down there,' down in the dark, moist depths? That's the soul's territory. It's no

1

wonder various spiritually inclined folk have been so keen to transcend the body, transcend this world, and rise above it all. If they had their way I'm sure we'd be little more than floating disembodied heads attached, at most, to a piece of string – *helium beings*. It's the body and its intrigues which gets us into one fine mess after another.

But I'd finally realised I wasn't a helium being and so, after being in a dry, next-to-no-sex relationship with a partner who rarely held my hand, let alone pinned me against the wall in an unbridled moment of knicker-ripping passion, the rest of my body – that wild, instinctual, feeling-led mass of wanton flesh – had decided enough was enough and signed me up, consciously/unconsciously, for a Tantra workshop.

Actually, before I continue, I'd better explain what I mean by 'consciously/unconsciously,' especially as it seems to be a recurring theme in my life usually with life-changing consequences.

When I signed up for the New York City Marathon four years earlier and, immediately after, the Rome and Athens Marathons, it was done with little conscious forethought – absentmindedly, you might say. Because if I had sat down and thought through the potential consequences for more than a fraction of a second, I'd have never submitted that application form let alone made a trumpet-accompanied announcement to my friends about my potential athletic endeavours.

But as I ran across the world I gathered up lost fragments of my being that had long been scattered and, for the most part, forgotten. Unlike Humpty Dumpty – who fared rather less favourably – I gradually put my broken, mostly loathed self back together again. In New York I unearthed a quiet sense of self-belief; in Rome, I regained a sense of humility and began listening and surrendering to my body's wisdom; and in Athens I realised 'I' wasn't quite so alone in my little psychic house.

In the months following my marathon pilgrimage, I sat with those fragments, puzzled over them, and pieced them together into, what would eventually become, my first book. Thinking back to how I felt while writing that book causes another head-hands moment. My confusion is apparent for all the world to see. But some implacable force compelled me to write it, insisted itself through me, bore down on me with an unbearable pressure until I finally relented and tried, as best I could, to make sense of what was attempting to be realised through me. In fact, my decision to write a book was another conscious/unconscious moment.

For someone who doesn't know when to stick a sock in it when it comes to talking or writing, I never aspired to be a writer, let alone an author. But writing is the only way I know how to make sense of my life – a life which compels me to make oddball decisions such as sign up for marathons for which I'm not prepared and write books with no prospect of being published and even less of an idea of what it is I'm trying to say.

But it's these conscious/unconscious decisions which have proved life-changing and upon which my life has hinged. And I don't use the term 'life-changing' casually or in a trite, clichéd way. These have been genuinely pivotal experiences which have lifted me up out of my narrowly circumscribed idea of life, demanded that I grow, and stretched me to breaking point (and then some), before dropping me back down to earth in the brace position mumbling: *There's no place like home, there's no place like home, there's no place like home...*

But no-one made me sign up for one marathon, never mind three. No-one forced me to write a book, either. I've naively galumphed into these experiences with all the grace of a lamb to the slaughter. So though I may have insisted, while doing them, that I couldn't do it – that I'm not big enough, not fit enough, not clever enough, not talented enough (let me tell you, I can wail and flail with the best of them) – when it came down to it, I've secretly relished every minute of every challenge I've ever stumbled into. Whether I've met these challenges as adequately and as proficiently as I could have remains to be seen. But I stepped up to the moment and finished what I started with as much grace and grit as I could muster – and that's all that matters to me.

So in January 2011, I fired off an email to an organisation called Shakti Tantra, consciously/unconsciously, enquiring about their Women's Invitation workshop which was being held in Liverpool at the end of the following month – a workshop I was now hurtling towards with *Death and All His Friends*.

A CHANCE ENCOUNTER

Sat on a bus, two and a half years earlier, on my way to my first date with Finn (Fallon), I'd been accompanied by another soundtrack – *Stepping Stone* by Duffy.

I'd first met Finn while working part-time at a supermarket when I was seventeen years old. I was drawn to him from the first time I saw him slink past the deli counter on which I worked. With a cocksure head and fair hair flopped over his forehead, he seemed laid-back – definitely not your run-of-the-mill manager. From what I could tell he garnered respect, camaraderie, and loyalty among his staff without having to resort to power trips.

I'm not sure whether I fancied him or whether there was just something about him I wanted to get closer to, something I admired. Regardless, my opportunity to change departments soon came with the arrival of a new boss who, although may have looked good on paper, was woeful when it came to managing people. With that, I put in a transfer request and was moved onto Finn's team.

Despite his apparent confidence I always felt there was an air about him which seemed somewhat removed from his work persona. I once saw him on a night out. He was alone (he later told me he was waiting for his friends). I felt sorry for him but couldn't understand why – and not in a patronising way or because he was alone. He seemed to me like a dying star whose core was shrinking – *sorrowful*.

None of this dented my attraction to him though and, soon after leaving the supermarket to pursue full-time employment elsewhere, we began dating. I can't, for the life of me, remember how we ended up dating, who asked who out. Neither could Finn. In fact it's at this point most of the details surrounding our brief affair fade to black.

The only common ground we seemed to have was work and now I'd left, we didn't even have that. If he wasn't at work he had his children. If he did have any other interests I never heard about them. My only other memory is of the last time I saw him. Irritated by what I called his 'slovenly' approach to sex I'd called a cab, left and with that, I ended our brief affair.

That said, there was never any ill will or animosity between us. So when I bumped into him again almost ten years later we struck up easy conversation. It was at that point I realised I'd often thought about him during the intervening years – his natural management style, his ease with people, his ability to really *see* staff and draw out and develop their innate talents. It was an approach I'd missed especially as I'd since been subjected to a succession of tyrannical bosses whose power trips knew no bounds.

Nothing came of our chance meeting aside from an exchange of pleasantries and me giving him my business card in case he fancied a coffee sometime. He later told me that because he knew he still liked me and because he was in a relationship, he didn't feel it was appropriate to go for a coffee with me and so he threw my card away. He said he deemed his ulterior motives a betrayal. But he also said he knew we'd see one another again. He just knew.

And so it was that, four years later, I bumped into him, yet again, while on a shopping trip with my mum. She'd been pestering me to take her to an out of town retail park (she can't drive). As I was living back home, for the sake of peace and quiet, I agreed.

The last time I'd bumped into him I was firmly rooted in a dark night of the soul – and that's putting it poetically. As far as I was concerned, I looked and felt like shit. It's probably a good job we never met up for coffee as my depression would've likely curdled the cream. But this time I was a whole different person both inside and out.

Though near penniless and living back with my parents, I was finally doing something that was a source of great joy – writing. I was also training for my third and final marathon in Athens. If I don't mind saying so myself, physically, I looked pretty good. In fact, as I got dressed and ready to leave the house, I remember wondering if I'd see him again; a strange thought, in retrospect, seeing as I hadn't seen him in four years and had also made a promise to myself to remain single for a year – a year which still had four months left to run.

What was curious about this encounter was not only was this a different store in a different area (of all the stores in all the towns in all the world, I walk into his), but he also later told me he didn't ordinarily work that shift and was supposed to have signed off when we ran into one another. But, if I'm being honest, it's at this point I felt ambivalence pool in the bottom of my gut.

There was a very good reason I'd taken a year-long vow of single living. My actual aim had been to remain both single *and* celibate but the more weight I lost as I trained for the marathon, the more I delighted in myself. Before long I was a one woman *Carousel* musical for whom spring was bustin' out all over.

Such revelling meant I'd lasted all of five months before I finally succumbed to the snare of a sexual encounter – or two. Despite this I continued my vow to remain single if only so I could take some time out without falling headlong into yet another relationship – something I was all too good at.

So when I sensed he was serious – indicated by him asking me out on a date that same night – I felt my stomach knot. Although I'd secretly hoped I'd bump into him a date was the last thing on my mind, least of all one that same night. What I didn't want to do was mislead anyone, give them the impression I was interested when I wasn't.

In a last ditch attempt to put him off me I told him I was living back with my parents, was now a professional writer (albeit a skint one), had changed my name, and was about to embark on the third of three marathons. Oh, and that I was going to write a book about my globetrotting, marathoning adventures and all they'd entailed.

But my cunning plan didn't work. On reflection I think it only served to highlight my attractiveness. However precarious my circumstances may have seemed to me at the time, I was still living my dream. And if you've ever met anyone who's had the courage to go after their dreams with all of their heart, you'll know just how attractive they are, how they radiate inspiration and hopefulness. They also embody something many seek but, often, dare not pursue for themselves – *change*.

I agreed to go for a drink with him that night, though on the way I couldn't stop listening to Duffy's crooning lamentations. Over and over I played *Stepping Stone*, as if trying to hammer home a message to myself. I wondered what, if anything, the song may have been trying to call my attention to.

WAITING FOR THE SIRENS' CALL

Rounding the corner on two wheels I screeched onto Liverpool's waterfront. Peering up through the windscreen I saw the Liver Birds perched high on top of the Royal Liver Building overlooking the vast sprawl of the River Mersey: a pair of giant, powder blue coloured statues – a cross between an eagle and a cormorant – who, with their backs turned to one another, look like they've just had a row and are about to take flight. Legend has it should they ever fly away Liverpool would cease to exist.

Another local fable says whenever a female virgin or an honest man passes by the buildings on which they're perched, the Liver Birds will flap their wings. Well, after driving up and down the waterfront several times trying to figure out which way I should be heading, they obviously had my number as there wasn't so much as a blink of an eye, let alone the ruffle of any feathers.

But now I was running late. And I was lost. Thing is, I don't get lost. I have a keen sense of direction which is one of several reasons why I won't entertain sat navs. Something in me refuses to hand over my sense of direction to technology no matter how expedient or efficient it professes to be. Old school, I much prefer a crinkled, dog-eared map which, once fully unfolded, fills the entire front cabin of the car covering everything and everyone in its wake. But on this occasion I didn't have one and the directions I'd scrawled in my spidery handwriting were frustratingly illegible. I wondered in an expletive-ridden out loud way whether I'd unconsciously tried to sabotage my break for sexual freedom, particularly in light of my uncharacteristic disorganisation. Berating myself I finally called my teacher.

'This number has not been recognised,' said a lady, 'please try again.' I tried again. Again it was the automated lady. *Nooooo, this isn't happening.* I briefly entertained a boo-hoo moment during which I hope someone will save me from myself. *I'm not meant to be here. I've been here before. I know the signs when I see them, forcing a situation that's clearly not meant to be.*

It's hard to know, sometimes, whether the Fates are trying to pull you back from the brink of disaster or if you're just flat-out resisting. This was one such occasion. And now, parked up by the side of the road, I was having a one-woman temper tantrum Liza Minnelli would have been proud of.

Sat contemplating the number for a few minutes it finally dawned on me it was one digit too long. Question was, which number was the one too many? Pondering my numerical conundrum I dropped the final digit. *Result!* It was ringing.

Apparently I wasn't too far away but as my teacher wasn't from these parts and, therefore, couldn't direct me, she put one of her assistants on the phone – her name was Sarah. For a moment I wondered if I'd been put through to a sex chat line. If I hadn't then this lady seriously ought to consider it. If she voiced sat navs I'd fast review my hard-line stance on them.

Whereas seconds before I was on the verge of throwing in the towel and turning round to go home, I now wanted to meet the woman from whom these sultry, soothing tones emanated. I kept her on the phone for as long as I could. 'Call me if you get lost again,' she purred, 'and don't panic... we'll make sure you get here.'

After hanging up the phone I sat for a moment as a thousand tiny hands burst into blossom all over my body, massaging my fearful psyche with their reassuring balm. Damn she sounded sexy. With my furrowed brow now straightened out I set off of in pursuit of the honey-voiced one and her horny cohorts.

Suffice to say I was back on the phone less than ten minutes later. It wasn't just me – this place really wasn't easy to find. But, once more, the honey-voiced one enchanted me with her come-hither tones, luring me down lanes and beckoning me across crossroads until, better-late-than-never, I arrived at the workshop venue.

As Sarah gathered me into a warm, melting hug, I realised we'd met before – three years earlier – at the Quaker Meeting House in Manchester. She'd co-presented a talk with Sue – Shakti Tantra's co-founder – about Tantra and the work they did which I'd attended. My friend, Lisbeth (Bert), who knew of my burgeoning interest in Tantra, had emailed me details of the event. (The same Lisbeth, incidentally, whose inspiring 10k endeavours was one of the reasons I'd signed up for the New York City Marathon. Here she was again planting seeds for the next stage of my initiation – albeit, unknowingly.)

During their talk, though, it wasn't so much Sarah's dulcet tones that had caught my attention as Sue's breasts. I've seen some knockers in my time – and my own pair aren't to be sniffed at – but this lady's were something else. They were magnificent – veritable mammary mountains. I couldn't take my eyes off them. Anyone who says women aren't as fascinated by boobs is lying, especially when they're as bountiful and buxom as this broad's were.

But it wasn't just Sue's boobs I was entranced by – it was an aspect of her presentation which I felt she was alluding to in ever decreasing circles and yet, for reasons I couldn't understand, wouldn't mention outright. *Why is she being so evasive? Why doesn't she just come right out and say it? Tell them*, I chunnered to myself, arms crossed in irritation.

Tell them about the sacred prostitute.

THE SACRED PROSTITUTE

I first came across the term 'sacred prostitute' in late 2006. Karl (Bacchus), an acquaintance I'd made on social networking site, MySpace, was plying me with book and lecture recommendations on mythology and analytical psychology – a school of psychology originating from the ideas of Swiss psychologist, Carl Jung.

Knowing I had a particular interest in Tantra he'd singled out two books for my attention: *The Sacred Prostitute* by Nancy Qualls-Corbett and *Dancing in the Flames* by Marion Woodman and Elinor Dickson – the latter of which introduced me to the Black Madonna and the Dark Mother.

The sacred prostitute, as the author described her, was a woman who embodied the union of spirituality and passionate love. She was a virgin – not in the sexually uninitiated way with which we, today, are familiar with the term (in Latin *virgo* means unmarried), but as 'one-in-herself': a sensuous, self-confident person who embodied the balanced union of masculine and feminine energies.

Before I continue I'd like to be clear as to what I mean by those terms – masculine and feminine – particularly as they've come to be so inextricably and unconsciously bound up with gender. Masculine energy is *not* the exclusive domain of males. Feminine energy is *not* the exclusive domain of females. Men *do not* have the monopoly on masculine traits. Women *do not* have the monopoly on feminine qualities. Regardless of our biological gender we are each a balance of seemingly opposing but, actually, complementary energies. Whether we call those energies yin and yang, spiritual and physical, Shakti and Shiva, King Sol and Queen Luna, doesn't matter.

What does matter, for the purpose of this book at least, is you mentally unhook the term *masculine* from males and *feminine* from females. When I write of masculine energy I am not thinking of males and when I write of feminine energy I am not thinking of females. What sometimes clouds the issue is, when working with dreams, masculine energy may occasionally be represented by male figures and feminine energy may occasionally be represented by female figures – the operative word here being, *occasionally*.

But as long as women continue to project their innate masculine qualities out onto men, and men continue to project their innate feminine qualities out onto women, we'll remain little more than half people living, at best, half lives.

So this sacred prostitute was a temple priestess who's said to have served such goddesses of love, passion, fertility, and sex as the Sumerian Inanna (whose Akkadian counterpart was Ishtar who was also known as the Mother of Harlots); Astarte (also known as Anath and Ashtart) who was revered by the Caananites, the Hebrews, and the Phoenicians; Isis (earlier identified with Hathor) in Egypt; Cybele in ancient Lydia; Aphrodite of ancient Greece and her Roman equivalent, Venus. According to Qualls-Corbett:

> **The sacred prostitute was the holy vessel wherein chthonic and spiritual forces were united ... a mortal woman who is devoted to the goddess. Her beauty, her graceful movements, her freedom from ambivalence, anxieties or self-consciousness toward her sexuality, all attributes of the goddess as well, derive from the reverence she holds for her feminine nature... Her beauty and sensuous body were not used in order to gain security, power or possessions ... in her embodiment of the goddess, she is the bringer of sexual joy and the vessel by which the raw instincts are transformed into love and love-making.**

> *– The Sacred Prostitute*

Whether these sacred prostitutes of the ancient world ever existed is subject to sharply polarised opinions. In the blue corner are various academics who, based on current evidence, refute the existence of such temple or religious prostitution. As far as they're concerned there's no data which can prove sexual services were performed in the name of any goddess in any culture at any time. Sacred prostitutes did not exist, period.

In the red corner are those who have gathered evidence from the writings of Enheduanna, an Akkadian princess and High Priestess, the Greek historian Herodotus, and from other sources including Quodoushka, a sacred sexuality practised among some Native American tribes. Locked at opposing ends of the spectrum theirs is less a both/and debate and more an either/or stalemate. But as Deena Metzger points out in her essay, *Re-Vamping the World: On The Return of the Holy Prostitute*: 'It is possible that neither view is correct, as each tends to inflate the physical activity and ignore or impugn the spiritual component. Our materialist preoccupation with form binds us to the content.'

Personally, I didn't care whether these figures existed or not. As a lover of myth, a paramour of parlance, I was more intrigued by the image conjured and language used to describe and give shape to such figures. More to the point I was intrigued with what these sacred prostitutes, real or not, may have *symbolised* – a symbol being something that communicates a meaning *beyond* itself.

So with this curiosity in mind let us consider, for a moment, the word 'prostitute.' Despite the word's negative connotations with which many of us today are all-too familiar, I discovered the notion of 'sex for hire' is not inherent in its etymological root at all. In fact, before you read on, pause for a moment and think of any other words which look or sound similar to prostitute.

Got one?

You may have come up with destitute, constitute, or substitute. I came up with institute. It was the 'stitute' part, in particular, which caught my eye and stems from the Latin, *statuere*, meaning 'to stand,' 'to set up,' or 'to establish.' As for the remaining part, *pro*, in Latin means, 'in front of.' So with this in mind, prostitute may suggest 'one who stands in place of' or 'one who stands for.' But stands in place of *whom* or *what*?

As we're imagining sacred prostitutes, let's now look at the word 'sacred.' Sacred finds its roots in the Latin, *sacrare*, which means 'to consecrate,' or 'make sacred.' Prostitution, as we're familiar with the term today, has come to be solely associated with the profane: profane deriving from the Latin word, *profanus*, meaning 'not initiated,' 'unholy,' 'outside the temple.'

It's this image of the prostitute as streetwalker, standing outside, propping up street corners, which most of us can easily envision. (Although the term 'sex worker' is the generally accepted term used today, the word prostitute still looms heavy in the imagination of the collective.)

But if someone was outside the temple, is it really such a stretch to imagine there may have been others inside the temple in service to something beyond themselves such as, perhaps, the divine as represented by a goddess – namely, sacred prostitutes? Why have one and not the other? After all, existence as we know it is rooted in duality – every light casting a shadow and all that.

Would it be so hard to imagine, then, that sacred prostitutes may have, at one time, existed? Temple priestesses who, having been initiated, stood in for – or in place of – sex, love, and fertility goddesses such as Inanna/Ishtar, Isis/Hathor, Astarte, Cybele, and Venus/Aphrodite? Sexual-spiritual priestesses who welcomed men and women into their temples and initiated them into the arts, practice, and mysteries of love-making? I'm just curious as to how the word prostitute came to be so inextricably bound up with sex if such women (and men) hadn't 'stood in for' these love and sex deities.

12

Putting aside our personal opinions and moral judgements for a moment, would such a thought be really so hard to conceive? Or is this combination of sexuality and spirituality – a process whereby individuals are initiated into the deeper mysteries of their spiritual nature by sexual means within a sacred temple space – really so alien to us? Or less alien and more repelling and morally incomprehensible to our modern inherited mind-set? As Marion Woodman says in her foreword to *The Sacred Prostitute*:

> To our modern minds, the words themselves seem contradictory – 'sacred' suggests dedication to a divine spirit; 'prostitute' suggests defilement of the human body. How can two words be related when mind is separated from matter, spirituality from sexuality?

As to what may have happened to these alleged Holy Prostitutes, Metzger continues:

> ... it is no wonder that from the beginning, the first patriarchs, the priests of Judea and Israel, the prophets of Jehovah, all condemned the Holy Prostitutes and the worship of Asherah, Astarte, Anath, and the other goddesses. Until the time of the priests, the women were one doorway to the divine. If the priests wished to insert themselves between the people and the divine, they had to remove women from that role. So it was not that sexuality was originally considered sinful per se, or that women's sexuality threatened property and progeny; it was that in order for the priests to have power, women had to be replaced as a road to the divine – this gate had to be closed.

– To Be a Woman: The Birth of the Conscious Feminine

The exception to this was in various eastern Tantra traditions in which women were still considered a doorway to the divine by means of rituals and practices.

Anyway, at the time of Sue and Sarah's talk the mind-body split was still a bridge too far for me and I knew it. I knew it up in my head but wasn't yet in a place where I was willing to sit in the same room as my body and talk terms with it. My head and body were at such a disjoint, they needed a satellite link-up just to communicate. I loathed my body – *loathed* it.

My dimply arse resembled the cratered surface of the moon. My thighs just didn't know when to stop jiggling. My acne-ridden back embarrassed me with its ceaseless, sore eruptions. With my flabby batwings doubling as a wingsuit, I could've BASE jumped off the top of the Empire State Building. As for my vulva? Don't get me started on that smelly, disfigured creature that looked like it had crept out of the sea 2.4 million years ago dragging its sorry entrails behind it. No man had ever dared look it in the eye for fear of being turned to stone, let alone pucker up for some pussy parlez. If they had, it was always, always, *always* beneath the sheets and with the lights out.

So this image of a sacred prostitute initiating men and women into the mysteries of love and love-making – whether or not it was true – appealed to me at an imaginal level. And, as I've come to learn these past few years, a metaphor – such as, for example, the sacred prostitute – can often be the key to unlocking something that has long been buried in the darkest, densest recesses of, what felt like at the time, an unresponsive lump of a body.

Despite Sue never directly mentioning the sacred prostitute, it was the presence of its absence which caught my attention; especially as it was an image I'd recently read about in Qualls-Corbett's book.

Much later, I asked Sue why she never mentioned the term 'sacred prostitute' itself. 'Prostitute is just too loaded a word,' she told me. 'The mere mention of it would leave people thinking that that's what we are. The situation, that day, was also somewhat constrained. But if I were to give that talk again I'd have no qualms whatsoever about mentioning her.'

At the end of the talk we were given a recommended reading list together with a schedule of their upcoming workshops. At that time it was the reading list I was most interested in especially as I was in the process of reclaiming my intellect. So when I scanned down the list and spotted Qualls-Corbett's book, I felt vindicated in my hunch she'd been alluding to such a figure in her talk.

Whereas the idea of a sacred prostitute – if it had been mentioned – may have left others with a bitter taste, it was probably the deciding factor in my eventual decision to enrol with their organisation. Being honest, I remember very little, if at all anything, about the rest of the talk. Besides Sue's boobs it was this image, this intriguing image, of women initiating men and women into the mysteries of the goddess of love, passion, and sex in a sacred setting, to which I was drawn.

This lot know their stuff – they're recommending Jungian texts. At the time that was important to me and, in my mind, lent their work an element of gravitas – that combination of the cerebral and the physical; mind and matter. It felt like a healthy balance. It also said to me they had depth; that they weren't one-sided and airy-fairy with their head in the clouds, nor all about the body to the detriment of logical, rational thinking. *These people embrace the depths, the darkness, the shadow. These people celebrate the soul.*

At the time, my sex life was the biggest, ongoing anti-climax of my adult life, so I wanted so much to learn about this idea of sacred sex, of meeting and merging with something *more*, something *other*, while in the passionate embrace of my beloved. And if I was to ever travel down that particular road I wanted to learn from women, with women.

But that wasn't the only time I'd heard mention of a prostitute within a sacred/profane setting. If anything, Sue and Sarah's talk had been the third and final 'knock on the door' (along with Qualls-Corbett's book). Just three months earlier, while at Delhi airport, India, I'd heard a story told by mythologist and storyteller, Michael Meade, which would change my life *forever*...

THE PROSTITUTE AND THE
PEARLS OF WISDOM

There was once a spiritual disciple who, after travelling the world to study with many different teachers, decided to return to the dwelling of his first teacher. On entering the village where the sage lived, he met a young man who was pulling a buffalo and carrying a sack of rice. Recognising the son of his old teacher, he went up to the young man, who looked a little down in the mouth and asked, 'Are you not the son of the great sage Ramananda?'

To which the young man said, 'Yes, I am.'

The disciple went on, 'Well, how is he doing? Where is he? Still in the same old place?'

And the son said, 'Well I'm sorry to say that my father – and my mother as well – have passed on to the other side.'

The disciple was saddened by the news but not surprised. They were already well into old age by the time they had given birth to their children. He looked at the young man and asked him, 'Well, how are you? How is it going?'

To which the son of the old sage replied, 'Well, since you ask, it's not going well. Here's the situation for me and it's been this way all along and it looks like it will be this way forevermore. All I have in life is this one buffalo and this one sack of rice. Every night I open the sack and share a little of the rice with my wife and our children. We eat as little as possible because we know there's not much in this world for us. That's how it's going. And I wish it was some other way but no matter what I do it turns out like this.'

He invited the disciple to his home. The disciple wondered what this dinner would be like when you add another person to an already paltry situation.

When he arrived at the home of the son of the great sage the disciple said, 'Listen, because of my love for your father and your mother, I have a suggestion to make. That is to say, tomorrow, take the buffalo and the rice to the market. Sell the buffalo for whatever you can get. Exchange the rice for whatever you can get. Then, take whatever money you make and spend it on the best foods and the finest wine and prepare the most delicious, the most sumptuous feast you can. Then call together all of your relatives, all of your friends, and a few people you don't like and feed everybody until they're abundantly fed and eat as much as you wish yourself. Make sure your children are full and satisfied, too. That's my recommendation.'

The son of the old sage sat and pondered the disciple's suggestion for a moment before saying, 'Easy for you to say. And I notice it's holy types like yourself who are always telling people to give everything away. In fact I think you're secretly hoping it'll wind up in your own hands.'

The wife of the son of the old sage, however, had been stood in the background, listening. Suddenly, she spoke up: 'Hold on. I hear something in the voice of this disciple that sounds a lot like your old sageful father. And because of that, I agree. I think you should do it. I think you should follow his advice.'

Well what could he do, you know? He was already depressed. And now the disciple and his wife were both telling him to give it all away.

So, the next morning, with great trepidation, he went to the market and sold the buffalo and exchanged the rice. He bought all the good foods he could find and he invited everybody over to his house. Everybody ate and everybody drank. It was a great feast. It was remarkable. It was exciting. It was only in the morning when the darkness was being chased away by the brightness of the sun glistening on the eastern edge of the world that the son of the old sage woke up and thought: *Oh my god, I've given away everything and now I've no idea what to do.*

Having developed a practice, every morning, of checking in on the shed where he kept the buffalo to at least be assured by the breathing presence of that one animal, weighed down with despair and doom, he walked in that direction where he feared he'd now see nothing but a wretched, empty shack. But – to his great surprise – when he looked into the shed, there was the buffalo again and there was a sack of rice.

He went right to the disciple and said, 'It's astounding! And it's amazing! I gave it away and now it's back.'

To which the disciple replied, 'Don't get too excited. I have more advice. Go to the market again, sell the buffalo, trade the sack of rice, get everything you can and use it to make a great feast. Invite all your relatives, all your neighbours, a few enemies, and have a great time. Do this every day.'

The son of the sage said, 'Well, I have no better idea. I think I will.'

So, every day, the son of the sage took the two things that fate had given him – the buffalo and the sack of rice – to the market. Each day he bought everything he could buy and each day he gave it all away. He became known for his great generosity and he also became very happy for, each day, they would be there again. And that became his practice, and that became his art, and that became his livelihood.

Pretty good, huh?

After a few days, the disciple, reassured that this advice had worked said, 'You know, I'm thinking a lot about your little sister. How is she and where is she?'

Suddenly, the son of the sage took on that depressive look again and he said, 'Well, she doesn't live here but in a town nearby.' He seemed pained and didn't want to speak any further. It was only when the disciple prodded him that he went on: 'Well, I have to tell you – and it shames me greatly – but she's a prostitute and each night she sells herself just to survive.'

The disciple said, 'Alright. Good luck with the buffalo and everything.' And, with that, he left.

He went to the nearby town and asked where the daughter of the great sage, Ramananda, was.

'Oh you mean the prostitute so-and-so?' said one man. 'She's in that hut over there.'

He went to the hut and knocked on the door. On opening it he said hello and introduced himself again at which point she welcomed him in. The daughter asked the disciple about his travels and the two of them lamented the loss of her father and mother. The disciple then asked the daughter of the old sage, 'Well, how is it going? How are you?'

'Well,' she said, 'to tell the truth, this is the most painful existence I could have ever imagined. For various reasons – and despite my best efforts – I became impoverished and reached a point where the only way I could survive, was to... well... sell myself as a prostitute. I do this every night and will do so tonight as well.' With that she hung her head in shame.

The disciple said, 'Well, I have some advice.' The daughter of the great sage listened as the disciple said, 'Tonight do not accept anyone or any payment. Do not give yourself away to anyone unless they come bearing a bag of pearls of the highest water. Is that clear?'

The daughter of the old sage thought this was strange and terribly unlikely. *On the other hand, living each night the way I live, what do I have to lose?* So, she agreed to do it. With that the disciple left.

Eventually, the end of the day arrived. The darkness began to creep throughout the world and remove all traces of light. When it became pitch-dark the first man came to the house of the prostitute – he was a regular customer. He knocked on the door expecting the usual things and expecting to pay the usual amount when she said from inside, 'I will not open the door to anyone unless they bring a bag of pearls of the highest water.'

The man thought: *She's gone mad*. He went back to town and told everyone what was going on, out there, at the hut of the prostitute. The next man came and she said the same thing and he went away. Then the next one came and again she refused until, after a while, no-one was coming at all. And the night was progressing and the stars were rotating and the darkness was gathering deeper and deeper into the depths of this long, dark night.

The daughter of the old sage was beginning to think: *Now I've really done it. Now no-one will come. Now I'll die in a simple poverty of utter isolation*. Meanwhile, in another part of the cosmos, there began to move a beautiful young man, dressed elegantly, carrying with him a bag of pearls of the highest water. By putting one elegant foot in front of the other he eventually arrived at the hut of the prostitute and knocked on the door.

'Go away! I know you don't have the price. I've made this stupid agreement to ask for a bag of pearls of the highest water and I won't open the door to anyone, even if it means dying alone on this very night.'

To which the beautiful young man replied, 'I'm here and I have the bag of pearls, and if you would open the door I would very much like to bring them in.'

She opened the door and beheld this beautiful man who she immediately welcomed in. And the night was spent the way a night is spent between a beautiful young man carrying a bag of pearls of the highest water and a woman who has waited until the exact right moment to receive them.

In the morning the daughter of Ramananda, otherwise known as the prostitute so-and-so, ran to the disciple and said, 'Wow. This was really a great idea. I thought it was sure to fail. But it worked! And you should see the beauty and the garments of the one who came, and the bag of pearls he brought are priceless.'

'Don't get too excited,' said the disciple. 'My next recommendation is that you take the bag of pearls to the market and give everything away to the poor. Take just what you need and go back to the hut and do the same thing again tonight. And then, and then, and then the same.'

The young woman was a little sad to see all of this wealth go right away. Nevertheless she did it. Later that night, at the very darkest moment, a tap came at the door. Once more she opened it to find a beautiful young man dressed in elegant garments carrying with him a bag of pearls of the highest water. Again she received him and again the night was spent in the way a night is spent between two beautiful souls who have waited until the exact right moment to come together in love and respect.

When the dawn came she took the pearls and gave them away to the poor and kept just what she needed. This went on night after night after night. Satisfied things had changed in a meaningful way the disciple began to walk on his way, saying goodbye to the daughter of the great sage.

As he walked along the road evening drew in and the shadowy darkness of night pushed back the light of the day. As the disciple was walking he saw a man pulling a buffalo and carrying, on his head, a sack of rice. He was moaning and groaning. The disciple went up to him and said, 'My friend, what is the problem?'

The man with the buffalo and the sack of rice said, 'I'll tell you what the problem is. Every night, I have to pull a buffalo to the shed of so-and-so and every night I have to carry a bag of rice on top of my head until I'm becoming bald. And this is going on and on and *on*. No sooner have I finished delivering the buffalo and the rice, I then quickly have to change my clothes and appear like a beautiful young man and take a bag of pearls of the highest water to the sister of this guy – THAT's the problem! And I'm weary to my bones. And, actually, now that I think about it, it's YOUR fault!'

It turned out the man walking the dark roads at night, carrying these gifts, was *Brahma* – the Hindu God of Creation – who had to enact the fate as a destiny when it was provoked by the disciple. Brahma continued: 'I'd like to make a deal. I'd like for you to release me from this bind for the requirements of the world are that I have to deliver what is fated to be theirs so long as they keep acting this way that disrupts the limits of time.'

The disciple said, 'I will do it... on one condition – that is, you will ease off the pressure of life on these two children of my beloved sage, give them some common happiness, some moments when the breath comes sweetly into the lungs, and give them some love in this life. If you will do that then I will not require you to keep the rules of the fate.'

Brahma said, '*Gladly* I will do that if you will take this burden off of me.' And so the deal was struck.

The disciple went back to the daughter and he went back to the son and said, 'Listen, things are going to change again. Though things have changed and are not the same as they have been this while, remember all you have learned. Don't become narrow again and it may all work out fine.'

They were grateful to him of course. Brahma was grateful to him, too. With that, the disciple began to walk onto the next place of learning. And there we will leave him – walking – unless, of course, you wish to go out onto the road and follow him along the way...

WAITING FOR A PEARL
LIKE YOU

For those of us who can't afford the luxury of therapists and analysts, life coaches and mentors, dreams, myths, and stories provide a sage and thrifty alternative – provided you know *how* to work with them.

Having worked with the story you've just read for several years, I cannot *begin* to tell you how much disruption – good and bad – this folktale has caused me. If you're ready, if your heart is open, and if you want a life-changing story, then look no further. It gave me wings. It was the runway on which I gained the momentum needed to make my eventual two-footed leap into Shakti Tantra's sandpit.

Okay, okay, I'm getting excited.

Still, if you follow such a path your *yes* must be total, a commitment made with all of your being. As the poet Miguel de Unamuno so eloquently puts it, 'throw yourself like seed' – for nothing less than a whole-hearted, two-footed *yes* will do.

What I've shared is only the second half of the tale as told by Meade on his brilliant, highly recommended audio talk, *Fate and Destiny: The Eye of the Pupil, The Heart of the Disciple*. I must have listened to it dozens of times. Or less listened to it and more clung to it for dear life all the while chanting: *Please let this be true, please let this be true, please let this be true.*

I first came across Meade in Santa Fe while staying with my then boyfriend, Sam (Corvus). He'd been to one of his talks and raved about him, buying me a couple of his lectures to listen to. After eventually attending one of his presentations at which he kept the audience rapt for at least two hours without dropping a beat, I dashed straight out into the foyer and bought all of his talks I could lay my hands on including the one above.

Meade's talk was in September 2007. But it wasn't until January 2008, at Delhi airport, while awaiting a flight to Goa, that I first consciously remember hearing this story. On hearing the part about 'waiting for the pearls,' it was as if I'd been struck with the Tuning Fork of Truth, such was its illusion-shattering resonance. I whipped out my earphones and garbled the story to Sam who was sat next to me. After listening he asked: 'Am I the man with the pearls?'

'NO,' clanged the split-second answer in my gut. Shocked and saddened by what I'd just felt, I made some excuse and sloped off in an attempt to avert further questioning.

Like dreams, the trick to working with myths and stories is to allow yourself to be caught by the story, listen into the details and see what jumps out at you, which details provoke a physical response. Wherever you find your curiosity piqued is where your inner work begins.

So, with this in mind, sit for a moment and think about which detail/s most struck you about the story. And remember, in dreams and stories there's no such thing as an insignificant, or a right or wrong detail. Age-old stories, such as this, are packed with more soulful wisdom than we could ever imagine – but only for those with the imagination and humility to heed the riches of their insight.

Stories, dreams, and myths speak the language of the soul. By 'soul' I mean that eternal part of us which is embodied. Or, we could say, the soul is the divine manifest as matter; or, even, our bodies are an expression of the soul. We have only to witness the birth of a child to see what was once a spiritual potential is now a soulful manifestation – the divine incarnate. It's not without good reason that self-confessed, non-spiritual folk who have witnessed the birth of their offspring have often described it as miraculous.

The soul, you see, doesn't think in a dry, cerebral way, wielding evidence and facts and figures to prove a point or drive its message home – it doesn't need to. It has a poetic, imaginative temperament. Its approach is crab-like: less direct, more sideways-on. Whereas the spiritual can be cool, lofty, and detached, often demanding perfection, the soul is warm, feeling, down-to-earth, and more accepting of human nature.

To use this story as an example, if you'd have asked me at the time whether I suffered from low self-esteem or lacked self-confidence, I'd have thought about it for a moment before answering, yes, perhaps I do. But the story, speaking the language of the soul, employs images and metaphor with which to convey its message, not cool clinical speak.

So when Sam asked: 'Am I the man with the pearls?' My gut resonated with an immediate 'NO' undermining any thoughts or opinions I may or may not have had on the subject. Because the story is on the soul's wavelength it cut through any self-delusory bullshit which may have been lurking and, whether I liked it or not, went straight to the heart of the matter.

That this truth hits close to home is one of several reasons why so many are unwilling to work with their nightly dreams, let alone stories such as this. Much better to unconsciously swallow the propaganda with which we're ceaselessly bombarded by individuals and corporations who profess to know what's best for us, than listen to our own souls, right?

And so it is that the psyche's nightly messages are dismissively waved away by our egos as 'just a dream' and 'not real.' I can understand this reticence at turning toward the within. The inner truths we're exposed to can, at times, be too much to bear – especially when, like me, you find yourself in a foreign country, one week into a nine-week holiday with a man you've just realised, deep down, you don't want to be with.

Damned stories.

During my stay in Goa I listened to the talk every single day trying to figure out whether I was the brother who, out of fear, is afraid to give away what he has in case he's left with nothing; or the sister who has to learn to hold out and demand a lot – or as the story puts it 'wait for the pearls.'

I'll explore each of these perspectives throughout this book but what I would like to say, right up front, is what I particularly like about the story is its lack of judgment or blame on the disciple's behalf regards the prostitute's situation. He already knows, when he makes his recommendation, she'll attract the attention of the divine as embodied by Brahma, the great Hindu God of Creation. But he doesn't say to her: 'Look, if you follow my plan to the letter Brahma's gonna rock up at your door. When he does, don't shag him you dirty bint. After all, a lowly prostitute, like you, has no right giving Brahma one. Just smile politely, take the pearls from him, and close the door.'

Instead, what this story shows in the pithiest, most poetic way I've ever come across, is how a profane situation, when provoked by conscious awareness and a genuine acceptance of our fated circumstances, may be transformed into a sacred one. In fact I'd go as far to say that, laid out within the delicate folds of this story is the essence of my journey, so far, through Tantra.

I find all this quite fitting, especially as this story hails from the Tamil Nadu region of India, that I first heard it while visiting India, and that it, pretty much single-handedly, provided me with the momentum, strength, and necessary means for my eventual journey with Shakti Tantra (with Tantra, itself, originally hailing from India) – though I didn't make any of these connections at the time.

But back to the brother and sister in our story. Honestly, at the time, I couldn't figure out which one I was more like. So I erred on the side of the sister. After all, it'd been this idea of waiting for the pearls that had caught my attention in the first place.

In his talk Meade says the condition of prostituting oneself has little to do with gender if you think of all the ways in which we sell ourselves cheap, all the ways in which we unthinkingly give of ourselves too freely and too easily to things, people, and experiences that don't have any real value, caring, or beauty: watching TV for hours on end, mindlessly surfing the Internet, reading trashy magazines and/or newspapers when we could be nourishing our souls with a good quality book, communing with nature, watching the stars, nurturing our creative talents, spending quality time with friends and/or loved ones. This idea of giving of myself too easily particularly resonated when it came to relationships.

So now, settled in Goa and newly single, I made a vow to stay that way – for a whole year, in fact – and to take this opportunity to reflect on why I'd spent my life going straight from one relationship to the next without so much as a pause for breath. Just what was at the root of this lack of self-esteem? Why did I not believe I was worth anything or, as the story says, a bag of pearls of the highest water?

Are You Loathsome
Tonight?

Well, I can tell you that took all of one-thousandth of a second to figure out – my relationship with my body; or, rather, *lack* of. I'd rejected my body so how could I ever expect anyone else to embrace it? Even if they did, I would never have felt comfortable about them doing so nor would I have been able to receive any love and/or tenderness they may have attempted to give me.

But now I was alone in India. If I was as loathsome as I felt I was, at least I could be loathsome thousands of miles away from where anyone knew me. Out here my body could be loathsome but free – free to feel the sun on its skin, free to slop over the top of my bikini bottoms, free to shake, rattle, and roll my wobbly bits maraca-stylee.

I took to stripping down to my bikini and striding up and down the beach on a daily basis. This was a giant step for me. HUGE. Normally, I'd be saronged up to within an inch of my neckline in an attempt to cover my hideous body. Gradually, though, I came to let it all hang out. I didn't know it then, but this time spent alone in Goa would mark a major turning point in my relationship with myself. In my own small ways I began putting down tentative roots into the ground of my being – namely, my body. Yes, I think it's safe to say that, in India, I began laying the groundwork for my Tantra journey.

Attuning myself to the rhythms of nature on my little plot of paradise also inspired me to come off the contraceptive pill. At that point I'd been on the pill since I was eighteen, give or take a year (I was thirty-one at the time). Coming off it was one of the best decisions I've ever made.

If you want to disassociate a woman from her body, putting her on hormonal contraceptives is the fastest way to do it. If you want to numb a woman to her body's natural cycles and dry up her libido, stick her on the pill. If you want to alienate a woman from the fullness of her being, put her on the pill. And I don't care how 'safe' it's said to be. There are countless corporations and individuals vested in keeping us as far removed from our bodies as possible – we'd do well to remember that. When we take the pill it's yet another way in which we unthinkingly give of ourselves to something that, however much it professes to, doesn't care for our wellbeing. When we take the pill we sell our bodies down the river.

Looking back on my time spent on the pill it felt to me like a form of repression which is ironic, really, considering it was originally supposed to be all about liberating women. On one level it did – but at what cost? One of my reasons for going on the pill was so I no longer had to think about my body. I also wanted to bring it under control, tame it to my will, have sex whenever I wanted without having to think about such pesky 'inconveniences' as condoms (although, I *always* practised safe sex). This 'not wanting to think' – there's the stealthy beginnings of your mind/matter split, right there.

That I even had that attitude saddens me – as though my body were a wild, unruly animal to be tamed and brought to heel by my supercilious ego demands. We have only to look at the relentless plundering of the earth's resources to see the arrogance of humanity in its attempts to bring nature under its control, submit matter to its will.

And here we are, women, mindlessly participating in this mass subjugation of our own matter every time we pop the pill. In fact the word 'matter' has feminine undertones deriving, as it does, from the Latin, *mater*, which means 'mother.' In light of this the much championed concept of 'mind *over* matter' takes on a rather suppressive hue.

In Jungian thought, the soul, in Latin, is called the *anima* and is depicted as a female. The soul as a female is also highlighted in a story called *The Tale of Psyche and Eros* which is contained within a novel called *The Golden Ass* written by Lucius Apuleius in the 2nd century CE. Psyche is the Greek word for soul. In the story Psyche is a mortal, human girl who falls in love with an immortal – namely Eros, the Greek god of love.

At the hand of an embittered Aphrodite, Psyche undergoes a series of trials culminating in a descent to Hades to visit Persephone, Queen of the Underworld. Thanks to the help of various aides – and much to the chagrin of Aphrodite – she successfully completes all the tasks and, reunited with Eros, is raised to the sublime heights of Olympus where their wedding is attended by all the gods and goddesses and where she's also granted divine status.

That Psyche is human (*humus*, of the earth) is yet another example of how the soul tends to be associated with all that's considered lowly and inferior, such as bodies – in particular, women's – sexuality, and the earth upon which our very lives depend.

Psyche's union with the divine, after suffering through her long, dark night of the soul, is also echoed in our Indian folktale with the prostitute's eventual meeting and merging with the god, Brahma, in a night (or several) of ecstatic embrace.

This upward movement of the soul – this 'raising up' of human matter so that it may be reunited with the divine – is also known as 'sublimation.' In Jungian thought, sublimation essentially means to 'raise that which is repressed.' The word derives from the Latin, *sublimis*, meaning 'high.' Jung drew inspiration for his concept of sublimation from the Royal Art as practised by the medieval alchemists.

In the spiritual practice of alchemy the process of *sublimatio* is an elevating process whereby a lowly, inferior substance is transformed into a higher, superior one. The reason for highlighting this idea of *sublimatio*, as the alchemists imagined it, is because it's often depicted in dreams as an upward movement. So whenever we find ourselves climbing mountains, flying, going up a ladder, ascending in an elevator or going up an escalator, for example, one of the associations we can make is that – psychologically speaking – something inferior within us (*inferus*, below) is being transformed into something superior (*superus*, above). Or, to put it another way, something unconscious is being made conscious.

But to bring these theories back down to earth, another reason I stopped taking the pill was because it inhibited my body's natural cycles. The concern I had – which gnawed at me in the image of a dam with hairline cracks – was what happens to our bodies in the long-term when you thwart and repress nature? I may not have had the answer but something in me felt this 'out of sight, out of mind' attitude wasn't good – least of all for my body.

Many women consider their monthly menses an 'inconvenience.' Prior to going on the pill mine had certainly felt that way. I knew that, once I came off the pill, the flow of my periods would return with a gushing vengeance – and I was absolutely right.

But since I've lifted the suppressive, pill-induced block, I've rediscovered the incredible, subtle shifts of my monthly cycle as played out in my body's mood changes, discharges, tender swellings, and the rise and fall of my sex drive. To be this subtly keyed in to nature as it makes its cyclical presence known through my body reminds me of how intrinsically connected I am to life itself – a walking, talking microcosmic reflection of the macrocosm.

So during my stay in India, when I didn't think I was doing much more than picking sand from my belly button, contemplating the meaning of life, and just *being*, I was actually learning to surrender to my feminine nature. As I said earlier just because I'm a woman, doesn't mean I was in touch with my innate feminine energy – and at that time, I definitely wasn't. By taking the pill I was effectively disassociated from my own matter (with its feminine undertones, remember?) – cut off from my very *soul*. But by no longer swallowing artificial hormones I was beginning the long process of 'raising up' my body which, for the longest time, I had so wilfully and unconsciously repressed.

Not just that, but by daily walking up and down the beach in my bikini, I was practising a form of self-acceptance. I was sick and tired of hiding, of being made to feel ashamed, of being made to feel misshapen, of not measuring up to so-called ideals. *This is how I'm shaped: with a jelly-like belly which wobbles and trembles to the touch, a spot-strewn back that would give the multitudinous stars in the night sky a run for their money, and bunion-deformed feet that look like Yoda's. Take it or leave it but this is me, warts and all.*

By stripping off the sarong-shaped layer of shame and allowing my body to be seen, I was releasing myself from years of self-loathing. By defiantly marching up and down the beach, music blaring on my iPod just in case anyone did have any wise-ass cracks to say about my body, I was taking something I'd previously deemed lowly and inferior, something to be despised and kicked about and, finally, began elevating it, raising it up for all the world to see – *sublimatio.*

SPECTRE REMORSE

Having said all that my trip to India always bothered me. While I was there it bothered me. When I came back it bothered me. For years I couldn't fathom why I went – it just didn't make sense.

I was in the middle of my marathoning Odyssey and still had two marathons to go. As I'd be travelling the length and breadth of India, this would obviously leave me with little-to-no time to train (although this had been my initial, albeit naïve plan) and on returning home I'd have just a few days before flying to Rome for my marathon there. Obsessed with all things Greek, I wasn't all that interested in Indian culture or mythology either – I was too busy learning all I could about Pan, Artemis et al, never mind contemplating Shakti, Shiva, and Co. I didn't even like Indian food for crying out loud.

Not that we necessarily *need* a reason for doing anything or going anywhere. But I do – I'm wired that way. Mum tells me when I was a nipper, I mithered her to death asking 'Why?' about *everything*. Exasperated, she thrust a book called, *Tell Me Why* into my hungry little hands. When I'd finished with it she gave me another, *More Tell Me Why*. And, when I was done with that, another one called, *Even More Tell Me Why*.

When I reappeared by her side tugging at her skirt with yet more questions, I'm surprised she didn't beat me round the head with said books. It's a pity she didn't know about the mythologist, Joseph Campbell's statement regarding life not having any meaning – that it's us who are supposed to bring meaning to it – as it would have probably stopped me dead in my relentless, why-asking tracks.

So why did I go to India for nine weeks? Especially after my original reason for going had fallen through the previous summer, largely on account of a conversation I'd shared with a market trader in Santa Fe; a man whose hugs were so warm, so reassuring, and so loving, he could've easily given up the day job and travelled round the world dispensing hug-shaped wisdom, giving Amma – an Indian spiritual teacher who does just that – a run for her rupees. But perhaps I shouldn't have been so surprised – he had, after all, spent years studying Tantra.

Sam had introduced us as he knew of his background in Tantra.

When I saw the clay-shaped, Venus of Willendorf-inspired goddesses he sculpted, propped atop long metal sticks like luscious lollipops, I squealed with delight. But what really caught my attention was his remark about *my* hugs.

'Wow,' he beamed after pulling away from our lingering embrace. 'You really know how to hug. None of this duck crap. You touch bellies. That is unusual.' He paused, surveying me the way an artist steps back to consider his creation. I looked at him, puzzled. He went on: 'People are afraid of connecting, of really touching one another. Next time two people hug, you watch – even if they wrap their arms around one another their chests barely touch, let alone their bellies – no heart-to-heart connection. And God forbid their crotches touch. No, they always arch their bodies away from one another – like ducks. But not you. It's unusual to receive a hug like that, especially from a non-Tantra person.'

I thought about this for a moment. He was right – we *are* afraid of fully embracing and truly connecting with one another, especially Brits. But I was more intrigued to hear of his experience with Tantra. He went on, telling me how he'd spent years living and studying in the community of an Indian spiritual teacher called Osho (also known as Bhagwan Shree Rajneesh – he's now passed away), when he'd been based in Oregon in the States. I told him I'd been thinking of studying at his ashram in Pune, India.

'Don't bother,' he told me. 'It's nothing like it was when he was alive. It's all commercialised now – a very slick operation.' I was disappointed to hear this, but not surprised. Especially when I'd seen the prices they were charging to stay at this place – he wasn't kidding about it being a slick operation.

The standard of accommodation they offered was nothing short of staggering. Although I wasn't keen on slumming it to the nth degree, I was shocked when I saw the polished marble floors and Mies van der Rohe's Barcelona armchairs in the reception area of this place. I had to check my browser to make sure I hadn't inadvertently clicked through to another page. If boutique hotel specialists, Mr & Mrs Smith recommended ashrams I've no doubt they'd include the Osho Meditation Resort.

But I'd be lying if I said I hadn't been a *little* tempted by the idea of staying in such a luxurious setting. And I know that attitude defeats the purpose of staying in an ashram on a spiritual retreat; that it's supposed to be a stripping away of the inessential so you can focus on what truly matters, reconnect with your divine inner nature and all that – I get that. But at the time this was all new to me. So if it had been offered, I wouldn't have said no to a few creature comforts such as, say, a comfortable bed and a mosquito net. And air-conditioning. Fresh coffee. (Just kidding! About the air-conditioning, anyway.) Seriously though, if there's one thing

I do need it's my sleep. Without it everything and everyone can go to hell in a hand-basket.

As for this Osho character? I first came across him in 2006. It was his books on sex, in particular, that had caught my eye. At the time I was finally emerging out the other end of a several year depression; or, rather, a dark night of the soul. And I don't use that expression because I want to dress it up, make it sound pretty, but because I have an issue with one-dimensional, clinical catch-all phrases such as 'depression.'

Not wishing to sound like a fan of morbidity and misery but, looking back, I now appreciate that there's a beauty to melancholy even if it did take every fibre of my being to keep myself from taking my own life such was the worthlessness, hopelessness, and emptiness that permeated my daily existence. Books such as Thomas Moore's, *Dark Nights of the Soul* were invaluable at helping me through that time in which he reminds us that, 'it is precisely because we resist the darkness in ourselves that we miss the depths of the loveliness, beauty, brilliance, creativity, and joy that lie at our core.'

So rather than attempting to suppress my feelings, get over it, or do something with it, Moore's book showed me how to be with my melancholic morass – ask it questions, listen to it, try and understand what it wanted *with* me. Although it didn't lift the interminable dark veil which hung over me most days, it did help me understand more about what was trying to happen to me and through me. Had it not been for books such as Moore's, that dark undercurrent would have probably pulled me under courtesy of a sudden swerve of my steering wheel at high speed straight into the wall of a tunnel during my daily commute, such was the magnetic pull it exerted.

It wasn't so much that I consciously wanted to kill myself; rather, it was as if my existence was underscored by a death wish which seemed to make every attempt to pull me away from life. It had started three years earlier when, night after night, I found myself sobbing into my pillow.

Outwardly everything seemed fine. I was living with my boyfriend who was handsome and thoughtful and generous – a really lovely guy. I had a stable, well-paid 9-5 office job which afforded me such luxuries as regular holidays, meals out, a couple of fancy watches and handbags. By and large my life consisted of things we're encouraged to strive towards and which are supposed to make us happy. But it was when I returned from a lunch-time shopping spree at Selfridges with a Louis Vuitton purse that things began to change.

A colleague asked me why I'd bought it. When I heard my reply, 'Because I can,' alarm bells went off. I didn't say I'd bought it because I loved it or because it was beautiful or because it filled my heart with joy.

No. I'd bought it *because I could*. The hollowness of this statement, uttered by my own mouth, was appalling to me.

Of course I didn't say any of this out loud. In the now bemused face of my colleague I maintained my pseudo defiant stance. But inside I was so deeply ashamed of this shallow, self-righteous attitude – *because I can*. If ever there was a statement to sum up the materialistic, consumer-driven problem of our culture that constantly strives to impress with its badges and labels, this was it.

I wouldn't mind but I didn't even like the thing. Design-wise it was dull and boring. I'd have probably been happier with something for a fraction of the price. But, as I'd soon come to discover, I didn't know what made me happy, what brought me genuine, heartfelt pleasure. I *thought* I did, but therein lay the problem – I was all up in my head. And most of the thoughts and opinions I had, they weren't even my own.

So now, night after night, I lay awake haunted by these shallow, meaningless words, haunted by the fact my life had no meaning. That's a hard thing to have to admit – that your life has no meaning. What's the point of being alive, I thought, if all I'm doing is getting by, getting through each day, week, with nothing more than the intention of earning money, taking holidays, buying, accumulating more and more *stuff* which, when it comes down to it, I don't even like? It just seemed so superficial and self-absorbed to me, particularly this attitude of thinking life owed me something. Soon I began to hate myself for it.

Although outwardly I kept up appearances, inwardly my self-loathing was gathering pace and beginning to eat away at me. It was at night, in the quiet of the undisturbed darkness, that the demonic voices really came into their own, mocking me, telling me I was worthless, that my very existence was pointless. *What's the point of you being here*, they'd ask? And they were right. What *was* the point of me being here?

During one of these never-ending nights I was – as had come to be the norm – stifling my tears into the pillow so as not to wake my boyfriend who was sleeping next to me. The voices were at me, yet again, with their perfectly reasonable, hard-to-disagree with question: *What's the point of you being here? Just take the pills. No-one will miss you.* When, finally – and for someone who wasn't remotely spiritual or religiously inclined, so this came as something of a shock – I said a line of a prayer I'd once heard: *Make me an instrument of thy peace.* Like a mantra, I mouthed it over and over, silently, into the darkness: *Make me an instrument of thy peace, make me an instrument of thy peace, make me an instrument of thy peace.*

It was hearing myself say these words, feeling this plea from the bottom of my heart that I realised – for the first time in my life – I wanted to *serve*. Serve what, I didn't know and at the time, it didn't matter. It was more the realisation I wanted to serve something *bigger*, something more important than me in the egocentric sense. That realisation did not, by any stretch, stop the seductive voices from taunting me, from attempting to suck the life from right out of me. But each night, when they'd ask me the point of my pathetic little existence, I'd reply: *Make me an instrument of thy peace, make me an instrument of thy peace, make me an instrument of thy peace...* until, finally, I fell asleep.

But it was only one morning – while sat on the toilet brushing my teeth – that my dark, barely conscious train of thought dawned on me in the outline of a suicide note I was mentally polishing. Its attention to detail was menacingly meticulous. I'd like to say I was so shocked and horrified at what was unconsciously unfolding within me, that I did something about it immediately – but I didn't. I think I was too ashamed.

It took the combination of my toady, two-faced boss at work to circulate a defamatory email about me to my colleagues behind my back (which, unbeknown to her, I'd discovered), together with a rousing, illuminating talk delivered to me by an electrician who was working on our house to bring me both to my knees and to my senses and make me realise that, unless I did something and soon, I was in real danger of dropping through the trap-door of death when no-one was looking.

I'd also just heard that one of the girls at the gym – a beautiful, newly engaged, happy-go-lucky girl with one of the sunniest dispositions I've ever known – had hanged herself. One minute she'd been giggling in the corner of the gym at the weight stack with her fiancé; the next, her radiant smile had been extinguished. But it was hearing several people's responses which really got my back up: 'How selfish. How could she do that to her fiancé and family?'

My own experience has taught me how seductive the death wish is, how it beckons you, lures you. Worst of all is how you may not even *know* you feel that way. Not everyone catches themselves as I did. Some succumb to the voices without realising. Unless you've been there – and I hope with all of my heartfelt being you never, *ever* experience what I did – I doubt you could ever truly understand how unconsciously insidious and slippery it is. If there's one thing I learnt from that period, it was the beginning of genuine, heartfelt compassion for another's suffering.

A week or so after catching myself polishing my death note, I finally made an appointment to see my doctor. Once in his office I proceeded to cave in on myself in front of the same kind and gentle man who'd known me all my life. The same man who'd peered down my throat at my swollen tonsils to tell mum that, yes, I had tonsillitis *again*. The same man who'd administered a sharp scratch of a vaccination, or three, while reassuring me with a red lollipop.

Doctor Fox didn't give me any lollipops that day. Instead, he listened quietly, holding the space while I broke down and explained, while snotting and snivelling through hiccup-ridden tears, that my life was a hopeless, meaningless heap of shit and how I was worthless, had nothing to offer the world, and had failed everyone. I felt both relieved to finally get it all off my chest and like a first-rate idiot – a first-rate idiot because I felt like a weak, pathetic failure who had copped out by running to the doctor.

'All the feelings you've described are the classic symptoms of depression. Right now,' he went on, 'your first priority is to take care of yourself.' And with that he signed me off work for a month. He also prescribed me anti-depressants. I took the prescription but dropped it in the bin on the way home.

What helped more than anything else was being given a safe, non-judgemental space in which to stop trying to be something I wasn't (strong, together) and just let it all out. Finally allowing someone to see the real me, hear how I really felt, I can't tell you what a relief that was. Dr Fox didn't judge me. Neither did he make me feel like I was an idiot. Saddened, perhaps, to see this young woman he'd seen grow up in a state of emotional disarray, but not an idiot. The voices that came night after night did, but they'd gradually disappear.

I never let anyone else see or know the full extent of the depths of my melancholy at that time. I've always been one to keep my cards close to my chest. Friends have since told me off for this – not saying anything, not opening up and sharing my heart when I'm suffering – but I can't help it. I know you're supposed to share everything with your friends but I'd have felt like I was burdening them had I laid *everything* out. I'd much rather speak to a neutral third-party who's trained and/or qualified to deal with such matters. I figure they've seen it all before so feel less embarrassed about sharing whatever it is I need to talk about.

Anyway, if you'd have told me I'd have another three years of this shitty state to endure and that it would get a whole lot worse before it got better, I may have thought twice about dropping that prescription in the bin.

It's not that I'm against anti-depressants – whatever gets you through the night and preferably alive, I say – but something in me wanted to understand what was happening to me. I was already depressed. I didn't want to further suppress the depression which I felt would have been the case had I taken pills.

One of the things that most helped was a Zen proverb I read in which a student tells their master they're discouraged and asks them what they should do about this. The master replies: 'Encourage others.' So, that's what I decided I wanted to do with my life – encourage others.

I knew I couldn't stop anyone else from experiencing the same darkness and hopelessness I had. But I could, at least, learn how to be present for them, hold the space, and lend an ear - just as Dr Fox had done for me.

A BIT TOO CLEAN-CUT

I spent the following year with my nose in books – spiritual ones, mostly. I also trained to be a life coach. Quiet study provided me with much needed relief from the interminable darkness which surrounded me most days. It also allowed me to step back and see the bigger picture. More than ever I realised I wanted to make a contribution to the community – preferably a meaningful one.

Looking back I now see my life was in the state of, what the alchemists call, *putrefactio*, which is the Latin, rather poetic way of saying, 'turning to shit.' My self, as I'd known it, was dying – *rotting*. As words go, it expresses more depth and richness than the word 'depression,' though, don't you think? ('Hey, Thea – how you doin'?' 'Ah, you know, *putrefying*.') I mean, it even comes complete with stench-ridden images.

Another term the alchemists have to express the breakdown of old or outmoded structures is *dissolutio* or *solutio*. The symbolism for *solutio* often shows up in dreams. It's one of the easier alchemical stages to spot as its symbolism is water. Flood dreams, in particular, may be showing us that the old order is being dissolved (hence *dissolutio*) to make way for a new order and/or way of being.

Those who don't work with their dreams may feel the urge to make a clean break, to come clean with themselves, or to clean out their lives so they can start over. What they're essentially expressing is this inner state of *solutio*. After all, when we feel stuck, we seek a solution so the situation can flow once more. It's interesting to note the countless flood myths in cultures across the world – even among desert people – such is the pervasiveness of this symbolism.

I knew little about working with dreams let alone alchemical symbolism but, looking back, I can see how important it was for me to cleanse my life (come clean with myself, you might say) and how, in particular, I became obsessed with my bathroom.

Many stories of depression and despair end up in the bathroom at some point. For anyone who's ever worked with their dreams they'll know the psyche's fondness for bathroom symbolism, particularly toilets. This is the room, after all, in which we get rid of our crap, clean up our act, and soak away – *dissolutio* – our stresses) – as without, so within.

When I split up from my boyfriend and bought my own house, no expense was spared on my bathroom which I designed down to the last hand-picked detail. Dark, sexy, and womblike, it became my sanctuary. Every evening, as soon as I got home from work, I'd light all the candles and retreat straight into the bath to read for hours on end. Other times my body felt so inexplicably sore and tender, bathing was the only way I knew how to support it.

So it was while enjoying one of my nightly 'bathathons' that I first read one of Osho's books (it just goes to show how indelible an impression his words left that I can remember *exactly* where I was when I first read him). And for the record, I don't care how many Rolls-Royces he was supposed to have owned, how many taxes he was supposed to have dodged, or what fraud he was supposed to have committed – the man's books offered food for thought and made me laugh out loud and for that alone I was grateful.

What particularly piqued my interest were his thoughts on sex, intimacy, the body, and women – the lattermost of which he seemed to hold in high regard. Although I wanted to serve others and had taken various steps in that direction, his words made me realise I would never truly be of help to another if my attitude towards myself and, in particular, my body remained unresolved.

Osho's teachings helped me understand my body was the bedrock of my existence. So no matter how sincere or enthusiastic I may have been about wanting to help others in a transformational capacity, it would ultimately amount to little more than hypocrisy if I hadn't first established a solid foundation of self-love and self-respect. After all, how could I accept others in their totality if I didn't fully accept myself?

Despite what someone says to us we instinctively know how they really feel by the signals they involuntarily give off. If studying body language had taught me anything, it was this: the body speaks the mind. So if someone professes to be totally accepting of others but, privately, berates their own body for not being good enough, thin enough, beautiful enough etc., their behaviour – however well controlled – will ultimately betray them.

This realisation was yet another wake-up call for me. Lay in the bath reading Osho's words, every so often I'd set the book down and contemplate my own body. Looking down at my thighs I realised I didn't like them. They were wobbly and ridden with cellulite. They weren't supposed to look like that. They were supposed to be lean and lithe. I was ashamed of them. In short, they'd failed me.

The one body part which had brought me more embarrassment and more shame than any other, however, were my vaginal lips; or, to be more specific, my labia minora. Or even, as they were affectionately known in secondary school, my piss flaps. During my teenage years I'd taken to calling mine my knicker lickers.

On the one hand I now find this amusing, but for the longest time they caused me so much pain and discomfort. Oh Lord, I can't believe I'm sharing this, out loud, in a book. But you know what? If this brings more attention to something I've since discovered countless women feel ashamed of, it can only be a good thing.

Because I'd never heard anyone – namely, women – speak openly and unashamedly about their muff/vagina/cunt/twat/yoni/vulva, I'd never quite known what to do with mine. That's not to say I hadn't already discovered the joys of self-pleasure at the ripe old age of eleven when, while in the bath one night, the shower head accidentally skimmed over my clitoris. All I'll say is, if cleanliness is next to godliness, by the age of twelve I was a veritable frickin' saint.

If bigger is better for men, thanks to the pervasiveness of porn, I was now learning that smaller was better for women. The more petite it is, the more it resembles a 'camel's toe,' the more attractive it's deemed. So when one side of my lips began to *grow* and *Grow* and *GROW* until it, eventually, resembled a cabbage leaf, it gave me cause for concern, shame, and much discomfort.

It chafed on my underwear (hence the nickname, 'knicker lickers') which, during hot weather, was nigh-on unbearable and difficult to readjust, especially while out in public. It got caught during sex which only led to further embarrassment and left me feeling tense and unable to enjoy myself. Half the time I didn't know whether the sounds I heard emanating from down below were the result of the bloke licking me or of me licking the bloke. But I just didn't know what to do about 'it' – a title I'd relegated it to as though it were something out of a horror movie.

So it was during this period of Osho-inspired body contemplation that I finally decided to take action. I'd read about a procedure on the NHS's website called a labia minora reduction. You could also have it done privately, but I didn't have the several thousand pounds necessary for such an operation. Besides, I didn't even know if there was anything necessarily wrong with 'mi nads,' as we refer to them locally (short for 'my nether regions').

I booked another appointment with my doctor – a female one this time. I'd figured Dr Fox had seen quite enough of depressed me these past few years without now having to stare into the depths of my now depressed vagina. As I was due a smear check-up, I seized the opportunity to ask her what she thought of my labia.

'I did wonder,' she said, staring up from between my legs, 'why you'd asked me to do your smear and not the nurse.'

'Tell me,' I asked, 'does that look normal to you? My outer left lip, I mean?'

She studied it for a moment. 'Erm, well, it is quite large. Why do you ask?' she said.

'Because it's done nothing but give me untold, painful grief since it started growing in my teens,' I said. 'Chafing on my knickers, getting trapped during sex – ' I can't tell you the relief I felt at finally being able to discuss this, openly, with another woman.

'Well,' she went on, 'there are surgical procedures available on the NHS, but only for exceptional circumstances. The emphasis isn't on aesthetics, on making the vulva look 'prettier' as is the current, rather worrying trend thanks to the proliferation of porn. It's about easing any discomfort the patient may have physically experienced as a result of its size.' She looked down at mi nads again before going on. 'But looking at yours, I'd say you easily qualify.'

You know, for the briefest of moments, I actually took umbrage with her comment that I'd 'easily qualify.' Then I realised she probably wouldn't have said anything had I not brought her attention to it in the first place. And if there was a chance something could be done about it, I'd be straight in there like a shot – which is exactly what happened.

Just six weeks later, I was in a bed on a hospital ward with a dozen other women who were also scheduled to have the same operation. Lying waiting for the surgeon to check in on me, I looked around at the other women who were casually flipping through magazines, chatting with their partners. *Gosh, so, we're all here to have our bits trimmed, eh?* And I don't mean to make light of the situation but, at the time, I was still deeply disconnected from my body.

After all, who do you talk to about such matters? We certainly weren't given the opportunity to at secondary school despite it being girls only. No one ever took us aside and recommended we whip out a mirror and take a good long look at our vulvas, celebrate their individuality, their unique beauty. And the first discussion I'd ever had about it, with my doctor, had resulted in me being recommended a surgical procedure which, being honest, I was only too pleased to accept, especially after suffering years of pain and discomfort.

In the weeks leading up to my operation I spent a fair bit of time closely scrutinising my yoni (Sanskrit word for vagina). With one leg hiked up on the edge of the bath, I squinted down at the mirror I'd carefully positioned so I could inspect the reflection of my hairy Mary. In fact, I have a before and after photo of her on an old Nokia camera phone – a phone I've kept in the hopes I'm able to charge it up, one day, and retrieve the images.

Back on the hospital ward the surgeon stopped off to chat with me ahead of my operation. It was a woman. I think I'd expected a man, so I was reassured by the fact I'd be operated on by a female (not that I'm ever 'happy' to willingly offer my body up on a surgical platter, but still). I was further reassured by the conversation we shared. She also told me this was a procedure which was becoming more popular.

'Popular?' I asked.

'Well, there's a fine line between this being a cosmetic procedure and there being a clear clinical need based on the physical discomfort caused to the patient. Based on the enlarged size of your left labia and the issues you discussed with your doctor and during the pre-op consultations, you clearly fell into the latter category. But we (NHS) don't offer labiaplasty for purely cosmetic reasons.'

This 'you clearly fell into the latter category' remark now made me feel I had a fleshy sail befitting the Cutty Sark stowed between my legs. She went on to explain how, thanks to porn, more and more women were seeking the tight and tidy look of the 'designer vagina.'

'What women don't realise,' she explained, 'is almost all of those actresses have had cosmetic surgery to "refine" and render the labia to make it more symmetrical. But what they also don't realise is just how brutal a procedure it can be. If performed incorrectly the irreversible effects are far, far worse than the symptoms they claim to have suffered from in the first place, including complete loss of sensation. Surgery should always be a last resort.'

She also told me about the increasing number of women, particularly east Africans, who were being sent to their doctors by their husbands who encouraged them to request the operation. Their 'complaint,' however, was usually related to their clitoris.

'What they're actually seeking is a clitoridectomy (removal of the clitoris). We turn them away, of course. But it's where they end up that worries me.'

I had my operation in 2006. I've since discovered more labia minora reductions were performed in 2006 (404) on the NHS than during the entire 2001-2005 period.

Despite not necessarily liking the look of my vulva, my reasons for going ahead with the operation were firmly rooted in the physical discomfort mine had caused me since being a teenager. That it could continue growing only further filled me with dread. But to have it operated on for purely cosmetic reasons knowing the potential risks? Not on your life.

The operation itself was swift and straight-forward. One minute I was being administered a general anaesthetic; the next I woke up on the ward where I'd earlier spoken with the surgeon. The nurse told me the procedure had been a success and that, after a brief rest, I'd be able to go home (no overnight stay – wham, bam, thank you ma'am). I only told a couple of friends about my impending procedure. So when my friend, Bing, realised I was up to my old tricks of trying to stay strong and look after myself she rollocked me, before making arrangements to pick me up and take me home.

Later that afternoon, as I tentatively made my way across the car park towards her car, she made some joke about me 'getting off my horse to drink my milk' courtesy of my John Wayne walk.

'What the bleedin' hell are you doing wearing a tight pair of jeans!' she asked.

'I didn't think when I left the house this morning.' ('Didn't think' – what a surprise.) When she asked how my 'mangy minge' was doing (if there's one thing I can always count on among my friends, it's their ability to bring a little levity, usually crass, to even the most serious of situations), I told her what was left seemed okay but that the other half was probably kicking around on the floor of an operating theatre somewhere.

Back home, sat on the edge of the bath, I positioned the mirror between my legs to inspect the surgeon's handiwork. Peering down, somewhat warily, I saw something resembling fish guts. I was told the stitches would eventually dissolve leaving me with something that, hopefully, resembled a normal looking vulva again.

I'm happy to report the operation was, indeed, a success and despite being left with two teeny-tiny holes on the left side of my outer labia from where the tissue didn't quite bind together properly, I've since suffered no problems whatsoever.

I can't tell you what an immense, life-enhancing relief this has been. No more chafing; no more numbness while riding a bike; no more getting caught during sex; no more awkward attempts at readjustment while out in public.

As mentioned earlier, I was *extremely* reticent to share this episode of my life as I didn't want to give the impression I was casually encouraging such surgical procedures. When I found myself – fingers poised over the keyboard – teetering on the edge of this sharing, my immediate reaction was: *Oh no, not that. I don't want to share that – that's waaaay too much information.* But something pushed me and insisted I share it. After pausing to consider it for a few moments, I realised this part of my journey was always meant to be shared with other women so that it may, perhaps, encourage debate.

With the alarming increase in these operations both in the US and UK, I feel more strongly than ever that these issues should be discussed openly and without shame – a view, I'd later discover, was also shared by Shakti Tantra.

So, to be very clear – because, seriously, I cannot stress nor say this enough – my reason for approaching my doctor was firmly rooted in the physical discomfort and distress I'd suffered since adolescence and *not* to make it look better. Like I've said, although I may not have necessarily liked the look of my vulva, I would never, *ever* have opted for cosmetic surgery just to make it look better. I just wanted to feel better.

After having the operation, I'm glad to say I did.

No More Ms Nice Gal

There's an old mythological idea that says whenever the body is cut into – whether by a surgeon's scalpel in an operation or a shaman's knife in a tribal scarification – from the soul's perspective an initiation has begun.

An initiation is a rite of passage ceremony which marks an individual's entrance into, not just the larger community but, psychologically speaking, an expanded sense of self which encompasses the play of opposites. Michael Meade describes this expanded sense of self as being 'double-minded.' We might think of this double-mindedness as one who is more balanced in their outlook on life, conscious of self and other.

An initiation typically consists of three stages: separation, initiation, and return. Initiation ceremonies include graduations, christenings, and such coming of age ceremonies as the Jewish Bar/Bat Mitzvah. If we take the secular example of a student we can see the process played out in their leaving home (separation) to embark on university life where they engage in several years of learning (initiation). After receiving their qualification the idea is they will then integrate what they've learnt during their years of study into their daily lives for the benefit of the greater community (return).

Whether or not we're spiritually or religiously inclined the soul is always seeking to be more deeply initiated into life. If we insist in our attempt to scratch out a superficial existence, sooner or later we may find our lives turned upside down and inside out as the soul drags us through the Great Round of Transformation that is life, death, and rebirth. Better to learn the steps and walk willingly, I say.

In his foreword to Mircea Eliade's classic book, *Rites and Symbols of Initiation*, Meade says:

> In dreams and dramas of initiation, death represents change for
> the entire psyche and life of the person. It means change inside
> and out, not a simple adaptation or switch in 'lifestyle.' Initiation
> includes death and rebirth, a radical altering of a person's 'mode
> of being'; a shattering and shaking all the way to the ground of

the soul. The initiate becomes as another person: more fully in life emotionally and more spiritually aware. Loss of identity and even betrayal of one's self are essential to rites of passage. In that sense, every initiation causes a funeral and a birth; a mourning appropriate to death and a joyous celebration for the restoration of full life. Without conscious rituals of loss and renewal, individuals and societies lose the capacity to experience the sorrows and joy that are essential for feeling fully human. Without them life flattens out, and meaning drains from both living and dying. Soon there is death of meaning and an increase in meaningless deaths.

If our idea of ourselves is outdated or no longer fits, the soul will start making all sorts of trouble for us. We may find ourselves drawn into a love triangle. We may find ourselves staring fifty in the face and suddenly realising our life doesn't reflect our inner truth in the least bit. We may have spent our life 'chasing the ace,' acquiring, accumulating before, one day, finding it (life) has no meaning – that the ladder we've spent our life climbing has been propped against the wrong wall. Illness, redundancy, depression, affairs, divorce, breakdowns, all these and more force us to consciously re-evaluate our lives.

The soul demands authenticity and, quite frankly, it couldn't give a flying Frisbee what your ego, with its narrow, limited idea of life has to say about it. By hook or by crook it will drag you to consciousness. Resist it and you'll only make the whole process worse – namely, for yourself.

So when I had my operation, unbeknown to me, from the psyche's perspective, I had triggered an initiation. Despite languishing and putrefying for three years in the stupor of a long, dark night, my operation marked a further deepening into the mysteries of the Underworld – a place known in Greek mythology as Hades.

Within months of my operation I was introduced to depth psychology and, in particular, the work of Carl Jung. After spending years acquainting myself with the lighter, spiritual end of the spectrum in an attempt to get my head straight and get some perspective, I now found myself intrigued with the darkness of the Underworld – which, psychologically speaking, is symbolic of the unconscious.

On reflection I now see I was beginning my descent from the bright heights of spirit down into the dark, dense depths of the soul with all its accompanying intrigues reflected by my obsession with my yoni and the rest of my body, and intimacy issues – in particular, my relationship with sex and sexuality. In fact, you might say this descent of the soul marked the beginning of my 'growing into myself.'

Throughout this time it may have seemed to outsiders that I was involved in little more than narcissistic navel-gazing, in which case they'd have been both right and wrong. Wrong, because I was less navel-gazing and more yoni-gazing, seeing as I'd spent most of the year fixated on my vulva. Right, because mythologically speaking, there was an element of narcissism involved – namely, in the shape of a narcissus flower. Author, Liz Greene was spot on when she said 'myth is the original self-help psychology.'

The myth involves the Greek goddess Persephone who is known both as the Kore (which means maiden) and as Queen of the Underworld. In the myth Persephone is playing in a meadow with the virgin (as in 'one-in-themselves') goddesses Artemis and Athena, when she spies a beautiful narcissus flower. As she plucks it from the ground the earth cracks open and out roars Hades, King of the Underworld, on his horse-drawn chariot. He snatches our butter-wouldn't-melt Kore and drags her back down with him into the Underworld (also called Hades) from whence he came. After they disappear the ground closes up and the virgin goddesses continue about their business as if nothing has happened.

When Persephone's mother, Demeter, gets wind her precious girl has disappeared she goes in search of her. Eventually, Hecate, the Crone goddess, who heard Persephone's cries as she was being dragged off approaches Demeter and suggests they go and see the sun god, Helios, as he's likely to know what's happened.

When Helios tells Demeter that Hades has had off with Kore in order to make her his bride she goes mad. To further rub salt in the wound, he tells her that her own father, Zeus, ignored her pleas for help and, in fact, it was him who sanctioned the whole thing in the first place. 'Hey, pipe down,' Helios tells Demeter. 'Hades is not an unworthy son-in-law, after all.' Well, as you can probably imagine, this does *not* go down well.

When she has no luck finding her daughter, Demeter eventually goes on strike. 'Strike' for Demeter, goddess of grain, means no crops grow, no water runs, and the earth turns barren. No crops mean no offerings can be made to the gods and goddesses up on Olympus. After much unsuccessful posturing by several of the Olympians, Zeus finally relents and sends the messenger god, Hermes, to retrieve Persephone. But – and here's the crucial detail – before Persephone leaves, she takes a bite of a pomegranate offered her by Hades.

On being reunited with her mother, Demeter immediately asks if she's eaten anything of the Underworld. If she hasn't, she'll be completely returned to her (Demeter). If she has, it'll mean she has to spend one-third of the year with Hades and the remaining two-thirds with her mother. So as not to upset her mother she lies to her saying Hades forced her to eat a pomegranate 'violently' and 'against her will.' Of course he'd done no such thing. Persephone was covering her tracks so her mother would think she was still the same butter-wouldn't-melt Kore who'd earlier been dragged off – except, she wasn't. Kore no more, she'd tasted the fruits of the Underworld – an Underworld she'd later rule as Queen.

My introduction to this myth came courtesy of the book, *Goddesses in Everywoman* by Jean Shinoda Bolen in which she brings the Greek pantheon to life, examining each figure from an archetypal, psychological perspective. If there's one book I recommend to everyone it's this and its counterpart, *Gods in Everyman*. As mentioned earlier, women are comprised of masculine and feminine energies; men, of feminine and masculine energies. So don't fall into the trap of thinking the goddess archetypes are only applicable to women and the god archetypes to men. As a writer, Hermes – the god of communication – is alive and well in my psyche.

As is evident from the brief snippet of the myth I've just shared, there are two distinct aspects to Persephone – her bright, innocent, topside (Kore) and her darker, not-so-innocent, Underworld aspect (Queen). Of all the Greek goddesses it was the duality of Persephone's archetype which most caught my eye.

When I first began the psychological process of seed-sorting, three years earlier, separating out what no longer mattered from what did, it never occurred to me to examine my close relationships – particularly familial ones. I was more focused on figuring out what I wanted to do with my life, what really mattered to me. Inner strengthening – that's what those years were about.

But now I realised that, if I wanted to go deeper, I'd have to examine my relationships – in particular, the psychologically symbiotic relationship I shared with mum. Although I no longer lived at home, I realised I was still very much dependent on her – her opinions still mattered, she held too much of a sway in my life. I couldn't tell where she ended and I began. She was still too 'up in my business,' as we say. Despite hurtling towards thirty I still sought to please her. I wanted her to approve of me because I was still a mummy's girl – nice, compliant, skipping through the meadows Kore.

If the recognition of three years earlier – that my life had no meaning – had sent me into a downwards spiral, this insight almost sent me over the edge altogether. *Just when you think you're making progress.* And I was. But even if we commit to living a more conscious life it doesn't mean we can deal with all of the issues in one go. The three years of inner work had been necessary. Now, it seemed, I'd reached a place where I was able to peel back a few more layers of the eye-watering onion of consciousness. Having said that, it's at times like this you want to shove the whole idea of 'coming to consciousness' up someone's arse.

But if there's one good thing about bringing such issues to light, it's that you can do something about them – or not. But I chose to. Especially as I'd realised this compliance didn't just apply to my relationship with mum, but to boyfriends too. If the former realisation irritated me, the latter *really* pissed me off. But as author Clarissa Pinkola Estés reminds us:

> **Compliance causes a shocking realisation that must be registered by all women. That is, to be ourselves causes us to be exiled by many others and yet to comply with what others want causes us to be exiled from ourselves. It is a tormenting tension and it must be borne, but the choice is clear.**

> **– Women Who Run with the Wolves**

Reading Bolen's description of Persephone I realised I'd been bending this way and that, being whatever they (men) wanted me to be – not that any of this was done consciously. Therein, however, lay the problem.

Whenever a man came on the scene I'd disappear into them, completely losing myself in the process. Deep down I was afraid if I didn't make them like me, I might lose them – I might be left, horror of horrors, *alone*. If I was myself, they might leave. Problem was, I didn't know who 'myself' was. I'd only ever existed as a reflection of others' expectations. Their thoughts became my thoughts, their opinions, mine. Whatever they wanted me to be, I was.

My aunt tells me that, from when I first started dating back in my teens, I'd say I was happy being single and alone. Then, before she'd even had a chance to turn around, I'd be in the arms of another man. She told me she once cried as she saw me going off up the street with yet another boyfriend without so much as a pause for breath. It wasn't for her to say anything, she said, but for me to figure it out for myself – she hoped.

Well now I was beginning to figure it out and I was *furious* with myself. But this figuring it out for myself was exactly how it was meant to be especially as I'm a stubborn so-and-so. If, for example, you'd have told me, to my face, that I was a good girl, nicey-nicey, always living my life through others, not grabbing hold of life with my own hands and attempting to shape my own destiny, I'm not sure it would have hit me with the same force with which it was now. Because now I saw clearly that I *was* a Handless Maiden who didn't have a grip on her life. I was a second-hand woman or, rather, a second-hand *girl*. The truth was, despite my age, I still hadn't grown up.

Moreover, because I'd always attempted to be all things to all men, I had no sense of myself, no sense of my innate sexuality. I was still sexually uninitiated. I may have been sexually active, yes, but this wasn't just about having sex – I had no idea of my innate pleasure. And because I had no sense of my own pleasure – of what I wanted, of what turned me on – I couldn't ask for it. The thing with this archetype – in its Kore aspect, at least – is its wishy-washiness, its compliance, always going along with what the other wants. For me, sex was no different.

In the myth Hades drags Persephone down into his realm and rapes her. It's easy to look at this myth in a concrete, literal way and throw our arms up in horror and say it's a typical patriarchal myth with its images of rape and what not. What we have to remember is, it's a *myth* and myths, like dreams, don't come from us, they come *through* us. As Joseph Campbell reminds us, 'myths are public dreams; dreams are private myths.'

If we look at the Underworld as symbolic of the unconscious, we might then reimagine this story as a too-bright, somewhat immature aspect of consciousness being pulled under and ravished by the unconscious. Why? Because this Kore-like attitude is one-sided: all light and no dark. And if there's one thing sure to tip the psyche into action, it's a lack of equilibrium.

If there's one thing about Kores, it's that they're all about being nicey-nicey. Believing themselves helpless they tend to resort to lies and manipulation as indicated by Kore telling her mother that Hades made her eat of the pomegranate 'violently' and 'against her will.' He did no such thing. He offered it to her. She ate it.

'The pomegranate,' according to The Book of Symbols, 'suggests, in a psychological sense, the bitter depths and majestic forces of the unconscious encountered in the taking in of the fertile, dreadful seeds of the self.' Let's stay with this image of the pomegranate for a moment because it's an interesting symbol – in particular, its bitterness.

The truth tends to be bitter. We talk of the 'bitter truth,' of something being a 'bitter pill to swallow.' Contrast this bitterness with Persephone's saccharine sweetness. It's no wonder she was given something bitter to incorporate (*in corpus*, to take into the body) in order to balance her too-sweet-for-her-own-good attitude. As mentioned earlier, the psyche can't abide the ego's one-sidedness. We are, after all, comprised of both the dark and the light. Those who are most obsessed with the light tend to cast the biggest shadows.

This is particularly prevalent in New Age thought and among spiritual, light-chasing folk. In fact, have you ever noticed how they often sign off messages with such sentiments as 'with love and light?' It's never 'with love and darkness,' is it? People go off on spiritual journeys in search of 'enlightenment' not 'endarkenment.' Why? Because everything associated with the dark is considered bad and negative. But how did this come to be?

For centuries the Judeo-Christian tradition has been splitting apart spirit and matter. Even before disobedient Eve with her apple and her friend, Snake, in the Garden of Eden, there was Lilith. Lilith was considered Adam's first wife. The name Lilith is derived from 'night' or 'evening' (darkness, surprise!) and she has come to be associated with sex, lust, death, demons, the unclean, and the animalistic – all things considered incompatible with living the good, clean spiritual ideals which were, in turn, exalted, raised up, and to which, if we wanted to go up to heaven, we should all aspire. Or, put another way, all things associated with the soul.

When you consider everything associated with spirit is light, perfect, and transcendent, and the soul with all that's imperfect, dense, and opaque, you may begin to see how the spiritual has, over centuries, become opposed to the chthonic (earthy). Persephone and her mother, Demeter, were chthonic goddesses (representatives of the earth). Hecate, too. In fact, these three goddesses are considered symbolic of the three aspects of the feminine: maiden, mother, and crone.

But when you continually emphasise one side of anything to the detriment of the other – the light to the dark, or spirit to matter, say – things become unbalanced. Keep this up and it's only a matter of time before its opposite is activated and the whole system swings into action in order to compensate the imbalance. In Jungian psychology this is called *enantiodromia*. This can happen at both a personal and collective level.

So if we take the case of Kore, sweetly skipping through the meadows, ignorant of her dark, lustful, earthy nature, it's only a matter of time before this imbalance is compensated by the sudden rise of the other – that 'other,' in this case, being the dark god Hades who drags her off to rape her.

As long as she remains unconscious of her chthonic, sexual nature – as symbolised by the Underworld – she'll remain a Kore: an uninitiated maiden lacking substance and depth. Unless she's consciously initiated into the riches of Hades' realm, she'll remain a maiden – a Sleeping Beauty unconscious of her sexuality, unconscious of her beauty, awaiting a prince to awaken her – and not the conscious, one-in-herself, sexually initiated woman and Queen of the Underworld she could be: a Queen who, having been initiated into the life-death mysteries, is now double-minded, consciously embodying both the light and the dark, holding the tension of opposites that are spirit and matter.

So the fact she ate the bitter fruit of the Underworld as symbolised by the pomegranate of her own accord – and not because Hades made her – shows a conscious acceptance of her earthy nature: the bitterness counterbalancing her sweet nature.

This Persephonic sweetness wasn't so much evident in my behaviour; rather, it showed up in my relationship with food. I had a raging sweet tooth. Still do. In fact, I should just come right out and say: 'My name is Thea and I am a sugar addict.' Conscious awareness of the situation has helped massively ease it but I'm still 'in recovery,' shall we say. Because I'm aware of what's going on, I don't beat myself up or berate myself for it. I don't deny myself sugar either, as I know that will only make it worse. For me, balance and constant awareness is key.

What has helped is looking at what this sweetness may *symbolise*. In light of this I've learnt to sit with it, ask it questions, try and understand what this yearning for sweetness may be about, what it may want *with* me.

When I first read about this myth, back in late 2006, my craving for all things sweet was titan. When I got home from work, rather than taking care of myself, cooking myself a nourishing meal, I'd eat a tub of ice-cream, a packet of biscuits, or a box of chocolates. I knew I was doing it, I knew it wasn't good for me, and I felt bloody awful after, but I'd still sit there mindlessly scoffing the lot.

I wouldn't say I had an eating disorder; more, a food complex – 'complex' being the operative word, not so much in the psychological sense but in the 'it's complicated' sense. It still is. I'm not naïve enough to think I'll ever be done with this issue – like alcoholics, once a sugar addict, always a sugar addict. If I was to ever take my eye off the ball I know I'd be in trouble.

Because I like both food and my teeth too much I've never been able to throw it (food) back up. (In bulimics, the constant onslaught of stomach acid in the mouth can, over time, cause excessive tooth decay.) And I won't deny myself food (anorexia) because, well... like I said, I enjoy it too much. Neither do I want to shit it out à la laxatives. Nope, I stuffed myself and my weapon of choice was sugar. But just *what* was I attempting to stuff down? And why sugar as opposed to starchy, bready products for example?

As mentioned earlier I was out of touch with my body, cut off from the neck down. This was evidenced by not knowing how much space I took up physically. It may sound strange but I had no spatial awareness. I didn't know how big I was. It was only when I saw my moon-sized face grinning back from a photograph that I finally got an objective – and somewhat shocked – look at myself.

But just because I wasn't physically in touch with myself didn't stop me (albeit, unconsciously) yearning for the sweetness we can only experience either by lovingly touching ourselves or from when another affectionately touches us. Why else do we long for the 'sweet embrace' of our beloved? Or sing of 'sweet love?' Love is sweet. *How Sweet It Is (To Be Loved by You)* sang Marvin Gaye. If we deny our bodies of such sweetness – its touch or its sentiment – we'll find other ways in which to fill up on it – namely in the form of sweet, sugary things.

So it wasn't sugar-laden food and drink my body was demanding; rather, it was a sweetness of touch. But the only way my body knew to cry out and call my attention to it was through demanding all things sugar – the literal, concrete version of sweetness. Because I was unconscious of this, though, in an attempt to keep it quiet I just kept stuffing my poor body's longing for a loving touch – its longing for sweetness – down with food.

Once I started reading about Little Miss Seff (aka Persephone), however, all this finally began to fall into place. Only problem was, I had absolutely no idea how to go about satisfying this longing for sweetness. As anyone who's suffered with addiction or body-related issues knows, if you've spent years abusing the body it takes a long time to regain its trust. Just because the head may finally be coming to terms with this mind-matter split doesn't mean it's all magically sorted out overnight.

But the more I thought about it the more it made sense, this sweet issue. It wasn't so much I was afraid of being intimate with another (although I probably was); rather, I didn't know *how* to genuinely connect with another because I didn't know how I felt from the neck down. How could I consciously receive the sweet, loving touch of another if I couldn't even feel into my own body? I'd made my body a whipping post. And if that's all I thought it was how could I expect anyone else to love it, offer it sweetness? Even if they did I still wouldn't be able to receive it because I wouldn't believe myself worthy of receiving it. And round. And round. And round it went.

What I didn't want to spend the rest of my life doing, though, was to sit on the sofa mindlessly filling my face with all the family-sized chocolate bars I could lay my hands on. Neither did I want to be alone. Though don't let me give you the impression I never had any intimate encounters – I absolutely did. Once I moved into my own place I took full advantage of it. But it was only once I began examining this Persephone archetype that I finally saw my pattern of compliance.

Always waiting for a prince to awaken me I only existed as a sexual being when there was someone else to reflect me, to rouse me from my unconscious sexual slumber. Without the presence of another in my life, however, I disappeared and so did my sexuality. So on the occasion when I did end up in bed with another, the focus was on what they wanted: their needs, their desires, their orgasm. In full-on Persephone pleasing mode I'd turn the equivalent of sexual back-flips in order to make sure I scored 'full points.'

I used to think that, if you're a bloke and you end up in bed with a woman like this (people pleasing Seff), it must be great. After all, he's getting everything he wants isn't he? He's bound to like me, right? But I now recognise there's a heavy dose of power play at work in a situation like that. I was seducing, manipulating men in order to make them like me – welcome on stage the *femme fatale*. Believing I had nothing to offer

I was using sex in an attempt to (indirectly) gain power. Unrelated to my body I was using it as little more than a tool.

So although I may have had all the 'right moves,' sexually speaking I was cold. I was also impenetrable. That may seem a strange thing to say seeing as I was being physically penetrated during sex, but I was only going through the motions. Deep down, I was afraid. I'd never truly opened up – not with my body, soul, and mind. Truth be told, I amounted to little more than a hole and a heartbeat. And if, deep down, I felt like that you have to wonder what the guys I slept with must have felt about me regardless of whatever wondrous moves and marvellous feats I may have pulled off.

Several years later I read something by Ginette Paris which nailed how I felt at that time:

> **Insisting on the beauty of Aphrodite, as one inevitably does, we risk forgetting that her mysteries are concerned with the whole body and not only with the eye. The woman who has the qualities of Aphrodite knows how to move, breathe, and vibrate, and is capable of generating as well as receiving high-intensity sexual energy.**
>
> **Some beautiful women give the impression that they are inhabited by Aphrodite's qualities. Their seductive appearance which promises of pleasure, however, leads to deception each time this promise is not kept by the body.**
>
> **But when competence at bodily love prevails over good looks, certain women, even though unsightly, may exert upon their lovers an extraordinary attraction.**

> *– Pagan Meditations*

Although I was good looking, appeared sexually confident, and was capable of turning impressive sexual tricks I was, ultimately, a pastiche of sexuality. I couldn't generate high-intensity sexual energy by myself, for myself, let alone with another.

This further realisation, regards my sexuality, made me feel like an awkward, inexperienced girl: a sexually uninitiated maiden who, despite being thirty years old, still hadn't grown into full womanhood; or, to borrow the image from our Kore/Demeter myth, Persephone, Queen of the Underworld.

But what I didn't want was to spend the next decade of my life in the same unconscious state as I'd spent the last. I wanted to feel the fullness of my sexuality, feel into the depths of my body, and generate high-intensity sexual energy by myself, for myself. I wanted to feel confident in my sensuality, really confident, not pretending to myself or another.

Split off from my body I'd narrowed my sexuality down to a genital-focused, well-rehearsed routine. But now I wanted to let go, to surrender, to be total – body, mind, and soul – to open fully, so fully but, at the same time, *consciously*. Not unconscious. Not with the lights out. I didn't want to hide. Goddammit, I wanted to consciously surrender to another, to be penetrated by them without fear or frigidity. In short, I wanted to be *ravished*. But how?

How, after being unconscious as to the wants and needs of my own body, to my own sexuality, would I go about discovering what I wanted? How would I bridge the gap between mind and matter? How would I deconstruct the emotional and physical body armour I'd carefully crafted in order to keep the world out? Bringing it to conscious awareness through reading was a start. But now what?

Aside from consciously eating the pomegranate what always bugged me about this myth is its lack of symbolism showing her transition from Kore to Queen. Although I've been able to re-vision her abduction and subsequent rape from a symbolic, psychological perspective – looking at the figures as representative of energies in the psyche and not literally as in a man raping a woman (for which there has never been, nor will ever be, any justification – rape is an abhorrent, inexcusable crime) – there wasn't much to go on which would help me understand just what she *experienced* down there in the Underworld that helped her transition from maiden to womanhood.

Well, I needn't have worried about this for long. What's that old saying? When the student is ready, the teacher will appear? Indeed he already had. Unbeknown to me it was the same man who'd introduced me to this world of mythology and depth psychology in the first place.

Remember the guy who bought me the Michael Meade talks in Santa Fe? Well, it was him – Sam. Sam was an artist. A poet, too. I'd met him on MySpace in late summer 2006, just a few months after my operation and right around the time I was getting interested in Tantra and my body. I'd not long turned thirty and had hit something of a nadir in my ongoing *nigredo*. As socialising still felt like too much of an effort for me, MySpace became a refuge of sorts. Every night, when I got home from work – and when not in the bath – I'd log on and check in with this virtual community from round the world.

Many of the connections I made on MySpace remain friends to this day – much loved, real-life friends. I'm not sure they realise but, back then, many of these new connections helped stop me from falling apart. It was them who read my first tentative attempts at writing via blogs and encouraged me, told me to keep writing as they enjoyed reading my work.

In alchemical symbolism there's a term, 'solve et coagula' which means to dissolve and coagulate. The idea is as one aspect of your life is dissolved, another new aspect is simultaneously formed or coagulated. Put another way, things fall apart so they can fall together in a new way. Many of these MySpacers formed a necessary and essential part of the foundations of my new life.

Sam mysteriously appeared at my very first blog – a piece I'd written encouraging people to go see Al Gore's documentary, *An Inconvenient Truth*. Talk about the universe whooshing in as soon as you open up and create a space for it. Soon we were engaged in an online dance which culminated in my eventual trip to Santa Fe where we met and embarked on a relationship. What I've not mentioned before is the effect he had on my writing.

When I first blogged I was finding my feet as a writer. Not that I'd ever fancied myself as a writer – I hadn't. And I certainly never aspired to be an author. That's why I'm grateful to those who told me they enjoyed my blogs and my writing style otherwise it would have passed me by altogether.

Anyway, when I started out it was the act of writing itself I most enjoyed. It was cathartic. Sharing how I felt with a close circle of others, albeit online, was healing. But because, up until that point, I'd spent most of my time reading New Age literature, I was also very light-oriented. I was all 'love and light.' This was reflected in my somewhat floaty, overly poetic style of writing. Long-term readers may disagree with that opinion but, looking back, I now see I was.

It was only once Sam started throwing the virtual equivalent of stones at me that I began questioning this. In his own way, he was tugging at my ankles to stop me floating off on my 'perfect purple cushion' as he put it and pull me back down to earth. In fact before he came along I'd say I was morphing into a helium being. It was him who tugged at my 'stringy body,' grounded me, reminded me I was a human being made of matter and never to forget that.

Not that he had the gentlest of approaches. Most of the time his remarks upset me. God, I was such a delicate little flower, but he was insistent, popping up on my blogs, leaving comments, emailing me. But though he may have upset me I was also intrigued by his observations. Did I really lack depth? Was I as insubstantial as he said I was? Was I all about spirit to the detriment of soul? Was I all sunny-side up?

Although it was an uncomfortable truth to face, he was right – I had become a spiritual light chaser. Skipping about with a one-sided, naïve perspective of life; thinking everything could be solved with little more than focused intention and the power of positive thinking. Oh yeah, I was disembodied alright.

Though I may have sincerely wanted to help others, so long as I maintained this one-sided perspective I'd only cause more harm than good. A dilettante, I'd spent my life skimming the surface, never sticking with one subject, never probing the depths – a *puella aeterna* (Latin for 'eternal girl,' aka Kore).

At the time, the video for Rhonda Byrne's *The Secret* had gone viral. The spiritual community I'd been hanging around with online were espousing the power of mind over matter with such dictums as: '*If you can think it, if you believe it, you can achieve it.*' '*If you can go there in the mind, you can go there with the body.*'

'You try telling someone to their face,' Sam once said to me, 'that they've somehow brought their cancer or heart attack on themselves through negative thinking. That it's their fault. See how far you get.' Suffice to say, he wasn't impressed with many of the light chasers I hung about with believing them shallow and lacking compassion for the human condition.

This is where I first saw a change in myself. So far I, too, had been all about love and light but now I was beginning, in my own small ways, to embrace aspects of the darkness. The tone of my writing reflected this shift in perspective – and it didn't go unnoticed.

Sam had been challenging the views of several of my more spiritually-oriented readers – *fiercely*. As you may imagine they didn't like this. They wrote to me in private telling me as much, telling me he was bad news, that I ought to stay away from him, that he wasn't good for me. A few even threatened to boycott my blog if he continued to show up.

Now, I don't know about you but if you'd just found out your psychological pattern was one of compliance, of people pleasing, of wanting to make everyone happy, bending this way and that, trying to be all things to all people, and you were presented with a situation where you have to choose between something 'good' and something 'bad,' for the record, I'd go for the 'bad' option – which is exactly what I did.

That may sound petty but, truth be told, Sam wasn't bad. He just stood for the soul and all that went with it. And now I wanted to learn more of the dark, wet, labyrinthine regions of the Underworld. I didn't want to be pigeon-holed as 'nice Thea' with her beautiful writing and her pretty pictures.

If I'd have continued playing along with what I felt readers expected of me I'd have ended up further split, a half person, but I now realised something in me wanted to embrace the 'other,' too. In short, I wanted to be whole. And whatever this guy stood for, I intuited if I followed it far enough and deep enough, it would lead me down into the depths of my body.

Sam also challenged me to stop presenting such a one-sided image of myself. Although I'd opened up online and shared how I felt, he encouraged me to come clean with the depths of my feelings and not to try and make nice of it. 'Stop trying to be something you're not,' he'd tell me. He encouraged me to read the works of Jung, Campbell, the late psychologist, James Hillman, and the poet, Robert Bly. 'You need more depth,' he'd say.

He also introduced me to his friend, Karl who, in turn, introduced me to the works of Marion Woodman, Marie-Louise von Franz, and Linda Schierse Leonard – all depth psychologists. I can't tell you just how different their work felt. After reading books by Eckhart Tolle, Neale Donald Walsch, Sanaya Roman etc., this was like wading about in the swampy, incomprehensible depths.

Despite, however, imagining myself to be a delicate little flower (a narcissus, if you will), I was also a tough one. So when he came a-huffing and a-puffing at my door, I stood my ground and took on board his observations however sharp they may have been. I was intrigued with what he stood for, this world of soul and depth of which he spoke, wrote, and painted about. More importantly, I liked the *feel* of it.

The arrival of Sam symbolised the constellation of the 'other' within my psyche – a real life Hades who'd come to drag me off to the Underworld and counterbalance my light-oriented one-sidedness. Only thing was, unlike Hades, he didn't have to drag me off – I went willingly.

But what exactly did Kore *do* once she was down in the Underworld to be eventually crowned, Queen of the Underworld? From what I could gather, she just sat around a lot, moping, crying for her mother – hardly the material of which monarchs are made. Suffice to say I found a clue in Bolen's, *Goddesses in Everywoman*:

> ... a sexual initiation that puts a woman in touch with her own sexuality is a potential of the Persephone archetype consistent with mythology. Once Persephone was Queen of the Underworld, she had a connection or a bond with Aphrodite, Goddess of Love and Beauty. Persephone may represent the underworld aspect of Aphrodite; Persephone is a more introverted sexuality, or a dormant sexuality. In the mythology, Adonis was loved by both Aphrodite and Persephone. And both goddesses shared the pomegranate as a symbol.

A 'sexual initiation' – now this was interesting. But just how does one go about being sexually initiated in this day and age? Sam knew of my intention to travel to India to learn more about Tantra. As our online dance developed into a real life relationship, we discussed the idea of going together – which we eventually did. By the time we got there, though, I'd given up on my original reason for going (to study Tantra) thanks, in large part, to the Tantric market trader I'd met in Santa Fe.

And that's what always bothered me: with no plan and absolutely no intention of doing anything spiritual just because I was in India, what exactly did I plan on doing once I got there? By this point I was as baffled by my own actions as anyone.

But here's the thing: by following Sam down the proverbial rabbit hole into the Underworld of dreams, mythology, depth psychology, and all things soul, my Tantra initiation had already begun. As Jung reminds us, 'The *road* is the goal.' I should have remembered this when I caught sight of the name of the Virgin airplane on which I flew to India: *Sleeping Beauty*. It caught my eye as I boarded my flight to Delhi, stuck in my mind like a splinter.

Little did I know, as I boarded that plane, that Beauty, here (aka yours truly), was about to get the Mother India of all wake-up calls.

THE GODDESS OF DISCORD

There's a figure in Slavic folklore who, should you find yourself lost and alone in the darkest part of the forest, you may be fortunate enough (or not, depending on your attitude towards her) to stumble across. If so, tread carefully, for this is the realm of the Baba Yaga – the great crowned Crone, also known as Queen of the Dead.

Her hut, in most stories, stands on a single, giant chicken's leg and continually spins, creaking and groaning all the while; or, else, it may stand with its back to you but always with its door open to the darkest part of the forest. Sometimes the hut is encircled by a fence made of human bones and topped with skulls whose eye sockets blaze in the darkness. In other stories there are twelve stakes set in the ground with men's heads stuck on eleven of them but with the twelfth noticeably empty. As you may have gathered, the rules of the ordinary world no longer apply here.

Among her loyal servants are the White Horseman, the Red Horseman, and the Black Horseman whom she describes as 'My Bright Dawn, my Red Sun, and my Dark Midnight.' She also calls upon three bodiless sets of rather creepy looking hands that appear out of thin air to do her bidding. But don't bother asking her about them because it's none of your business. In fact, don't ask her about anything – it's not for no good reason that curiosity killed the cat.

As old as time she's seen all that was, is, and will ever be. And despite legs as spindly as a skeleton's, she maintains a ferocious appetite. Often seated in a mortar which she rows through the air with an oar-shaped pestle, she's not one for company. As such, she has little patience for unexpected visitors such as yourself, so you'd better make sure you give her the correct answer when she asks:

Are you here of your own free will or by compulsion?

It's worth pondering this for a moment or you may just find your thigh bones lining her white picket fence and your skull filling the empty spot. Almost all who gamble with her invariably lose for, despite seeming straightforward, hers is a paradoxical question which, therefore, demands a paradoxical answer.

But don't think too long or else it'll be your bones she'll pulverise to a pulp in her mortar. And don't even *think* of trying to charm your way out of there because her skulls can see straight through your nicey-nicey smile and/or your little girl/boy lost act. Their fiery eyes will burn you to cinders which she'll then sweep away with the broom she keeps by the door – because she's tidy like that. Moreover, the merest whiff of a smart-arse answer and she'll have your guts for garters.

I first came across the Baba Yaga in the Russian fairy tale, *Vasilisa the Beautiful*. In the story, Vasilisa is a sweet, beautiful girl who lived with her mother and father – the latter of whom is a merchant.

When the girl was eight years old, her mother suddenly took ill and called Vasilisa to her deathbed. 'Listen, my dear child, these are my last words and don't forget them. I am dying and leave you with my blessing and this doll. Keep it with you always, show it to nobody, and whenever you are in any trouble, ask it for advice.' Then she kissed her daughter for the last time and died.

After a period of mourning, her father eventually remarried a widow who had two daughters of her own (unless you've never heard or read a fairy tale in your life, I think we can all see where this one's going).

Soon, the stepmother was giving her all the crap jobs and generally doing all she could to make sure Vasilisa's beauty was spoilt to the point where, she hoped, the girl would resemble little more than a poor-looking peasant girl.

Like her more famous cousin, Cinderella, Vasilisa went about her daily chores without so much as a grumble and, much to the irritation of her stepmother and her stepsisters, grew even more beautiful with each passing day. Her stepsisters, meanwhile, who sat around doing nothing but bitch and moan, grew uglier on account of their envy. What the stepmother and stepsisters didn't realise was, Vasilisa had a pocket-sized friend her mother had given her and it's this wee doll who did most of the work for her.

Things went on like this for a year or so until, when the merchant went away on business, the stepmother moved to a house at the edge of a great forest – the same forest in which the Baba Yaga lived. One night, having finally had enough of Vasilisa's sweet, compliant nature and knowing full well the Baba Yaga lived in the forest, the stepmother and her daughters conspired to send Vasilisa to ask the old witch for a spark with which to light the fire they'd deliberately extinguished. To quote from Clarissa Pinkola Estés' version of this story, 'Oh, they all clapped and squeaked like things that live in the dark.' Despite being afraid, Vasilisa's doll advised her to go.

Just before dawn, as she walked along, a man dressed in white galloped by on a white horse. Soon after, as the sun was rising, a man dressed in red riding a red horse trotted by. Vasilisa schlepped on until she eventually arrived at the strange old hut of the Baba Yaga. Just then another mysterious man, this time dressed all in black sat on a black horse, rode by her and straight into the house of the Yaga. As he did, night fell. It was at this point Vasilisa saw the skulls with the fiery eyes, glowing eerily, peering at her through the darkness.

Rooted to the spot with fear, Vasilisa asked her doll companion if this was the place she sought to which the doll replied, yes, it was. Just then, the trees rustled and the mighty Baba Yaga appeared, hovering mid-air, in her mortar-shaped vessel which she rowed with her pestle, carrying a broom she used to sweep away her tracks.

'What do you want?' Yaga hissed down at the girl through her crooked yellow teeth.

Trembling, Vasilisa replied, 'Why Grandma, I've come to fetch a fire. My house is cold and if we don't warm it soon, my... my family will die.'

Considering the girl for a moment, Yaga stroked the hairs on her crescent-shaped chin before replying, 'Hmmm... light eh? Well, you useless girl, it's your fault it went out in the first place. Why do you think I should help you?'

Vasilisa quickly consulted the doll her mother gave her. Looking the Yaga straight in the eye she answered, 'Because I ask.'

On hearing her response, the Yaga smiled to herself. *This one has a little gristle.* 'Very well,' said the Yaga. 'I will give you your light. But you're going to have to earn it.'

'Yes, Grandma,' replied Vasilisa who, heaving a sigh of relief, was just thankful her skull hadn't gone to join the others at picket fence hell.

Through narrowed eyes the Yaga continued, 'Stay with me a bit and you shall have your fire... '

And so in they went to the hovel where the Yaga lay down upon her bed and demanded Vasilisa bring her everything that was cooking in the oven. Despite there being enough for ten people the Yaga scoffed the lot, leaving only a crust of bread and a thimble of soup for the young girl.

On finishing, she wiped her mouth and turned to Vasilisa saying, 'Tomorrow, when I go out, I want you to wash my clothes, sweep the yard, clean this hut from top to toe, prepare my meal, and separate the mildewed corn from the good seed. And I want all this done by the time I get home or I'll eat you. Is that clear?'

Vasilisa nodded.

When the Yaga was sound asleep, evidenced by her raucous snoring, Vasilisa fed the little bit of food she had to her doll-shaped friend before asking it what she should do. 'There's so much work,' she panicked, 'I'll never be able to do all that on time!' The doll told her not to be afraid and to say her prayers and go to bed, for the morning was cleverer than the evening.

In the morning Vasilisa awoke to find the doll had done everything for her. All she had to do was cook the meal. Suffice to say, she couldn't thank her little friend enough.

Later that night the Yaga returned and asked Vasilisa whether everything was done.

'Look for yourself, Grandma,' said the girl.

The Yaga inspected the place and was furious she wasn't able to find any fault saying through gritted teeth, 'Yes, it's alright.'

She then called her loyal servants to grind her corn at which time three pairs of hands appeared out of thin air to carry out her bidding. The Baba Yaga filled her face with as much food as she did the night before. Before she went to bed she told Vasilisa she wanted the same jobs completed by the time she got home the following day. But, this time, she also wanted her to sort out the poppy seeds in the granary and clean the dirt away.

Once again Vasilisa asked her little friend what she should do, whereupon the doll told her to do exactly the same as she did the night before. That night, when the girl and the Baba Yaga were asleep, the doll completed all of Vasilisa's tasks for her. Later the next day, when the old woman returned, she looked everything over and, satisfied, albeit irritated, summoned the three pairs of hands once more – this time to press oil from the poppy seeds.

While stumbling and mumbling about the place, the Yaga saw the young girl gawping at her.

'What are you staring at without saying a word?' barked the Yaga. 'Are you dumb?'

'If you would allow me to do so, may I ask you some questions, Grandma?'

'Ask,' ordered the Yaga, 'but remember, not all questions are wise and too much knowledge can make a person old too soon.'

Vasilisa said she just wanted to know about the riders.

'Mmm...' smiled the Yaga, peering down her nose at Vasilisa, 'that first is my Dawn.'

'Who was the red man on the red horse?'

'Ah, that is my Red Sun,' she said, now moving closer to the girl.

'And the man dressed all in black on the black horse?'

Rubbing her hands together as she moved even closer the Yaga replied, 'That is my Night.'

'I see,' said Vasilisa who was now wondering about the three pairs of hands.

'Come child,' said the Yaga, now so close Vasilisa could smell her odious breath emanating from behind her thin, crooked smile, 'why don't you ask more?'

Just as she was about to ask the Baba Yaga about the hands, the little doll jumped up and down, tugging at the inside of her pocket warning her not to.

'That's enough,' said Vasilisa. 'After all, you said yourself, Grandma, not all questions are wise and too much knowledge can make a person old too soon.'

'Hmm...' said the Yaga, 'you, my girl, are wise beyond your years. You were right to ask only about what you saw outside the hut. But now I have a question for you: just how did one so young come to be so wise?'

'Why, by the blessing of my mother,' chirped Vasilisa through a beaming smile.

'Blessing?!' screeched the Yaga. 'Blessing?! In that case, get out! I don't want any blessings in my house. C'mon, out, out! It's high time you left, young one,' she said now hustling Vasilisa towards the door and out into the darkness of the forest. It was night-time now.

As the Yaga hurried the young girl down the garden path, she took one of the skulls, whose fiery eyes were now ablaze, from her white picket fence made of thigh bones, put it on a stick, and gave it to Vasilisa.

'Here! Take this home with you and use it to light the fire for your stepfamily. Don't say another word. Just be on your way.'

Just as Vasilisa was about to thank the Yaga, the doll, jumped up and down again, warning her not to. Heeding its advice, Vasilisa took the fire and ran home through the dark forest, her little doll guiding her and the light from the skull's eyes illuminating her path.

As she ran, the skull grew heavier and its light more eerie, both of which frightened Vasilisa. Nearing home, she wondered if she should throw it away when, all of a sudden, the skull spoke to her telling her to be calm and that, when she got home, she must give it to her stepmother.

Meantime, the stepmother and her daughters, whose house had been plunged into darkness ever since Vasilisa left, saw a strange glow in the forest which seemed to be heading towards their house. Soon, they saw that it was Vasilisa and, for the first time, ran out to greet her in a friendly way such was their gratitude for the light.

The stepmother told Vasilisa they'd had difficulty lighting any fires or lights since she'd been gone. However hard they'd tried, they'd always gone out. On hearing this Vasilisa felt triumphant for she had survived her dangerous journey, looked the Yaga straight in the eye, and brought the fire home.

'Perhaps your fire won't go out,' said the stepmother to Vasilisa, who took the skull on a stick from her.

The skull watched the stepmother and her daughters closely – so closely, in fact, it was able to see right through them and all the way down into the rotted roots of their souls. Aware their every move was being watched, they tried to hide from the unceasing stare of the skull, but it continued to burn holes through them. The following morning, when Vasilisa came downstairs, she found the wicked trio had been burnt to ashes.

The story continues, but we'll leave it there.

On first reading this fairytale, although familiar with both stories, I didn't see the similarities between Persephone and Vasilisa; Vasilisa and Cinderella, yes – but not Persephone. It was Marie-Louise von Franz whose psychological exploration of the Baba Yaga in this tale alerted me to the Persephone-Vasilisa connection:

She is full of the powers of destruction, of desolation, and of chaos, but at the same time is a helpful figure. Viewed historically, she probably represents the surviving image of the late antique Greek Hekate, the queen of the underworld. In Hellenistic times this goddess of Hades became more and more identified with the Neoplatonic world soul, and as such she became the feminine spirit of the universe, a goddess of nature and of life as well of death, who was even praised as Soteira, the feminine saviour. Her daughter was Persephone, with whom she was secretly identical. This throws a light on the heroine of our story, who is called Vasilisa. This is identical with the Greek Bassilissa, which means queen and which was one of the titles of Persephone. Russian fairy tales have been deeply influenced from the south by the late Greek civilisation, and thus we have in Baba Yaga and Vasilisa really a survival of the great cosmic goddesses Hekate and Persephone.

– The Feminine in Fairytales

The idea of the Baba Yaga being a survival of Hecate is further echoed by Jung who says of Hecate, 'she is sometimes shown riding a horse, and in the Hesiod she is counted the patron saint of riders.'

In the Greek pantheon, Kore/Persephone, Demeter, and Hecate represent the three aspects, or faces of the same chthonic goddess: maiden, mother, crone. They also represent the three phases of the moon: waxing, full, and waning. What I've always found interesting about the Persephone myth was why Hecate, despite hearing Kore's cries when she was dragged off, made no attempt to help her. She later helped Demeter look for her, but at the moment she was being dragged off, she remained curiously quiet.

This motif, of a Crone-like figure appearing somewhat unhelpful, also appears in another fairytale – the Handless Maiden. In one variation of that story the Handless Maiden was in a forest with her two babies, one tucked under each arm as she had no hands with which to hold them. After wandering for many hours, she finally stopped to rest so she could drink some water and give some to her babies. But on finding a source of water she couldn't drink any as it would mean her dropping her babies. By this time both were crying from thirst and the Maiden was also near exhaustion.

Just then, she saw an old woman stood nearby and appealed to her for help. But the woman did nothing, saying only, 'Get it yourself.'

To which the Handless Maiden said, 'You don't understand, I have no hands. I can't get it myself because if I reach down, I'll drop my babies. Please, you have to help me.'

Unmoved, the old woman said once more, 'Get it yourself.'

Exasperated, the Handless Maiden lowered her mouth towards the water but, on doing so, her worst nightmare was realised when *both* her babies fell into the water. Now desperate, she cried out to the old woman once more. But just as before, she remained unmoved simply saying, 'Get them yourself.'

'But I can't,' cried the Handless Maiden, 'I have no hands!'

'Then plunge in your stumps,' said the old woman.

Having no other choice, the Handless Maiden plunged her stumps into the water to save her babies. To her surprise, as she drew her arms out of the water, she found her stumps had been replaced with hands – hands with which she saved her babies.

When the Handless Maiden looked up to thank the old woman, however, she was nowhere to be seen...

On first glance it may seem these mysterious old women are being rather mean-spirited in their refusal to help the various 'damsels-in-distress.' But these Crone figures have been initiated into the life-death-rebirth mysteries of the deep feminine. So whereas a Too-Good Mother, as Estés calls her, would rush over and help her little girl, the wise old Crone knows it's better to stand back, watch, let the young maiden figure it out for herself, and allow her to reconnect with her own innate instincts and intuitions. In the case of the Handless Maiden, she must first learn to 'plunge in her stumps' so she can discover, for herself, that she has hands of her own. In short, she's encouraging the maiden to 'get a grip' of her own life.

If Demeter would have been near the scene of Kore's abduction into the Underworld, you can bet she would have fought the mother of all battles to stop her little girl being dragged off. But, like the Crone who refused to help the Handless Maiden, Hecate also knew that if Kore was to become a mature woman – a woman who is one-in-herself, able to stand in her own power – she'd have to be initiated into the mysteries of the Underworld.

Unlike the Too-Good Mother (aka Demeter) who can be sentimental and over-protective, the Crone retains a level of discernment and is less attached. That doesn't mean to say she doesn't love – she does. Only difference is, her love is fierce, instinctual, and not sentimental.

Like a wolf, she's not afraid to bare her teeth to her cubs when necessary, scare them a little, teach them how to fend for themselves rather than them getting too cosy and overly reliant on her.

From a psychological perspective this Crone wields a sharp Sword of Discernment – also known as the Logos-Cutter – with which she cuts to the chase, cuts through the crap, cuts to the heart of the matter. Of this crap-cutting Crone figure, Marion Woodman remarks, 'To the Crone, detachment is not indifference. It means she has lived, and suffered, can draw back, and see with her heart.' One thing's for sure, she won't mollycoddle you.

This sharp Sword of Discernment the Crone carries appears in alchemical symbolism too, where it shows up as *separatio*. *Separatio* symbolism, as you've probably guessed, is all about separating one thing from another. It also indicates the first stage of the initiation process I mentioned earlier: separation, initiation, return. Again, to quote Woodman, 'The Crone has seen enough to be able to separate irrelevance from essence. She has neither time nor energy to waste on superficialities.'

All the stories I've shared, so far, have an element of *separatio* symbolism. In the case of Vasilisa, she's first separated from her mother when she dies. Next, she's separated from her stepfamily when they send her off into the forest to face the Baba Yaga. It shows up when the Yaga asks her to separate out the mildewed corn from the good seeds and, again, when she asks her to separate the poppy seeds out from the dirt. Finally, for good measure, she's separated from the Yaga when she's kicked out and sent home again. In the myth of Kore-Demeter, Kore is separated from her mother when Hades abducts her into the Underworld. Fine-tuning – that's what this is all about.

A similar motif appears in the myth of *Psyche and Eros*. In the myth, Psyche, a mortal, has married Eros, except she doesn't know he's a god. He's warned her never to look upon him at night. If she does she'll never see him again. As far as their relationship's concerned he'd much rather keep her in the dark.

Psyche, however, has two older sisters who, jealous of the fortunate circumstances into which their youngest sister has married, tell her she's married a beast who is plotting to kill and eat her. Between them they hatch a plot in which they convince her to kill him first. One night she takes a knife and lights an oil lamp with which to look upon the beast she believes is her husband. When she looks down at her lover, however, she finds not a beast, but a god. When she accidentally drops some of the hot oil on Eros, he immediately flies off leaving Psyche heartbroken.

As you can imagine, it doesn't get much worse than being left by the god of love. Now alone and completely in the dark, she's about to drown herself in a moment of suicidal despair when the goat-footed god, Pan (well, well, look who it is...), talks her out of it and encourages her to face the issue head-on and set about winning Eros back. But in order to do this it means she must go and see her mother-in-law, Aphrodite, face-to-face.

Aphrodite, *furious* at what she believes has been Psyche's attempt to steal her thunder (people have been worshipping Psyche and neglecting Aphrodite's temples), tortures the girl with her handmaidens, Trouble and Sorrow, then sets Psyche a series of seemingly impossible tasks to complete – the first of which involves her separating and sorting out a giant pile of seeds. If she doesn't, she'll die. After dissolving into a wailing, flailing heap of despair, a colony of ants mysteriously appear and help her – much like the little doll who helps Vasilisa.

This image of seed-sorting also shows up in versions of Cinderella where her stepmother leaves her a pile of lentils to sort out from ashes. In her case two white turtle doves appear, followed by all the birds in the sky, to help pick the lentils from out of the ashes.

During the three years which marked my *nigredo*, like Vasilisa, I spent my time cut off from the world, deep in the heart of the Forest of Symbols, deep in introversion, seed-sorting, separating this from that, what mattered from what didn't. I wouldn't know it then but this period marked the beginning of a Great Round of Transformation that would take ten years to come full circle.

Throughout that time I existed in a liminal state of betwixt and between – no longer in my old life, but not yet in my new one. Now living alone, I'd been separated from my former existence but had no idea of what my new life might entail. I could fully empathise with Psyche wanting to throw in the towel when confronted with such an overwhelming task. Her initial attempt to drown herself may seem like something of a cop-out. But we might look at this symbolism from another perspective: as being temporarily overcome by the waters of the unconscious – *dissolutio*.

Like Psyche, I seemed to spend most of my time in one helpless heap of despair or another. When I wasn't crying I was in the bath. When I wasn't in the bath I was in bed. Overwhelmed, I just gave up most of the time. I took vegging to a whole new level. But this giving up and vegging out was necessary. This is the moment when an addict in a twelve-step programme recognises they are powerless and surrenders themselves to a 'power greater than themselves.'

Like Vasilisa, Psyche, and Cinderella, the task they face is not one their ego consciousness can face by itself. They consciously surrender and 'turn their lives and will over to God' - and it's at this point Vasilisa's doll, Psyche's ants, and Cinderella's birds all take over. Each of these motifs symbolise those aspects of the psyche which go about dismantling our old lives beneath the surface level of consciousness. During this period, there's little our egos can *do* - rather, the emphasis is on *being*. We have to wait and see or, as in my case, make like rotting vegetation and 'veg out.' The biological counterpart of this act is the repeated division of a single fertilised egg during pregnancy, which is why this motif of 'seed-sorting' is commonly associated with the feminine.

Although the tasks these women set the young maidens may seem harsh and somewhat severe (*severe* sharing its etymological roots with *separate*), this separation is a necessary stage for growth and development. Things must be rent asunder so they can be put back together in a new way. In my own life I had to undergo a *separatio* from my mum in order to figure out who I was. One of the issues I realised when the fog of my *nigredo* rolled in and took up residence was I couldn't tell where she ended and I began. Of this symbiotic state, Woodman remarks:

> **The extent to which mother and child believe they belong to each other destroys psychic growth. At the deepest levels, most children know they do not 'belong' to their parents; they feel their sense of unity with all life. In a world in which people possess each other, however, not to belong makes the child feel like an outsider. While the resultant 'orphan' psychology may be a source of fearful anxiety, in reality it is an affirmation, from the beginning, of spiritual freedom.**

> **– *The Pregnant Virgin***

Despite being in my mid-twenties and living away from home I still hadn't made the cut. The umbilical cord may have been cut at birth, but the psychic umbilical cord was still very much intact and now it was beginning to feel it had caught around my neck. It was time for me to break free of the too-tight swaddling blanket. Of this symbiotic state, Edward Edinger remarks, 'to the extent that the opposites remain unconscious and unseparated, one lives in a state of *participation mystique* which means that one identifies with one side of a pair of opposites and projects its contrary as an enemy.' And this is exactly what happened with me.

I rebelled against mum, made an enemy of her and everything else which symbolised Mother - all actions of the uninitiated girl, the Kore. I got secretive, drew a protective arm around my life, and did things by myself, for myself without ever telling her. I'd spin elaborate yarns to cover my tracks so she didn't know what I was up to. I wanted to strike out, see what happened when I lived life on my own terms. Sure I'd make mistakes, but at least they'd be *my* mistakes. I had to stop caring about her opinions, her approval. I'd played at being her little girl – 'doll' was my childhood nickname – too long. I now realised I was protecting an outdated image of myself – namely, an innocent one. But this innocent little girl act was stifling me and, in particular, my burgeoning sexuality.

One telling moment came when I was about twenty-two. I had an office at work – the first time in my life I'd ever had a private space of my own. I also had a Polaroid camera which, let me tell you, was a lot of fun. One afternoon, when I knew I'd be undisturbed, I decided to explore my sexuality by taking some racy photos of myself. I loaded up my lips with a scarlet red lipstick and struck several sexy, sultry poses in nothing but my black underwear. A one woman romp, I had a whale of a time. I loved seeing myself in that way, spilling over like the Trevi Fountain, splashing my sensuality up the walls. I kept most for myself, gave one to a guy I was seeing at the time, and binned one I didn't really like – or so I thought.

Later that evening I heard mum *bellowing* my name, summoning me up the stairs where I found her, on the upstairs landing, holding the photo in her hand, asking, 'What's *this?*' I thought I'd screwed it up and hid it at the bottom of the waste bin. Not well enough, it seemed.

To my mind I hadn't done anything wrong, but she went to town on me. I was now a dirty bitch, a slut, 'just like all the rest of them.' She wanted to wash her hands of me. The loathing, contempt, and scorn with which she attacked me was off the scale. I put my sexuality 'in the bag' that day. It would be another thirteen years before I'd get it out again.

In the tale of Vasilisa, her mother dies leaving her alone with her father. I consciously had to sever ties with my mum. But if you don't have a mother – say she's died, you never knew her, or you just weren't particularly close to her – don't for a minute think you're free of the all-pervasive power of the archetypal Mother; she also shows up in relationships where's she's just as capable of stifling sexuality and, in fact, often does as Woodman reminds us here:

> **Take, for example, the man who projects Great Mother onto his wife. He tends to take her unconditional love and service for granted, because on some level he is a child and mother is always there. Mother in that situation has no personal identity. She is merely an archetypal caretaker. Like the daughter unconsciously bound to her father, he is tied to his mother-mate by an umbilical lifeline that he trusts she will not cut. At the**

same time his childishness blinds him to his own shadow who fears, perhaps even hates, the woman he is bound to.

It is not uncommon for such a man to have an ongoing affair with another woman and yet to be genuinely shocked when his wife says, 'Choose between us.' He may claim his love for one enhances his love for the other. He loves them in different ways. He may blame his wife for not activating his sexuality. If he looks at his dreams, however, he may realise that part of him craves the protection and comfort of mother, and another part lusts for the mistress with whom he has contacted the life force. If he and his wife are committed to consciousness, both may become aware of the overbearing mother within themselves; then, through the relationship, they may find the liberated virgin who brings lust and love together.

– The Ravaged Bridegroom

Once I became aware of this pattern I saw it *everywhere*. The number of son-lovers hanging off the teats of their mother-mates is staggering. A male friend once shared something with me his wife said: 'I just want to look after my two boys.' She had a teenage son from a previous relationship. Her husband – my friend – however, was in his mid-thirties. He seemed oblivious of what she'd said. I hadn't yet been introduced to depth psychology but, on hearing this, I knew there was something very, very wrong. *I just want to look after my two boys?* It made me shudder. But despite admitting he was sexually unsatisfied, he just couldn't leave her – such is the power of unconditional Mother love.

The Crone who has been consciously initiated into the life-death-rebirth mysteries, however, won't tolerate this unconscious, ouroboric state of existence. She won't tolerate it between a symbiotic maiden-mother dyad (Kore-Demeter) and she won't tolerate it between women and their son-lovers, or women and their daddy-lovers either. This is probably why she's seen as threatening, destructive, deadly even, as she goes about wielding her Sword of Discernment, separating this from that, cutting cords here, there, and everywhere.

I mentioned the Yaga had seen all there was, is, and ever will be; this is because she stands at the beginning, middle, and end of time. In one of her three-faceted forms she may be imagined as *Atropos*, one of the three sisters of Fate also known as the *Moirai*. In Greek mythology, the Fates were *Clotho*, who was believed to have spun the thread of a mortal's life; the second sister was *Lachesis*, who measured its length; finally was *Atropos* who ended the life by cutting the thread with her 'abhorred shears' – *separatio*. Atropos's Roman equivalent was *Morta* – the goddess of death – and from whose name we get such words as morgue and mortuary.

In another of her forms, she stands at the beginning of life as midwife to newborns – this time as Artemis: Greek goddess of the hunt and moon. Cast your mind back to the Kore-Demeter myth. We could excuse Hecate for not helping Kore when she was being dragged off by Hades as she was elsewhere and only heard her cries. But Kore was playing with Artemis and Athena. Now, doesn't it strike you as a little odd that they were both nearby and yet neither of them did anything to help her? It did me. Particularly as Artemis is also considered the feminist of the Greek pantheon as she always surrounded herself with nymph-companions.

Artemis, however, was also considered the goddess of childbirth and midwifery for, as soon as she was born, she immediately helped her mother, Leto, birth her twin brother, Apollo, in what turned out to be a nine-day delivery. But the connection between Artemis-Hecate-Yaga and Persephone-Vasilisa becomes all the more clear when we read the following by M. Esther Harding:

> Torches, candles, and fires are burned in honour of the moon and are used as fertilising magic, being carried, for example, round the newly seeded fields to aid the germination of the grain, just as Hecate's torches were carried around the freshly sown fields, long ago in Greece, to promote their fertility ... there is another primitive myth, which states that an old woman, probably the moon herself, who is often called the Old Woman, made the first fire by rubbing her genitals ... Thus the goddess was, as it were, the flame latent in the bundle, waiting to be brought to life again by certain rituals. In Italy they named her Diviana, which means The Goddess, a name that is more familiar to us in its shortened form of Diana. For Diana, the Huntress, was none other than the Moon Goddess, Mother of all animals. She is shown in her statues crowned with the crescent and carrying a raised torch. The Latin word for torch or candle is vesta, and Diana was also known as Vesta. In her temple a perpetual fire was kept burning and her chief festival was called the Festival of Candles or of Torches.

– Women's Mysteries

Both Artemis (who the Romans called Diana) and Hecate are moon goddesses. One stands at the beginning of life as symbolised by the waxing crescent moon; the other stands at the end of life as the waning crescent moon. Demeter, as mother, is symbolised by the full moon.

When Kore was abducted into the Underworld, both Artemis and Hecate understood the necessity of her abduction as essential to her growth from the nameless maiden (Kore) to Persephone, Queen of the Underworld.

In the story of Vasilisa we can see Yaga handing the torch to her youngest self so she might be deeper initiated into life. After her stay at the Yaga's hut, she is not the same naïve girl she was when she left her stepfamily. She has a touch of the Yaga's fire about her as symbolised by the lighted skull she now carries. As she heads back through the forest, torch in hand, she is almost identical to Artemis, goddess of the hunt, who also carried a raised torch. Like the virgin goddess, Artemis, Vasilisa is now becoming one-in-herself.

Another way we might imagine the torch is as a symbol of consciousness that has been wrested from having spent time in the dark of the Underworld. This 'phosphorescent wisdom,' a fruit from the Forest of Symbols, means she now sees more wholly than she did before. Yes, she's still a sweet girl with a kind heart, but she can now see in the dark. No longer easily fooled, she can see straight through the pretence of her stepfamily's act. This depth of sight can intimidate those not acquainted with the life-death-rebirth mysteries.

From the soul's perspective, we're not just born once when the umbilical cord is cut and we're separated from our mothers. As we continue through life we experience many psychic deaths and rebirths. This is how it should be. Death is only feared by those who are unacquainted with the life-death-rebirth mysteries. Those who have consciously surrendered to the fires of transformation, not just once, but again and again as Hecate has – and as Vasilisa is now beginning to – recognise the necessity of such initiations.

The Crone understands that life is not the opposite of death – *birth* is the opposite of death (or, rather its counterpart). Life encompasses both birth *and* death – something many would do well to remember. This is why the virgin goddess Artemis stands at the beginning of life as the goddess of midwifery and Hecate, who is the older, wiser version of Artemis, stands at the other end as goddess of crossroads. Interestingly, Jung says there is a Hecate Aphrodisias whose symbols are the key, the whip, the dagger, and the torch.

As goddess of the crossroads, she is present whenever we find ourselves having to choose between this path and that; between our wife and our mistress; between our boring job and our dreams. Which road will we take? Will we take the road less travelled or will we stick to the path we've always known? Will we choose life or death? Will we walk willingly or be dragged? As the Crone has spent her life cutting away what no longer matters, consciously submitting to the fires of transformation, surrendering to soul, she doesn't seek power over you, to control or manipulate you. Neither does she have the will nor the wherewithal to play games. You want the truth? Speak to an initiated Crone.

And don't for a minute think that because someone is older that they're necessarily wiser. Age alone does not an elder make. The culture is filled with men and women in their fifties, sixties, and seventies who, psychologically speaking, remain stuck at the level of Kore (*puella aeterna*) and Peter Pan (*puer aeterna*) in the negative sense (every archetype has a positive and a negative side, after all). Little boys and girls who refuse to grow up, looking for mummy, in one form or another, to rescue them from the apathy of themselves, to take a hold of their life for them, to make everything better – *Please mummy because I can't do it for myself!* Arrested in their development they fear dying into life.

The Crone, however, is an initiated elder who, with her discriminating, unsentimental Sword of Discernment has stood at crossroad after crossroad after crossroad in her own life. Her life is now surrendered to soul. No longer afraid of death, she's even made her home there as evidenced by the skull and bone picket fence surrounding the Yaga's hut. Although this may seem morbid, by repeatedly dying into life she's shown her willingness to live no matter the consequences. She's not afraid to let it all go, give it all up, throw it all out. By repeatedly surrendering to the life-death-rebirth mysteries, she's said *yes* to life with all her heart and both her feet. Throwing herself like seed, she is like the self-germinating virgin forest in which she's often found: untrammelled, one-in-herself, empowered in her aloneness.

* * *

As fate would have it, after writing the last paragraph I stopped to have a coffee and a chat with my aunt – one of the few initiated Crones I'm fortunate enough to know. I call her the 'don' of the family as she contains it, keeps it together – not because she necessarily wants to, but because her energy and presence is such that it couldn't be any other way. Should there be any trouble or disputes in the family you can guarantee it'll end up at her door.

To many outsiders my aunt is in intimidating figure. Growing up, I watched as the truths she uttered would lacerate anyone who tried it on with her or any of her loved ones. She's always had an uncanny ability to see straight through people, call them out on their hypocrisy and game playing, reducing many a grown man and woman to tears in the process. Not that this has ever bothered her. She couldn't care less whether you like her or not. She's not interested in being liked. She is the way she is because that *is* who she is – one-in-herself. Now seventy-one, I can see how she's matured from an archetypal Artemis into a magnificent Crone of a Hecate.

Despite having the names Dorcas and Morgana lined up as possible names for me, as soon as she heard me roaring my way down her birth canal, mum immediately named me after her sister instead. Growing up, I didn't think I was the least bit like my aunt. Even when I first came across the Greek goddess archetypes Artemis was the last figure I'd have identified with. I was Kore through and through and I knew it.

As a child, though, it was my aunt who took me out with her on 'adventures.' Together we roamed far and wide, swimming, walking, going to the gym. She thought it was important I get out and see more of the world. Today I see she was wielding a sword, cutting me out of what she believed was a too-tight swaddling cloth, nurturing my wildish instincts.

So we were stood in the kitchen when she showed me a newspaper headline highlighting the 'big freeze' the UK is experiencing as I write.

'Big freeze? D'you know,' she said waving the newspaper about in exasperation, 'I watched a programme the other day on the winter of '63. Now *that* was a winter. Except, I don't really remember it being that bad; probably because everyone mucked in together and just got on with it – none of this namby-pamby crap like today. I mean, the schools won't even let the kids play out in the snow in case they throw snowballs and hurt one another. What's *that* about? No wonder they're all bleedin' mard. Life's tough – deal with it.'

I grabbed a pen, told her to hold that thought.

'Why, what are you up to?' she asked.

'Writing,' I answered.

'And I tell you what else,' she went on, now on a roll, 'I also read the other day that the kids in school are refusing to drink milk. They want sugary drinks instead. Now, you tell me – whose fault is that? I'll tell ya whose – their parents. They're not eating fruit either. No wonder they're all bleedin' fat. Next thing you know, they're having these gastric band operations.'

Scribbling this down, I thanked her, kissed her on the forehead, and scuttled straight back to my laptop.

That's the Crone, right there, cutting through the too-tight cloth that swaddles our culture. As she spoke I got a picture of Demeter not letting her little girl play out in case she hurt herself. From an archetypal perspective, there's no difference between this and our culture's preoccupation with stopping kids playing out in case they cop for an ice-laden snowball in the chops – a theme echoed in the Mother Goose rhyme:

73

'Mother may I go out to swim?'
'Yes, my darling daughter.
Hang your clothes on a hickory limb,
But don't go near the water.'

The smothering, over-protective Mother (an archetype known as the Terrible Mother – every archetype having both a positive and negative aspect) who wraps our scaffolding poles in foam sleeves in case someone walks into them and hurts themselves can, if we're not careful, do more harm than good. In its attempt to protect us from life's hard knocks it over-softens and makes wimps out of all of us.

Others, meantime, are drowning in materialism (materialism, *mater*, mother), buying all they can, padding out their lives, padding out their comfy, cosy nests with more and more stuff. They're being swallowed up, devoured by another aspect of the Terrible Mother. *Make yourself at home*, she whispers to people as they mindlessly wander around shopping malls, hand in hand, looking for more stuff to buy. *Settle down. You don't want to go out into the big bad world. Stay here with me where it's nice and warm. Here, have something to eat...* It's like the author Chuck Palahniuk says, 'The things you own end up owning you. It's only after you lose everything that you're free to do anything.' And it's this willingness to lose everything that the Crone stands for.

Yet others are over-filling their faces (food being another form of matter), padding out their bodies. But the sweetness they seek in the form of sugary drinks and chocolate etc. is a poor substitute for the sweetness of the mother's nourishment they really want and which they desperately lack. So long as our culture remains split off from matter in a positive sense we, both men and women, lose touch with the sweetness inherent in our bodies.

When we don't genuinely cherish our own bodies we can't provide our children with what it is they need to, in turn, nurture a positive relationship with their own matter; in other words, so long as we remain unable to mother ourselves, mother our bodies in a positive, life-affirming sense, our children don't stand a chance either. And just to be clear, I'm talking about an archetype here. I'm not blaming anyone and I'm certainly not launching an attack on mothers or men who provide maternal care to dependants.

I've known many men and women who lacked this nourishing, cherishing relationship with their parents and, so, compensated for this loss by seeking solace in food (food as matter, *mater*, mother). As my aunt has always said, 'What baby see, baby do.' So even if a child's caregivers may have appeared to take care of themselves if, deep down, they loathed their own bodies, this will be felt and echoed by the child in the form of the relationship they themselves will later go on to have with their own bodies.

Like my aunt says, before you know it they're drowning in matter (fat) and the only way they can be freed is by the surgeon's knife. Whereas once upon a time the hero fought against and slayed the dragon (symbolic of the Terrible Mother) with his sword (*separatio*) that guarded the treasure hard to attain, the dragon we modern folk face is this excess of materialism in whatever form it shows up: be it too much food, the accumulation of more and more stuff, or too-fat bodies which weigh us down and hold us back.

But if there were more initiated Crone figures in our culture, it wouldn't get that far. My aunt is the first to step in and say something if she thinks my mum is buying too many sweet, sugar-laden foods. ('You can stop that crap, right now,' she'll say. 'Don't think you'll be making a habit out of that. We're not gonna get fat.') The Crone, in the positive sense of the archetype has been lost to us in the West, driven underground, despised, and denigrated. But she is still very much alive and well in myths and in other cultures – as I discovered in India.

It's easy with folktales and suchlike, to dismiss them, say they're not real, that they're just a figment of the imagination. But on arrival in India I discovered there's more truth to these myths than one might imagine – especially when, on stumbling out of the airport and into the disorienting maelstrom that is Delhi, I came face-to-face with the dark-faced sister of the Baba Yaga – *Kali*. Two words summed up my reaction to my Meeting with the Goddess in her dark-faced aspect: *Holy. Fuck.*

As black as night (often blue-black), Kali, like the Yaga, has an affinity for skulls, wearing, as she does, a necklace made of fifty human heads.

In common with the Yaga, Kali, too, has a penchant for hands. In fact she has an entire girdle made out of them (is it wrong to say a part of me rather likes the sound of that?). She's also often seen with four arms (sometimes, two, six, or eight). Of these many hands, Ajit Mookerjee in his book, *Kali*, says 'hands are the principal instruments of work and so signify the action of karma or accumulated deeds, constantly reminding us that ultimate freedom is to be attained as the fruit of karmic action.' In other words, you reap what you sow – so plunge in your stumps and make the most of what you have, right here, right now.

With one of her other four hands she's often seen holding a severed head and a sword in one of the others with which, as Mookerjee says, she 'cuts the thread of bondage' in much the same way the Crone cuts through the too-tight swaddling cloth and Atropos/Morta cuts the thread of life. As I've said, these ladies don't mince their words or their actions as Mookerjee goes on to tell us:

In her absolute, primordial nakedness she is free from all covering of illusion. She is Nature, stripped of all 'clothes.' She

gives birth to the cosmos parthenogenetically, as she contains
the male principle within herself ... Her three eyes indicate the
past, present, and future. Her white teeth, symbolic of sattva,
the translucent intelligence stuff, hold back her lolling tongue
which is red, representing rajas, the activating quality of nature
leading downwards to tamas, inertia ... In this form she is
changeless, limitless primordial power, acting in the great
drama, awakening the unmanifest Siva beneath her feet.'

– Kali

Both goddesses also have the colours red, black, and white in common.
In medieval alchemy these colours parallel the alchemical stages of *nigredo*
(blackening), *albedo* (whitening), and *rubedo* (reddening). One way we may
look at these colours is as symbolising the cyclic life-death-rebirth
mysteries.

Beginning with black we learn from *The Book of Symbols* that:

Black envelops and swallows, is cave and abyss, the holes of
space and the bowels of the earth, night, melancholy, and death.
Black is foulness, decay and dirt. But the black dirt can be the
soil itself, the fertile covering of the earth from which life arises.
Black encompasses the terrors and beauties of the underworld
and its tenebrous precincts of healing and initiation. The 'black'
deities are ambiguous, chthonic and fateful. The dark ground
of Kali, the Black One, absorbs the blood of sacrifice and
nature's slaughter and nurtures the seeds of return. Black Mary,
Isis, Persephone, Artemis, Hecate possess the black womb of
uncanny darkness and new moon.

From the same book of white we learn:

On the one hand white was childlike naivety, unawareness,
immaturity and a lack of experience. One might need to sacrifice
such whiteness and tincture one's matter with substance and
individuality. On the other hand, white represented the ash or
salt of bitter suffering and hard-won wisdom, and the white hair
of the knowing old man or crone ... Some deemed the albedo
the attainment of the goal. Others believed the opus reached
fulfilment only when dawn turned into the ruby brilliance of
sunrise, the roundness of an integrated, creatively embodied life.

And finally of red we learn:

Symbolically, red is the colour of life. Red attracts us, conveying vitality, warmth, excitement, passion, but also warns of danger, calls for attention, says 'stop!' In China, as well as in Stone Age Europe, red pigment was buried with the bones of the dead for renewal of life. The colour red stands at the centre of our images of libido – life energy – whether sexual passion or aggression and rage. The slinky red dress, the scarlet-robed Whore of Babylon, the Scarlet Letter (of adultery), the red hearts on valentines, 'red-light district,' all strike the sexual chord. But we also 'see red' when we are enraged and connect the 'red planet' Mars with the god of war.

It's worth studying the symbolism associated with these colours as, not only do they appear in numerous myths, but they also appear in the nightly dreams of modern-day individuals. Having said that, it's well worth studying the symbolism associated with all colours as dreams often employ them in various, imaginative ways. The thing about these particular colours – from my experience anyway – is they often provide us with an insight into the psyche's movements. When we're aware of the symbolism behind such colours, we're able to catch sight of what might be occurring within our psyches.

In sharing those particular excerpts from *The Book of Symbols* (a book I highly recommend), I wanted to highlight how both the Baba Yaga and Kali incorporate the cycle of life-death-rebirth within their mysteries. You may recall the Yaga's three horseman symbolising her Bright Dawn, her Red Sun, and her Black Night; colours which are reflected in Kali's black skin, her white teeth, and her red lolling tongue. Like the Yaga and Artemis-Hecate, Kali simultaneously stands at the beginning and end of time as both womb and tomb.

That 'she gives birth to the cosmos parthenogenetically,' also reflects her virgin state, her one-in-herself fruitfulness. This sentiment is echoed by author Erich Neumann when he says:

The Great Mother is a virgin, too, in a sense other than that intended by the patriarchate, which later misunderstood her as the symbol of chastity. Precisely in virtue of her fruitfulness, she is a virgin, that is, unrelated and not dependent upon any man. In Sanskrit, 'independent woman' is a synonym for a harlot. Hence the woman who is unattached to a man is not only a universal feminine type but a sacral type in antiquity.

– *The Great Mother*

77

Though I may not have known much about Kali prior to my visit, you need only walk down the street in India to see, feel, hear, and smell the presence of this chthonic goddess everywhere. India, like Kali, is a paradox whose streets teem with an endless, relentless abundance of life, pouring forth in a never-ending stream, threatening to overwhelm you should you stop still long enough.

On the other hand, suffusing the air you breathe is the stomach-wrenching, suffocating scent of death whose presence is witnessed in the animal carcasses rotting by the road, the haunting, emaciated faces of abject poverty reminiscent of the walking dead, and the ashes of bodies on funeral pyres drifting by on the breeze which, you suddenly realise, you've just got a bit of in your mouth. Life and death, together, in your face – deal with it.

Being in India made me realise just how little we in the West know about death; how we're afraid of it, shut it away, and pretend it doesn't exist. Not that I had any romantic delusions of India to begin with. It had never particularly appealed to me unlike, say, the Middle East, with which I've always felt a more soul-stirring resonance. I knew right from the get-go the place would be tough going. But never had I been among a culture in which life and death sit side-by-side so openly.

So when India asked me 'Are you here of your own free will or by compulsion?' I stood my ground and scrambled for an answer lest she add my skull to her necklace. *I'm here because I want to be and because something compelled me.* Because that was the truth – no-one had made me go and, yet, I'd also been intrigued by Tantra (thanks to Osho's books), even if I'd long since shelved that idea.

But that 'both/and' answer as opposed to an 'either/or' answer is the correct one for it is 'double-minded,' reflecting the mysteries of both the Baba Yaga and Kali. So when I looked this wild Life-Death goddess, that was India, straight in the eye, accepted her exactly as she was without judgement and without sentimentality, she shared with me her wisdom. I may have been reeling from culture shock but I remained composed. And when she ripped my nicey-nicey idea of myself from me, turned it on its head, and initiated me into my deeper, instinctual nature, I held my nerve.

It wasn't until I settled into her rhythms that I realised I absolutely had to be there. In the fiery crucible of the Indian goddess was forged the beginnings of a less naïve woman. She put starch in my shirt, forced me to stand up straight, take care of myself. But she also accepted me for who I was, celebrated my body, took me into her arms, and told me I was beautiful exactly as I was.

In an essay in *Tantra in Practice*, June McDaniel interviews a priest who worships Kali and meditates upon her. One of the priest's practices involves feeding skulls. Of these skulls McDaniel says:

Skulls are widely used in Bengali folk Tantra. They empower buildings and grounds, like the relics in early and medieval churches. They are buried in temples, under the altar or in a corner, and they turn the building into sacred ground. They are also buried at the foot of sacred trees, and they make ordinary ground into an empowered meditation seat.

Although skulls and images of death are normally inauspicious in Hinduism, certain skulls bring good luck and fortune in meditation. Skulls give protective energy (sákti) and support the sadhu in his efforts. They are often painted red, to show that they are alive and auspicious, and to protect them from mould and the Bengali weather. They are ironic images, which represent death yet encourage the spiritual rebirth of the holy man or sadhu. Skulls are not old bones, but relics that mediate the supernatural world, calling down the goddess Kali to help the practitioner. Skulls are not really dead but alive, companions and friends of the sadhus.

- Interviews with a Tantric Kali Priest:
Feeding Skulls in the Town of Sacrifice

Like the skulls who draw down the protective, feminine energy of sákti (Sanskrit for *power*) in order to support the sadhu's efforts, I imagined the skull given Vasilisa by the Yaga as representative of a similar energy. The skulls being painted red also called to mind the red pigment being buried with the bones of the dead in China and Stone Age Europe to ensure the renewal of life - in other words, a rebirth (*rubedo*).

McDaniel goes on to share the transcript of an interview she has with the priest himself, called Tapan Goswami, who tells her:

There are many forms of Tantric sadhana. There are three major styles (bhavas): the sattvika, rajasika and tamasika bhavas. The sattvika bhava is devotion (bhakti), and that is the best path to follow. The tamasika bhava can give one the presence of the Goddess, but it does not last long. It stays for a little while, and then it ceases. It is very brief, and very fickle. Devotion lasts longer. One cannot really get close to the Goddess without devotional love. *Only bhakti justifies Tantra.* [Italics mine.]

There it was - the reason I'd gone to India. I'd even left a clue for myself in my first book by way of a chapter I'd called *Bhakti* in which I wrote of the devotional practice I'd spontaneously engaged in during my time there. In Hinduism, bhakti, a movement founded in Tamil Nadu - the same place our folktale *The Prostitute and the Pearls of Wisdom* comes from – emphasises the mutual emotional attachment and love of a devotee toward a personal god and of the god for the devotee. The word bhakti comes from the Sanskrit root *bhaj*, meaning to 'share' or 'participate.'

It may also help to further clarify the priest's comments by sharing something Jung says about 'the loving and the terrible mother,' Kali. He says 'in Sankhya philosophy, there are three fundamental attributes – *sattva*, *rajas*, *tamas*: goodness, passion, and darkness. These are three essential aspects of the mother: her cherishing and nourishing goodness, her orgiastic emotionality, and her Stygian depths.' ('Stygian' – River Styx in the Underworld.) This neatly sums up my experience of Kali: in Delhi and Varanasi, I'd been confronted with her dark and hellish Stygian depths, no doubt about it. But in Goa, I met her cherishing, nourishing aspect.

Prior to my visit, I'd never considered myself a religious person. I'd never engaged in any spiritual or religious practices. I wasn't raised in a religion. Mum believed if I wanted to follow a religious path then that was a decision I should make for myself and not be one thrust upon me. After being attuned to Reiki I'd practised the rituals my teacher had recommended, but that was because I'd been told to.

In India, although you couldn't swing a rat without bumping up against a religious building, shrine, or individual practising some form of devotional, I still flat out refused to participate in anything with even the faintest whiff of sacrality. I even refused to go to yoga classes. Just because I was in India didn't mean I was suddenly going to come over all spiritual and start floating about in a kaftan.

But once I was left alone with myself and settled into Mother India's rhythms in Goa, what had first felt like a harsh and difficult experience gradually transformed into one of the most blissful, most life-affirming experiences I'd ever had. It was in my concrete room which resembled a prison cell with its tiny barred window and barely enough room for my bed, a table, and a chair, that I had, what can only be described as, my first conscious encounter with the divine – or, what I prefer to call, the Self.

Perhaps I should explain why I use the term 'Self' and not God.

For me, the word 'God' is just too loaded. It also feels too far removed and abstract for me to relate to. I can't get close to God. It also has masculine undertones which, as a woman, I feel alienated from. And it's for the same reason I don't use the term 'Goddess,' as I feel that alienates men.

Self, on the other hand, is a term Jung used to describe God. Self, when capitalised, as opposed to self with a little 's', refers to something bigger than me in the egoic sense. As I have an orderly way of thinking, this appeals to me, this big Self and little self. It feels like the bigger, wiser version of me. I look up to the Self, respect it. In my mind I envision myself walking alongside the Self, aspiring to be whatever it calls me to be. I also like the fact it has no gender connotations. Neither do I have any picture of what it looks like. It's everything and nothing. For me, it's just a presence. And it's this presence I experienced for the first time in India.

Lying awake at night I began to feel 'I' wasn't quite so alone. Something else was present. I'd stare around the room at night, looking into the corners wondering what it could be. I felt something enveloping me, guiding me. The only way I can describe it was it felt like love – pure, unconditional, I-love-you-just-the-way-you-are love.

After experiencing this for several days, I felt compelled from the inside out to answer. The only way I knew how, was to kneel on the concrete floor, put my forehead to the ground and say, 'Thank you.' And when I said 'thank you' I said it from the bottom of my heart. There was nothing showy about it. I wasn't doing it because someone told me I should or because I was trying suck up to it. There was nothing rote or contrived about it. I just wanted to let this quiet, steady presence know I was grateful with all of my being. I wanted to let it know, in my little human way, that I loved it back, that I would do anything for it, that I was *devoted* to it – *bhakti*.

In the archetype of the Hero's Journey – or the Great Round of Transformation as I like to call it – there comes a point during the initiation stage when the hero has, what Joseph Campbell calls, The Meeting With the Goddess, of which he says:

In the Tantric books of medieval and modern India the abode of the goddess is called Mani-dvipa, 'The Island of Jewels.' Her couch-and-throne is there, in a grove of wish-fulfilling trees. The beaches of the isle are of golden sands. They are laved by the still waters of the ocean of the nectar of immortality. The goddess is red with the fire of life; the earth, the solar system, the galaxies of far-extending space, all swell within her womb. For she is the world creatrix, ever mother, ever virgin. She encompasses the encompassing, nourishes the nourishing, and is the life of everything that lives.

She is also the death of everything that dies. The whole round of existence is accomplished within her sway, from birth, through adolescence, maturity, and senescence, to the grave. She is the womb and the tomb: the sow that eats her farrow. Thus she unites the 'good' and the 'bad,' exhibiting the two modes of the remembered mother, not as personal only, but as universal.

The devotee is expected to contemplate the two with equal equanimity. Through this exercise his spirit is purged of its infantile, inappropriate sentimentalities and resentments, and his mind opened to the inscrutable presence which exists, not primarily as 'good' and 'bad' with respect to his childlike human convenience, his weal and woe, but as the law and image of the nature of being.

– The Hero with a Thousand Faces

And so it was, on my little paradisiacal beach in Goa, on my own Island of Jewels, beneath a 'grove of wish-fulfilling trees,' that I felt for the first time, the unconditional love of what Campbell calls, the Queen Goddess of the World 'within the darkness of the deepest chamber of my heart.' To put a mythical spin on it, it was here I began my heartfelt devotion to the goddess. And as the Kali priest said, only bhakti justifies Tantra.

Of bhakti, the Bhagavad Gita – an ancient Indian sacred text – says in the ninth chapter, 'Fill thy mind with Me, be My devotee, sacrifice unto Me, bow down to Me; thus having made thy heart steadfast in Me, taking Me as the Supreme Goal, thou shalt come to Me.'

Reading this I realised that, despite my best attempts to avoid anything spiritual, I'd experienced what I now affectionately refer to as a spontaneous 'attack of the bhaktis.' I didn't need to *do* anything spiritual. By simply *being*, by surrendering, I'd had a personal, authentic experience of the Self.

After splitting from my boyfriend, like Vasilisa, I continued alone into the dark undergrowth of India. I could have easily given up and flown home. But I didn't. Like Vasilisa, I listened to the little voice of my intuition and stayed with the process even when it scared the shit out of me. After being struck through with terror when I first met the Yaga in the form of her dark sister, Kali, on the streets of Delhi, I surrendered to her initiation. In doing so, I was purged of my 'infantile, inappropriate sentimentalities and resentments.' I said *yes* to life – both its dark and its light side. And life said *yes* to me. And with that, she gifted me a presence I could carry forth – a renewed sense of self with eyes that could see in the dark.

The Rose Gave Honey to the Bee.

THE INVITATION

Three years to the month after my trip to India, I emailed Shakti Tantra about a workshop I'd seen advertised on their website. The workshop was called Women's Invitation about which they had this to say:

> Women's Invitation – this two-day residential workshop provides an opportunity for women to start to heal inhibitions and negative feelings they carry around their bodies and sexuality and to feel vibrant and energised. This workshop allows women to share their experiences and support each other in a safe and nurturing way.

Before contacting Shakti Tantra, however, I looked to see if any of Marion Woodman's BodySoul workshops were being held in the UK. During my time in Santa Fe I'd befriended a woman, called Ira, who was being trained by Woodman herself. Despite running a closed group for women that had already started, Ira welcomed me to join them during my time there. This was the first time I'd done any form of body work with a group of women and I *loved* it.

At the time, I was being initiated into the realm of *logos*, you might say – a realm traditionally associated with the masculine (remember, I'm talking about energies not biological gender) as author Maureen Murdock reminds us here:

> When a woman decides to break with the established images of the feminine she inevitably begins the traditional hero's journey. She puts on her armour, mounts her steed, leaves loved ones behind, and goes in search of the golden treasure. She fine-tunes the skills of logos. She looks for clearly defined routes to success. She sees the male world as healthy, fun-loving, and action-oriented. Men get things done. This fuels her own ambition.
> This is an important period in the development of a woman's ego. Our heroine looks for role models who can show

her the steps along the way. These male allies may take the form of a father, boyfriend, teacher, manager, or coach, or the institution granting the degree or salary she seeks, or of a minister, rabbi, priest, or God. The ally may also be a male-identified woman, perhaps an older childless woman who has played by team rules and successfully made her way to the top.

– The Heroine's Journey

This was exactly what I'd done: boarded a plane and decamped to the States for the summer to be with my artist boyfriend, Sam, where most of my days were spent studying mythology and depth psychology. I was devouring all the books on these new subjects with which I'd fallen in love as fast as I could. But as much as I loved it, I still intuited an imbalance. I was all up in my head. What I also noticed from watching and speaking with others with whom I regularly met to discuss these topics was how disembodied some of them seemed – particularly the men. They knew their onions, no doubt about it, but several of them seemed a tad 'stiff' to me.

What I hadn't realised, up until this point, was just how bright I was. I'd dropped out of college as the style of psychology (cognitive) I'd chosen to study wasn't my cup of tea. As such, I never went to university. Since then I'd rarely read anything. But now, alone and away from everything and everyone I knew, I was reading and studying at a rate of knots. My hungry little hands and inquiring mind had finally found subjects about which I was passionate and of which I couldn't get enough.

But it was a conversation with Ira, one day, which made me look at myself in a new light. We were having a coffee after her class and discussing psychology. I was sharing my thoughts with her about a Woodman book I'd recently read.

'Hold on a minute,' Ira said, 'you've read that book?'

'Yeah,' I said. I proceeded to tell her the others I'd read too.

'And you understand it all?' she asked.

'Well, not quite *all* of it,' I said. 'I'm still acquainting myself with Jungian terminology, so some of it gets lost in translation. But, yeah, I'd say I understand about eighty per cent of what she's saying. Why do you ask?'

'Woodman isn't the easiest of writers to understand. It took me a long time to fully grasp what she's saying in those books and I've been doing this work for years *and* I have an analyst. In fact, I have learned friends, professors and such like, who don't even understand her books. How old are you?'

'Thirty-one,' I answered.

'Wow,' she said leaning back to take a good look at me. 'Marion's always saying the goddess is returning. When I talk to young women like you – particularly ones who are embracing her work – it gives me hope. Even your figure – my god, girl, you even look like a goddess!'

Her comments made me blush. But what always stayed with me about that conversation, was someone affirming my grasp of the subject matter to which I was still fairly new. She wasn't blowing smoke up my arse, she was pointing out a fact – I *was* intelligent. Sam had been telling me this, but I couldn't receive it from him. But from Ira, I could. But Sam was also telling me not to get lost up in my head. 'You have a body, too,' he'd say, 'don't forget that.'

Marathon training had been a great help at keeping me grounded and in my body, but Ira's classes were much more fun. She was a Nia dance teacher (Nia stands for either Neuromuscular Integrative Action or Non-Impact Aerobics and is a sensory-based movement practice which can act as a pathway for self-discovery and personal transformation), but she also incorporated elements from the work she was doing in the BodySoul training programme about which the Marion Woodman Foundation website says:

The core of this work is the exploration of dreams, movement, voice, masks, creative expression, and ritual. The safety of the temenos (sacred space) created in the structure and format of the programs allows the healing of old wounds and the emergence of new energies. We pursue the inner marriage as we honour the positive feminine in our bodies and the positive masculine in our creative pursuits.

It was this balance between the masculine and feminine energies which appealed to me, this idea of pursuing an 'inner marriage.' If possible, I wanted to continue this combination of body work together with my ongoing studies. I didn't want to be 'top heavy,' all *logos* to the detriment of *eros*; all spirit to the detriment of soul. I was well aware I'd neglected my body for long enough otherwise I wouldn't have had the wild and crazy idea to run off to India to study Tantra in the first place.

But when I'd looked on the Woodman Foundation website in January 2011, they had no upcoming workshops. The ones they did have were over in the States and I couldn't afford those, let alone the plane fare, the accommodation, and all other associated costs such a trip would entail. I didn't have a bean – I was absolutely and utterly *skint*. So though I fired off an email to Shakti Tantra I had no idea how I was going to pay for their workshop. It was thanks to Finn and the wisdom tucked away in the story of *The Prostitute and the Pearls of Wisdom*, that I was able to find a way.

In the first part of the story, the brother tells the disciple that all he has is a buffalo and a sack of rice. The brother bemoans the fact he's been carving out the same narrow existence, day after day, surviving on the little he has. So when the disciple recommends he sell the buffalo and exchange the bag of rice, this doesn't go down too well. The brother's fear is, if he gives away what he has, he'll be left with nothing. What he doesn't realise is if he gives away the little he does have and shares it with others, only then will he know abundance.

It's one thing hearing this wisdom in stories; it's quite another applying it to your own life. I'd first identified with the sister in that I'd always sold myself cheap – particularly in relationships – because I believed, deep down, I wasn't worth much. If I didn't take what I could get I'd end up alone, beggars not being choosers and all that. But Meade says you can't be both (brother and sister) at the same time. So someone is either afraid to give away what they have in case they wind up bereft, or they sell themselves cheap instead of holding out for something with real warmth, beauty, and value ('bag of pearls').

What I hadn't realised is we can shift between the two at different times in our life and also in different situations. So, unbeknown to me, I'd become a lot like the brother who refused to give away his buffalo – my 'buffalo' being my writing.

When I first started blogging I shared my writing freely. I didn't do it with any expectation; I wrote because it was the only way I knew how to make sense of my life. Soon, though, others were writing to me to say that, not only was my writing helping them, but they also liked my writing itself. This is a sentiment that's been echoed down the years.

It's at this point I could have got all Ms False Modesty about it, but just two years after I started writing I was being paid for it. And just a year after that, I wrote my first book. So I obviously had a talent when it came to this writing malarkey. This, however, was where the problems set in.

As I never aspired to be a writer, let alone an author, I didn't realise what a big deal this was (writing a book). In fact, it turns out it's a big deal to a lot of people. But it wasn't a big a deal to me. It was just a means to an end, a way to share 'the story so far' with others.

But after my book came out, hubris crept in. In fact, it probably crept in as I was writing it. If there's one thing I've learnt, it's don't *ever* say or pretend to be something you're not. Furthermore don't make promises you can't keep. This is a lesson I've had to learn the hard way.

Sam was the first person to point out my hubristic tendencies, this pretending to be something I wasn't. Despite it being a bitter pill to swallow, I knew he was right. It was him who'd say that until I got paid for my writing, I wasn't really a writer – I was an *aspiring* writer. But there was also a part of me that believed you have to 'fake it 'til you make it.' So by telling people I was a writer, I was feeling my way into the role, trying it on for size. Eventually I *did* grow into one – a professional one – but his sentiments about being honest and not to get too inflated or too ahead of myself, stayed with me.

So when I bumped into Finn in the supermarket, rather than pretend to be something I wasn't, I told him the truth about my situation. After all, I figured, how many people would want to date someone who's just started writing and, as such, doesn't have a penny? Not just that, but they're also back living with their parents? It's not the most attractive of propositions. Many a woman has run screaming the other way on discovering their prospective thirty-something partner still lives at home with their parents. But Finn didn't.

That this *didn't* deter him, however, perplexed me. If anything, he seemed insistent in his pursuit – *very* insistent. But this was where the sister in our folktale sneaked into my behaviour, because on a very deep level, unconscious even to me, I was *flattered*: I was flattered that someone would be interested in me enough to want to pursue a relationship despite the fact I had nothing. Or did I (have nothing)?

In our culture, self-worth is inextricably bound up with net worth – you are what you earn. You are your house, your postcode, your car, your position at work; you are all the stuff you've ever accumulated. The more you accumulate, the more you're worth. The flipside is, the less you have, the less you're worth (or, at least, that's the general consensus). So if you give it all up and go back to square one, you're worth nothing – or, at least, that's what I believed. You're a failure. After all, what do you have to show for your life?

Despite sacrificing everything to pursue a dream – even if I didn't know what that dream was besides writing a book – because I earned peanuts I believed I had nothing to offer the world. (Unless you really make it, most writers are paid a pittance.) As such I believed I was worth very little, if anything. So when Finn pursued me, although I initially spurned his advances in order to fulfil a promise I'd made to myself (completing the Athens Marathon by myself, for myself), he didn't give up.

Putting the brother and sister aside for a moment, this motif – of being pursued – forms part of an even larger archetypal pattern. In the Hero's Journey, Joseph Campbell calls this pursuit the Magic Flight. My problem was, despite detecting the faint outline of this archetype (Hero's Journey) at play in my life, I didn't think of myself as a 'hero.' So I never for a moment suspected I was being 'pursued,' even though that was exactly what Finn was doing.

The motif of the Magic Flight appears when the hero crosses the threshold back into the Ordinary World after their initiation in the Special World. It's one of several motifs which marks the beginning of the third and final stage of the Hero's Journey called the Return (separation, initiation, return). And there was I thinking such events only ever happened 'once upon a time' in myths of old. How wrong was I?

My particular initiation consisted of, what Campbell calls, The Road of Trials, which usually has three tests or trials – pretty apt considering I ran three marathons. Again, when I signed up for the marathons I had no idea of this. Yes, I'd been introduced to Campbell's work, but my reason for signing up for three marathons was hardly the stuff of heroes. In fact, today, when I read back my third and final deciding factor for signing up for the marathon (Sam telling me an ex had run the New York City Marathon), I laugh out loud. But, hey, that was where I was at the time. Of this Road of Trials, Campbell says:

> Once having traversed the threshold, the hero moves in a dream landscape of curiously fluid, ambiguous forms, where he must survive a succession of trials. This is a favourite phase of the myth-adventure. It has produced a world literature of miraculous tests and ordeals. The hero is covertly aided by the advice, amulets, and secret agents of the supernatural helper whom he met before his entrance into this region. Or it may be that he here discovers for the first time that there is a benign power everywhere supporting him in his passage.

> *– The Hero with a Thousand Faces*

When I read this now, it makes *so* much more sense. But I would have missed it altogether had it not been for Christopher Vogler who says, in *The Writer's Journey*: 'It's most common for heroes to be chased by villains, but there are other possibilities. An unusual variant of the chase is pursuit by admirers. It's a chase scene with a twist: Rather than hero fleeing villain, hero is being pursued by his admirer.' It was only while writing this book that I joined the dots and spotted this motif.

After Athens I remember thinking that if I really was in the middle of a so-called Hero's Journey and the three marathons formed my initiatory ordeal, then they weren't that bad. But as the Sibyl says to Aeneas in *The Aeneid*: 'Easy is the descent to the Lower World; but, to retrace your steps and to escape to the upper air – this is the task, this is the toil.'

As tough as they were, running those three marathons felt like an adventure. They took me across the world and helped put me back in the story of my life. In retrospect, they were great fun. As the Sibyl says, however, that's the easy part, crossing into the Special World/Lower World. But the question The Return asks of us all is are you able to incorporate the lessons learnt in the Special World on your return to the Ordinary World? From an alchemical perspective, this is where the abstract principles of the ambiguous dream-like world (*albedo*) are grounded in the flesh-and-blood reality of our daily lives (*rubedo*). Or, as the bible puts it, The Word (*albedo*) is made flesh (*rubedo*). In other words, what this stage demands of us is we now walk our talk – easier said than done.

By the time I got to Athens I was much more aware of my innermost fears and insecurities, so I used that particular marathon as an opportunity to face those issues head-on. Up until that point I'd been afraid of travelling alone, doing something by myself, for myself. I'd always needed to do things with others – usually boyfriends. Truth be told, I wasn't even sure I'd like my own company. Who *was* I when I was left alone with myself? I was a stranger even to myself.

But crossing the finish line in Athens I'd been gifted with a similar, but more powerful experience than those I'd had in India – an awareness that 'I' wasn't so alone in my little psychic house. There was something else, something greater than me that was always with me, guiding me, looking out for me. For the first time in my life, I felt this *something* – which I've since realised is the Self – had my back: but only so long as I continued to surrender to it and trust it.

For someone whose greatest fear was being abandoned and left alone in the world, this was a powerful realisation. Up until this time I'd clung onto others for dear life: mum, boyfriends, institutions. I'd tried to make myself fit their idea of me, appease them. But now my ego consciousness had done a one-eighty about turn and was now firmly focused on something within.

The question asked of me, on my return to the Ordinary World, was would I be able to continue my allegiance to this inner Self, to surrender to it, to trust it in the face of my mundane, day-to-day reality? Despite the experiences I'd had in India and Athens, surrendering to and trusting in something as tenuous as the Self in our modern culture with all its distractions and temptations was the biggest challenge I would face. As Campbell says, 'Can the ego put itself to death?'

Would I be able to stand by myself, for the Self, even in the face of fierce outer opposition? Even if it meant the withdrawal of others' support, friendship, and love? My greatest fear was abandonment – that no-one would love me or want to be with me if I didn't stack up to their idea of who they thought I should be. Could I stand to my innermost truth even if it meant no-one liked me? This was what The Return asked of me. But as we all know, old habits die hard.

Despite trying my damndest to embody (*rubedo*) as many of the lessons I'd learnt in the Special World of my marathoning initiation on my return home to the Ordinary World (aka Manchester), I still managed to slip up good and proper. It was one error, perhaps the only one, but it would be enough to take me to hell and back – *literally*.

Because I believed I had nothing, when Finn pursued me it momentarily disoriented me. I was coming straight out of a two-year adventure and my feet had barely touched the ground when we started dating. So when he gave me a set of keys to his house and a debit card to one of his accounts, I was completely blindsided. This is what some women nag men years for and here he was handing it me on a plate. I thought I must have come a long way in my development to have wound up with someone as generous as him. *Hmmm...*

For the first six months of our relationship things went well. I was still living at my parents but Finn asked me to stay over with him several nights a week. Despite having a set of keys to his house what I didn't want to do was muscle in on his territory or ask to move in with him. But it was on 25 June 2009 (I remember the date because it was the day Michael Jackson died) that I had, what turned out to be, a pivotal conversation with him.

During our first six months together we'd discussed our future. Much of this future, however, rested on the success of my writing – in particular the book I planned to write. Finn was unhappy in his job at the supermarket and wanted to leave, travel, and pursue his creativity. After being in his job for most of his adult life, he himself admitted he'd become 'institutionalised.'

Now, first of all, whatever possessed me to think I'd ever be a successful writer, let alone one who's in a position to support both myself and another is beyond me. You want delusions of grandeur with a side serving of naivety? There it is. But something else was gnawing at me about our relationship. I wondered what sacrifices he was willing to make in order to pursue his dreams because, if there's one thing I've learnt, it's that dreams demand sacrifice. I also wondered how he was willing to support me, if the plan was I would eventually support him. Yes, he'd given me the keys to his house and a debit card with some emergency cash should I ever need it (which I only ever used to buy food shopping when I stayed at his), but I was still living at my parents half the week. Considering the scale of the plans we'd discussed for our future together (me assuming all financial responsibility so he could pursue his dreams), I didn't feel particularly supported in the here and now.

What I'd also noticed, when I returned to Finn's after being away, was his house was untidy – nothing had been washed up since I'd left, for example. Now, of course, it was his house, he was an incredibly busy man who worked long hours, and he could do whatever he pleased in his private living space, but I was beginning to feel like a glorified housemaid. I felt he had the best of both worlds – a part-time girlfriend who tidied his house and who would, one day, help him leave his job. Deep down, my concern was he didn't see me; rather, he saw me as a *stepping stone* – a way out.

Rather than festering, I decided to talk to Finn, share how I felt. I admit, I was emotional and more than a little nervous about having such a discussion – after all, this was the first time I'd ever stood up for myself and my dreams. But I felt strongly about these issues. So I wrote down everything I wanted to say and rehearsed the points over and over. I wanted to be clear and articulate. Gone were my days of unnecessary dramas and histrionics.

Finn was surprised to hear I felt the way I did. He said it hadn't been his intention to treat me as a 'glorified housemaid' and he certainly didn't see me that way. On this, I believed him. He also said he appreciated my clarity, that I made all my points in a calm and dignified manner. But, as I've said, there was no need for drama.

The upshot of that conversation was he asked me to move in with him there and then. That was a happy moment. He admitted he was nervous about the prospect as he'd lived alone for six years or so. It would take some readjustment on his behalf. I understood his concerns. But I reminded him that dreams demand sacrifice and it *has* to be conscious.

A week later, while on a night out, he also told me he'd pay for the publication of my book. This was another sweet moment. When he did that, I really felt supported, that he had my back. I felt proud of myself for standing up for what I was beginning to believe in – myself. But this was also the moment – the one effin' moment – I slipped up.

Despite taking a stand on behalf of my dreams, I still wasn't fully able to *receive* his offer without feeling obliged to do something in return. So what I did, as a kneejerk reaction, was promised him the Christmas coming (2009) would be his last in the supermarket and that, thanks to my book, I'd have him out of there before the end of 2010. Again, on reflection, I don't know who was dumber for believing such a wild and fanciful statement – me for saying it or him for believing it. I've come out with some absolute *howlers* in my time, but that has to rank up there as numero uno.

Who did I think I was? JK Rowling? Not just that, but what was this all about, this heroic attempt to sweep into someone else's life and save them from their unhappiness? What I should have said was: 'You know there's every possibility this might not work out? I know I've risked everything to pursue my dreams, but we should also bear in mind I could well fail. This could all be for nothing. Then what will you do about leaving your job?' Like I said, there are some lessons we have to learn the hard way.

I wrote my first book in late 2009, submitting it to my publisher just before Christmas. It was released in April 2010. I'd say our relationship reached its peak around this time (summer '10). I'd even asked Finn to marry me in the February. Neither of us had ever been engaged before, so I don't know if I was falling back into my old pattern of being in love *with* love or I just wanted to prove a point that Finn would marry if it was the right person ('see, look, *I'm* the special one,' purred the still slightly insecure cat that thought she'd got the cream).

As I'm a romantic with mythic tendencies it was a beautiful proposal even if I may say so myself. He said yes and we planned to marry in Melbourne (St Kilda) on Beltane the following year. But I sensed there was something rotten in Denmark right from the get go. In fact, looking back, I now see there were problems even before that.

In May 2009 my friends Sylvie (Zippora) and Jerry (Treebeard) came to visit from the States. While they were over Finn and I took the opportunity to meet up with them. Sylvie's a stunner, no doubt about it. So I wasn't surprised when he made a comment to me about her fabulous figure. But it wasn't this that bothered me. This comment marked the beginning of something so subtle, that it took me a long time to see the pattern: he'd compliment and praise everyone and everything else for a whole manner of things, but never me.

In fact, thinking back, I can count on one hand the number of times he acknowledged, let alone complimented me for anything. What had changed for me, since Athens, was I no longer sought anyone's approval regards what I did – for example, my work – nor did I need to be reaffirmed in what I looked like. In that respect, the marathons had turned me back on myself and made me more self-sufficient and at ease with myself. But what did strike me as odd was, despite being so encouraging of his staff at work, he couldn't muster up two words of encouragement about *anything*, for me, his partner.

Like I said, I didn't spot this straight off. Though what I did notice was he never told anyone about our plans to marry. Meantime, during the spring and summer of 2010 he blossomed. I introduced him to running which he'd never believed himself capable of doing. When he got home from work he took up painting and began churning out some mature, mythically-inspired pieces with real depth and beauty. He drank less, watched less TV, ate better (by this time I'd stopped pretending I couldn't cook and assumed responsibility for all meal preparation). I introduced him to nature trails and paths in his neighbourhood of which he'd previously been unaware (very Artemisian of me, going off to explore the local countryside and landscape).

He also blossomed, I believe, because of my ceaseless encouragement and enthusiasm for his artistic endeavours. As a creative, I know how challenging it can be when you're first finding your 'voice.' So it's a massive help when you're with a fellow creative who's already established themselves as a professional in their respective field (even if they are penniless).

Sam had been a wonderful creative mentor to me. My editor, George, had also given me numerous tips and advice. But what both these men also did, in very different ways, was to say 'toughen up cupcake' and that I'd better get used to the inevitable knocks, criticisms, and failures that would inevitably come my way. Most people aren't doing what they love so when someone does have the courage to stick their neck above the parapet and pursue their dreams, the world will come screaming after you taking a thousand nasty cuts and swipes along the way – and they weren't wrong.

When I first started writing for the online magazine my articles were often criticised and, on occasion, ripped to shreds. It was George who told me never to enter into dialogue with anyone regarding their comments or opinions about my work. Corn. Chickens. Do your work. Let it go. Move on. For a recovering Persephone, this was grist for the mill, toughened me up, even if it sometimes left me in tears.

But it was this potential criticism Finn was unhappy about. In his work environment he was top dog. But in the world of creativity, he was starting over. I loved his work and I'm not just saying that because he was my partner – he had a genuine talent. Self-taught, his work was reminiscent of Sam's (who was also self-taught). If he nurtured it he could have done well. Only problem was, it's hard enough practising and nurturing your own craft when you're still a relative newbie, let alone providing ceaseless support and encouragement to another fledgling creative – support which, I'd noticed, didn't flow both ways (it took him a year to read my book about which he said nothing).

So when folk across the world didn't camp outside bookshops overnight in order to be the first ones to read my book and I didn't sell 100 million copies – in fact, I didn't sell 100 copies – and it was fast becoming clear Finn would have to work another Christmas at the supermarket, things soon began to deteriorate between us.

One particularly heart-breaking and humbling moment had to do with a book reading I'd arranged in Manchester – a book reading which, despite advertising it, no-one turned up for. Just as the Rome Marathon had brought me to my knees in humility, so too did this empty room (the same room, incidentally, in which I'd heard Sue and Sarah's talk two years earlier) bring Icarus, here, back down to earth with an ego-shattering *bang*.

I gathered up my books and took my sorry arse back home. It was at that point my naivety hit me – *hard*. Just what did I think I was doing making such hubristic promises? More to the point, how was I going to tell Finn I'd failed?

Christopher Vogler says of the setbacks the hero may face during The Return (or, as he calls it, The Road Back):

> Another twist of The Road Back may be a sudden catastrophic reversal of the hero's good fortune. Things were going well after surviving the Ordeal, but now reality sets in again. Heroes may encounter setbacks that seem to doom the adventure. Within sight of shore the ship may spring a leak. For a moment, after great risk, effort, and sacrifice, it may look like all is lost ... Almost every story needs a moment to acknowledge the hero's resolve to finish, and provide her with necessary motivation to return home with the elixir despite the temptations of the Special World and the trials that remain ahead.

– The Writer's Journey

Hindsight's a wonderful thing, isn't it? Today, when I read this I go, 'Ooh, would you look at that? They're not wrong.' Thing is, we're usually exposed to the archetype of the Hero's Journey in a movie, a book, or a myth – not in someone's life. So though I spend most of my time with my nose buried in books on myth and, as such, am familiar with these patterns, doesn't for a minute mean I believed they ever actually happened to everyday folk.

Even if I was aware such a pattern was both circumscribing and suffusing my life, doesn't mean I could *do* anything to speed it up. This isn't the movies. This is real life. And in real life these patterns can take *years* to unfold. You only have to look at the great Hero's Journey in which we're all participating: birth (separation from the mother – or the unmanifest, if you really want to take it back); initiation (life – or perhaps 'ordeal' may be more appropriate here, depending on your perspective); death (return).

Anyway, back to my failure. Or was it? As Vogler says above, 'every story needs a moment to acknowledge the hero's resolve to finish.' Looking back, this was my moment – or, rather, my *turning point*.

While I'd been working on the book, Finn had supported me financially. We'd agreed this: he'd support me in the short term while I pursued my dreams so that, eventually, I'd be able to support him in pursuing his dreams. This trade-off felt fair to me and right.

While I worked on the book it meant I didn't write for the online magazine so I wasn't earning any money. But now it was summer 2010 and I hadn't earned anything for more than a year. As it became clear my book wasn't about to earn us a penny any time soon, Finn turned up the pressure that I get a job so I could contribute towards the bills.

'You must have had a Plan B?' he said to me one day during a walk. It was on hearing this comment that I first felt something very deep, very quiet, and very resolute kick in.

'No,' I said quietly, 'there is no plan B. It's plan A or die.' I don't know where it came from (well, I do *now*), but even though I'd failed, even though I still had no idea whatsoever where any of this was heading, something in me refused to give up and, as such, would *not* be moved. As a manager, he couldn't understand this.

'What do you mean, there's no plan B? You always need a contingency plan in case your original line of action doesn't work out,' he replied. 'You're going to have to start earning some money.'

'If I had a plan B, it would mean that, on some level, I'd doubted plan A. If I doubt plan A, it means I doubt myself. And I've come too far and sacrificed too much to give up on myself now. Therefore, there is no plan B. I'm not giving up on myself.'

'But nothing's clearly happening with the book,' he said, 'so now what?'

'I don't know. But I'm not gonna give up on myself now,' I answered.

I wouldn't mind, but I was hardly a lazy so-and-so who sat on her arse all day watching TV and running up debts on his cards. I spent all my time reading, learning all I could on the subjects I loved. When it comes to studying I am *incredibly* self-disciplined. As such, I never went out, never bought any clothes – only ever my beloved books. But Finn never saw that. According to him, all he saw was someone who sat around all day on the laptop. *Well, isn't that where most writers spend their time?*

What I did agree to do was return to writing for the magazine. Again, because I was an author now, Ms Hubris, here, had decided she didn't *do* articles anymore. But what was it Churchill said? 'In the course of my life, I have often had to eat my words, and I must confess that I have always found it a wholesome diet.' Seems I was going to have to eat a few million more of them.

But something interesting happened. Now I'd written a book I noticed I had much more confidence as a writer. I'm not saying I was a better writer, but what the book had done for me was helped strengthen my 'writing vessel,' if that makes sense? I was able to contain more. I wasn't as intimidated by writing as I had been before the book. I was less fazed.

Just as the marathons had helped me 'get bigger' physically – endure more, stay the distance no matter how hard it got – so had writing a book. In fact, if it hadn't have been for the marathons, I doubt I'd have had the confidence or the discipline necessary to write a book in the first place.

But now the book had acted as the psychological equivalent of the marathons. By running the marathons and, now, writing a book, I'd been expanded. And no matter what else happened from here on out, there was no going back to my former small idea of who I thought I was.

Though I may have written the odd article here and there, I still earned peanuts. Finn turned up the heat that I get a 'proper' job but I refused. I'd been down that road already. I knew all too well where it led. And I wasn't going back. It was at this point where our stand-off really kicked in. But it wasn't done through arguments – it was done through a physical and emotional withdrawal.

Back when he was pursuing me he'd been physically demonstrative, holding my hand, being affectionate. But, when I think about it, that wore off during our first year together. Along with the lack of compliments and acknowledgement, I'd noticed a dwindling in his affections towards me. In fact, I felt more like a friend or a sister than his girlfriend. And it was this brother-sister dynamic that alerted me to the archetype of Artemis and her twin brother, Apollo, who was known as the 'far-distant one.'

In the myth, Artemis was the first-born of Leto. As soon as she'd been born she helped her mother deliver her younger brother (as you do). This detail, alone, provides a clue as to what we're dealing with here. Whereas in the myth she helps physically birth him, psychologically that was exactly what I'd been doing – helping birth Finn out of his old life at the supermarket and into a new life as an artist. Of this Apollonian archetype, Jean Shinoda Bolen says:

> The Apollo archetype favours thinking over feeling, distance over closeness, objective assessment over subjective intuition ... Living in his head, rather than either in his body or emotions, the Apollo man is not a lover. There's characteristically a lack of passion in his relationships with women. Also a relationship with him often doesn't have much emotional depth, for he prefers to maintain his usual emotional distance ... Living in his head, rather than his body or his imagination, the Apollo man is a stranger in the realm of Eros. He knows little experientially of the ebb and flow of sexual attraction, or the ongoing need to be touched and communicated with on a body-to-body level (or of intimate verbal communication either). Thus, if he wins the woman who roused him and then 'goes away' as a lover (which is typical of an Apollo man), she may be unfaithful in his 'absence.'

> **– Gods in Everyman**

At the time I got together with Finn, I was a very different woman to the one who'd lined up at the start of the New York City Marathon a year earlier. Gone was the Persephone-like woman who couldn't get a grip on her life, who hid behind others, and never finished what she started. In her place stood a woman who'd had the courage to strike out alone and follow her dreams, go the distance. After previously believing myself to be insubstantial and lacking core conviction, I revelled in the centred, focused energy of the go-getter energy of Artemis. But now this sole identification with one archetype was beginning to irritate a few of the others – namely, Aphrodite.

By taking aim and hitting my self-oriented targets again and again – first with the marathons, then with the book – I'd proved myself to myself several times over. These were necessary qualities I'd had to cultivate. Problems arise, however, when we solely identify with one archetype at the expense of the others. So though I was initially able to overlook the gradual demise of Finn's affection towards me as I was focused on other areas, once I'd finished writing the book his lack of tenderness and warmth really hit home – this was when the Ice Man Cometh.

My problem was I pretended it didn't bother me. But it did. And now I was beginning to experience the shadow side of archetypal over-identification. Every archetype has a positive and negative side. So far, I'd identified with those Artemisian qualities which were the most fitting of all the Greek god and goddess archetypes to complete the tasks at hand. It wasn't conscious. I didn't sit there and think, 'Oh, I know who'd be perfect to help me complete three marathons and focus on writing a book – Artemis.' It'd happened naturally as I progressed through the marathons. My actions had constellated (activated) her, strengthened her presence within my psyche.

But now I'd completed those tasks and was in a relationship – the realm of Eros (the Greek god of love and relatedness who you may remember from our story of *Psyche and Eros*). Eros's mother is Aphrodite, goddess of love and beauty. And if there's one thing the myths tell us, it's that Aphrodite does not appreciate being ignored. After all, we've already seen how pissed she gets at Psyche for stealing her thunder. In fact, there's a line from the movie, *Fatal Attraction* – a movie I hadn't seen for about twenty years – that sprang to mind and summed up the energy of this archetype I felt building inside me.

In the movie, Glenn Close's character, Alex Forrest, confronts Michael Douglas's character, Dan Gallagher, in a scene in which she tells him she's pregnant and that she 'just wants to be a part of his life.'

'What am I supposed to do?' she says, 'you won't answer my calls, you change your number, I mean, I'm not gonna be *ignored*, Dan.' That my psyche was able to reach into the depths of my personal unconscious and retrieve this particular scene is testament to its ingenuity at highlighting how I felt. And now I was beginning to learn how 'hell hath no fury like a goddess scorned.' Aphrodite was *not* going to be ignored.

Despite always having had an eye for beauty – the arts, interior design, and so forth – I'd never really known how to cultivate my inner Aphrodite. Apart from mascara and a little eyeliner, neither my mum nor my aunt wore any make-up so I never played with any as a child. The one time my grandma gave me some red lipstick to play with, mum snatched it straight off me saying something along the lines of 'What you giving her that shite for? Only tarts wear that.' Being a good little Persephone, I wore the dresses mum picked out for me. She washed and braided my hair. But when it came to self-expression I'd never had a say in my personal appearance.

As I got older I favoured more of a tomboy appearance. I think this was a combination of playing down my looks as I was uncomfortable about drawing any unnecessary attention to myself as I didn't know how to 'hold' compliments and so forth; not feeling comfortable with my body so, therefore, hiding it in drab and shapeless clothes, jeans etc.; and not having the slightest clue as to what suited me. As I'd not played 'dress up' as a child like most of the other girls, I had no clue as to what I liked and what my own style might be. So as an adult, I just didn't know where to start. I felt lost. And this feeling, of being lost, left me feeling intimidated and like an outsider when it came to, well, *girly* things. In a culture which is all about appearance, I didn't know what I was doing and, as such, felt awkward. So I'd always erred on the side of simple and neutral.

Physically, I also wondered whether there was something 'wrong' with me. When your partner hardly ever touches you, you begin to wonder if you're somehow repulsive.

As we neared the end of 2010 all these factors coalesced – Finn's continued lack of tenderness and affection towards me, his emotional withdrawal and increasing frostiness; the failure of my book, the fact I was making no money, the overall lack of beauty, and love in my life – until they were impossible for me to ignore. I could feel it breaking me. The things I once thought, in my Artemisian aloofness, didn't matter, did. They mattered so *very* much.

I longed for romance and imaginative gestures. Although I have no interest in Valentine's Day (commercial crap), doesn't mean I'm not a sucker for spontaneous, romantic gestures. For example, I've always loved being bought flowers. When I once mentioned this to Finn, he said 'You'll only think I've done something wrong if I buy you flowers.' This remark stunned me. I have *never* believed that, let alone said it to anyone. He may have heard it from someone else, but he'd never heard it from me. Consequently, he never bought me any. Instead, I'd grab some along with the weekly shopping. They never failed to lift my spirits arranged in a pretty vase in the living room.

I also wanted to be desired and lusted after. In short, I wanted sex – hot, wanton, up-against-the-wall, I-want-you-now sex. I wanted down-and-dirty sex. I wanted throwing about the bedroom, not a polite peck on the lips when my partner got home from work. Yeah, the sex was okay at the beginning of our relationship – quite the turnaround from years earlier – but it wasn't *passionate*. It was lights out, underneath the duvet sex. And now I wanted fucking with a breathtaking fervour.

But I knew I couldn't lay the blame for the lack of love and lust solely at his feet – I had as much a part to play in this dearth of desire as he did. I was still afraid to surrender, to let go, to be vulnerable with another. And if there's one thing Artemis isn't, it's vulnerable. Persephone is – after all, she's dragged off into the depths of the Underworld. But Artemis was never raped, ravished, or taken advantage of in any way, shape or form – she was an invulnerable goddess, immune from falling in love. But she could be – she's an archetype, an immortal. But I'm not. I'm a mortal, a vulnerable flesh and bones human being. And if there's one thing I should have learnt by now, it's that I shouldn't *identify* with an archetype – *relate* to it, yes, but don't identify with it as though I were the archetype.

So, yes, I'd re-established a relationship with my body, but I wasn't *in* it. I still had no idea about my own pleasure. So even if we had been having sex, I wouldn't have known what to ask for. And even if I had known what I wanted, I wouldn't have been able to receive him – not *consciously*. That fear of years earlier, of being physically penetrated, hadn't gone away. But it takes two to Tango – whether vertically or horizontally. I couldn't do anything about his actions (or lack of), but I could take responsibility for my own. So this was when I began looking for some form of body work. But how to afford it?

I started back writing for the online magazine in August 2010 but soon realised I no longer wanted to write about food and drink. The thing with me is, if I'm not enthused by a subject, I'd rather not write about it at all. This may seem like a picky attitude for someone cutting their teeth as a writer, but I was now in a position with the magazine to write about whatever I wanted.

Except there was one problem – the budget for freelancers such as myself was dwindling. If I wrote about food and drink, I'd be paid. But I didn't want to write about food and drink. My initial gig with the magazine had been to write about cocktails. This had been fun and my column popular but I'd quickly spotted the metaphor – I was writing about spirit in its concrete, literal form. Now I wanted to write about it in its symbolic form. I no longer wanted to go out drinking. I wanted to write about the soul.

But in order to write about soul (mind and body, too), I'd have to write for a different arm of the magazine called *Body*. George told me if I wrote for *Body*, though my articles would be published, I wouldn't be paid for them. With Finn piling on the pressure to start earning I was faced with a choice – write about something which brought me no joy and paid me a little money or apprentice myself freely to the craft of writing about mind, body, and soul?

When I opted for the latter this didn't go down well. By this time it was less a crack between Finn and I, and more a gaping chasm. Besides the rote peck he gave me on arrival home from work, he never held my hand let alone showed me any warmth. Relations were of the polar variety. But I couldn't sell out on myself. I didn't want to be a writer per se; I wanted to write about personal transformation and soul. The writing itself was just the instrument. And seeing as I'd only been a professional writer, in the paid sense, for a little over two years, I now realised – thanks to the spectacular failure of my book – I still had a lot to learn when it came to the craft itself.

The upside of writing about mind, body, and soul however was, although I wouldn't be paid for my writing, I would be in a position to negotiate experiences and products in exchange for articles. Whenever we reviewed food and drink we did so anonymously and it was paid for by the magazine itself to ensure impartiality. Neither restaurants nor bars could buy our favour.

Of course, this would require integrity on my behalf. Just because I was negotiating experiences and products didn't mean I was about to sell out for any old freebie. I felt a strong moral obligation to honour the readers' integrity too. But for the first time I also recognised I had a sizeable platform with which I could do some good. I felt I was returning to my original blogging roots – writing freely, sharing things I genuinely felt would benefit others. In fact, going back even further, it felt the same as when I first climbed on stage in secondary school, as an eleven year old, and gave a public speech on the deforestation of the rainforests and its resultant impact on the ozone layer. After hearing the second year students during their public speech competition talk about their personal hobbies and what not, it irritated me that they hadn't taken the opportunity to share something of meaning with their audience, something that could make a difference, especially when they had several hundred of us listening.

My first article was about a yin yoga and Pilates teacher whose ethic and approach I admired and who'd helped keep me on the road during my marathoning pilgrimage (and who has, since, sadly passed away). But when I submitted it to George, he told me *Body* wasn't his area, it was Sally's – the editor of *Body*.

I'd seen Sally in the office whenever I'd dropped by to see George, but I'd never spoken with her. Tall and lithe with an elegant demeanour, she reminded me of Queen Nefertiti. She'd always seemed aloof, unapproachable. George had affectionately nicknamed her his Work Wife. But she was also known as the Tough Nun. I got the impression she didn't take any crap. So when George told me I had to submit my piece to her, I was nervous.

So far, when it came to my creativity, I'd solely aligned myself with male mentors. But now I had to realign myself with a female mentor and I wasn't sure how I felt about that. Mostly because every woman I'd ever worked for had been a tyrannical, power-wielding psycho who couldn't keep her emotions out of the task in hand. I'm not saying all women are like that, just the ones I'd worked for. Furthermore, none of them had particularly liked me. And now I was in front of one nicknamed the Tough Nun.

Looking back, I now see I was beginning the process of what Maureen Murdock calls Urgent Yearning to Reconnect with the Feminine, of which she says:

If a woman has spent many years fine-tuning her intellect and her command of the material world while ignoring the subtleties of her bodily knowings, she may now be reminded that the body and spirit are one. If she has ignored her emotions while serving the needs of her family or community, she may now slowly begin to reclaim how she feels as a woman. The mysteries of the feminine realm will appear in her dreams, in synchronistic events, in her poetry, art, and dance.

– The Heroine's Journey

And indeed, they already had. During summer 2010, I had a dream which, to this day, remains one of the most magnificent I've ever had the privilege of experiencing. I won't go into detail here about the progression and development of my dreams since I began working with them in 2006, otherwise I'd never finish this book. Suffice to say by 2009 Barack Obama was a regular dream fixture, followed in 2010 by his wife, Michelle. Together, they were a lot of fun to hang out with. But it was a dream in which I was at their private residence as symbolised by an all-white space (representative of the White House) which really caught my imagination.

Michelle, as always, greeted me warmly and welcomed me in. Downstairs, watching TV in a den with glass doors which led out onto a garden, Barack waved up at me. Michelle led me further into the house. Then she nodded over my shoulder at someone and gestured for me to go. When I looked I saw an old black woman shrouded in a hooded outfit who I'd never seen before. Despite being old and as black as the earth itself, she was *radiant*. As I walked towards her I felt nervous. But she took hold of me, pulled me into an embrace, and kissed me on the lips. All in that moment I felt such unconditional love, such acceptance. She seemed *so* incredibly proud of me as she took a moment to survey me. It'd be no exaggeration to say her kiss felt like a blessing.

I awoke from that dream feeling I could touch the sky. Despite my recent failure with the book, despite the sadness I felt about my relationship, that dream, that one dream, lifted my spirits and carried me for weeks.

The thing about dreams is they don't all have a meaning – some of them just *are*. Attempting to ascribe meaning to this particular dream would have been like attempting to ascribe meaning to a beautiful sunset – it has no meaning, it just *is*. When a gorgeous stranger walks into a room and takes your breath away, makes you blush, do you attempt to slap a meaning on them, or does your heart and all of your being resonate with an absolute *yes*? That's what this dream felt like – it was a bodily knowing. She was the Dark Mother and she'd just given me her blessing.

In another corner of eternity it was the Tough Nun's blessing I was now waiting on. So when I received an email back from her of the 'Yeah, no worries, that's great thanks,' variety, I was relieved. Then, during our correspondence, something transpired that made me realise I had more in common with Sally than I'd had with any of my male mentors so far – our mutual love and frustration of decent products (or lack of) for our afro-European hair.

Unless you have hair like ours you have no idea of the problems we face in trying to track down products which won't dry it out, won't weigh it down, and don't cost a fortune. So when I mentioned something about a product I was investigating, that was it. Soon, emails were flying back and forth in which we lamented our mutual frustration, sharing products, tips. And with that conversation – a conversation which endures to this day and to which George always responds with, 'Oh god, you girls and your hair,' before putting in his headphones to shut us out – I was back in the realm of 'girly' things. I was writing for *Body* and back in my body.

I think Finn thought I'd lost the plot when I mentioned I wouldn't be paid for my articles. My seeming irrationality was, I suspect, getting on his rather more rational goat. Not that he ever got angry. In a typically Apollonian manner, there was never any drama. We never argued. But just because we didn't argue didn't mean everything was alright between us. All that happened was passions got pushed down. Except mine was now banging to be let out.

After a Christmas and New Year (it was now January 2011) during which I could feel the underlying, unspoken tension between us building to intolerable levels, I set myself a challenge to arrange us a holiday for his birthday which was at the end of the month. But, of course, I had no money. So, like the brother in the story who doesn't believe he has anything, I had to take my buffalo and my bag of rice (aka my writing) down to the market-place and trade it for something I believed was gargantuan and beyond my scope (a holiday for the both of us).

This sort of thing goes on all the time in the world of media, but I'd never done it before. I was really nervous about it. It meant I had to learn how to put myself out there, hustle, negotiate, and be pushy – especially as I had less than a month in which to pull this off. This, of course, would inevitably entail rejection – something I still had to learn to deal with. But it also had to abide by my personal standards for a green holiday (sustainable travel). If I'm going to endorse or put my name to anything I have to agree with the company or individual's ethics. I stick by my principles whether anyone's looking or not.

When I managed to pull it off I ran screaming through the house in jubilation just as I had when I'd raised the necessary fundraising amount to run the New York City Marathon. In a situation analogous with Sam who, four years earlier, had peered down the webcam at me when I'd been wailing about how I couldn't do it and told me he 'expected more of me' and to 'get to it,' Finn had, in a roundabout way, done the same thing. He'd put his managerial head on, come down hard on me, but, in the end, I was grateful for it. But that wasn't the only thing that was about to come down hard.

During our short break, while sitting out in a hot-tub beneath the stars, Finn made a move on me. It was the first affectionate move he'd made on me in months; well, if you can call it affectionate – he just came up on me and attempted to initiate sex. This was when I had my first experience of what's known as *vagina dentata* – the vagina with teeth. Despite trying to go along with a moment which my heart just wasn't in, my body said 'NO, I'm not letting you in' – and it bit him.

His vajra (a Sanskrit term for penis) was sore for *days*. He was in agony. As you can probably imagine his attempt at sex was unsuccessful. It was then I knew something was broken (and I'm not just talking about his cock, either). Our relationship was broken.

I knew it was irrevocably broken because, holed up together, we had nothing to talk about. All we did was play a card game he taught me. His world, his whole world, revolved around the supermarket – a world about which, as much as I pretended, I just didn't care about. And now, holed up in a Scottish hideaway, the truth was coming at me in surround sound – we were very different people who had long since grown apart.

When I arrived back home I discovered an email from the originator and founder of Shakti Tantra, Hilly. While firing off emails in my search for eco retreats, I'd absentmindedly fired one off to Shakti Tantra. But when I received a reply, albeit a cautious one, I wasn't so sure how I felt about it. If I was wary of the Tough Nun, I was more wary of this Tantric business. So, I conveniently 'forgot' about it.

But a few days later Hilly was back. I could feel my resistance building as we got into a game of email tennis. I was making excuses. I was busy. I'd catch her later. Though you could tell she must have been used to folks getting cold feet as she wouldn't let up. Finally, on her third knock at my fearful door, I let her in.

Though I wasn't the only one who was suspicious – she was too. She was suspicious as to my motivations. After all, I was a magazine writer. In her experience writers usually have agendas, particularly when it comes to Tantra. She wanted to know mine. I told her I didn't have one. I explained how I'd heard Sue and Sarah's talk three years earlier in Manchester, that I'd read *The Sacred Prostitute*, and that I was now looking to do some body work in order to counter the inordinate amount of time I spent up in my head.

She said she'd need to speak with her co-founder, Sue, but, based on what I'd said, the fact she felt I was sincere and not out to pull a fast one, she was prepared to do a deal with me down at the market-place, and accept my buffalo and sack of rice in exchange for an invitation to her workshop.

Thanks to the advice the disciple offers the brother, to give away what little he perceives he has so he might know abundance, and a little pressure from Finn (albeit of the silent variety), I was now learning that I did have something to offer – my skills as a writer. And my pocketful of words were, as I was about to find out, worth more than I could ever imagine.

GOING BACK TO MY ROOTS – AN ODYSSEY

I'd like to share a wee bit of synchronicity which happened while writing this book. So I finished the last chapter on the same day the movie, *Flight*, opened. I'd seen the trailer months earlier and patiently awaited its UK release. In the movie, Denzel Washington plays a pilot who successfully crash-lands a malfunctioning plane saving most of the passengers on board. Only problem was, he was overtired and intoxicated with drugs and alcohol when he did so.

On the way to see the movie I was mulling over this chapter and its focus on descent. At Women's Invitation in Liverpool, we descended into a basement to do the workshop itself. I'm not sure if anyone else spotted this symbolism – descending into the Underworld for our initiation – but it sure wasn't lost on old mythic eyes, here.

Anyway, after watching the movie I wrote a few lines about it on my Facebook page saying it was about the highs and lows of spirit in the literal and symbolic sense – flying high in artificially induced states, before coming back down to earth with a bang as reflected by the lead character's struggle with alcohol and drugs. I won't say any more in case you haven't seen it, but I thought it a clever use of metaphor.

I also wondered whether there was any symbolism which linked it with what I was about to write. Then I got to thinking about alchemy and the idea of being grounded, because that was what we were about to do at the workshop – come back down to earth by reconnecting with our bodies. Curious, I opened Edward Edinger's book on alchemical symbolism and, lo and behold, in the chapter about *coagulatio*, I came across this:

> **Dreams of planes crashing or objects falling generally refer to coagulatio.**
>
> *– Anatomy of the Psyche*

One of the reasons I'm fond of alchemical symbolism is because its motifs continue to show up in dreams whether we're aware of them or not. If you're familiar with its symbolism it can provide you with one of the most useful insights into what's going on in your psyche. I've already introduced the colours black (*nigredo*), white (*albedo*), and red (*rubedo*) which often show up in dreams and may in turn be linked to the stages of separation (blackening), initiation (whitening), and return (reddening).

Typically, when everything turns into a dark shitty mass of confusion and despair and we find ourselves lost and in a liminal state of betwixt and between, it's usually associated with separation and the blackening of *nigredo* (the Black Dog being a term for depression).

It's then that we seek knowledge, illumination, spiritual insight ('my Bright Dawn,' says the Yaga of her horseman). This is typically associated with the whitening (*albedo*). The dark night of the *nigredo* lifts and dawn (*albedo*) breaks into our consciousness.

The third stage, the reddening (*rubedo*), is where many stumble and is analogous with the Return. After the illumination of working with your dreams and gaining knowledge or spiritual insight, this is the time to bring it back down to earth – a stage in alchemy known as *coagulatio*.

If *sublimatio* pertains to the air, spirit, and the psychological function of thinking (gaining a higher perspective of our situation), *coagulatio* pertains to the element of earth, soul, and the psychological function of sensation. So after the high-flying, enlightenment seeking whiteness of *albedo*, what we're finally asked to do is ground our lofty, up-in-the-head knowledge, our intellectual theories and spiritual illuminations, and bring it all back down to earth – in other words, walk our talk.

The medieval alchemists talked about tincturing the white with the red (poetically referred to as the *blushing*). It's because red is symbolic of the instincts, of passion, of the base chakra – the *muladhara* – which roots us here on earth, of the blood of experience, of nature red in tooth and claw, of the life-giving emotions. What they were saying was, now it's time to animate – to bring to life – courtesy of the body, all that intellectual, spiritual stuff you've learnt. So long as it all remains up in the head, it doesn't count for anything. If we don't ground our beliefs in our day-to-day actions, we'll remain little more than helium beings – all up in the head, nothing but gas and air, all talk and no action.

For many, this coming back down to earth and reconnecting with the body can feel more like a crash landing. Anyone can be perfect when they're espousing spiritual and intellectual truths they've acquired while hanging out in the head: meditating, cogitating, theorising, day-dreaming. But you try living them out. This is why consciously reconnecting with the body can be the most painful part of this journey. The Apollonian highs are great, but the lows, the depths of Hades, can come as a shock and, for many, are to be avoided at all costs, as highlighted in the above movie: gotta stay high whatever the cost, even if it costs us our lives.

To come back down into the body means to *feel*. And not everyone wants to feel into their body's depths – its sadness, its anger, its fear – especially if they've spent most of their lives neglecting them, abusing them, poisoning them. Or what of those whose bodies were never held, loved, and cherished by their parents or caregivers – what then for those individuals? How do they relate to their own matter if their bodies were never physically affirmed and unconditionally loved? Alienated from their own bodies they feel alienated from the world. Insecure in their bodies they are unable to love themselves. In turn, they believe themselves unlovable. For them, to come 'back down to earth' – that earth being their matter (*mater*, mother) – is to bring this dearth of love and affection to conscious awareness.

Then there are those Kore-like individuals, one-sided, spiritually identified light chasers of whom author Monika Wikman, speaking of such a woman says:

> Yet introverted puella attitudes can be biased towards spirit, and discovering the coagulatio mysteries of spirit indwelling and committing to forms can be difficult. Relationship with spirit came more naturally to her than relationship with form. Coming down the mountain a little and learning the mysteries of embodiment was another story. This began her confrontation with her shadow.
>
> That shadow was impatient with the facts of ordinary life and the slowness of things on the material plane. It also had not let her come into the kind of power that comes from embodying limits. What was calling her now was making peace with the facts and limits of outer life. She needed to die to life, submit to the fact of living in the material world and make peace with form so that her life and work could flourish, and she could find soul harmony. And this meant paying simple attention to the mysteries of incarnation in the lowlands, in the simplest of ways.

> – *Pregnant Darkness*

If they don't descend willingly into the Underworld that is their body and accept their limits and their humanness, such individuals may be dragged down by illness, disease, and symptom. The body will not tolerate ongoing abuse and suppression – it is not a machine. It will eventually break down.

I once asked an archetypal Apollo man (a high-flying Peter Pan of a *puer*) how he felt about something. That was all I asked: how he felt about it. Well, he spun into a free-fall. Visibly irritated, he squirmed and accused me of 'psychologising' him – and all because I asked him how he felt. He finally admitted he 'didn't do feelings.' But feelings are what the body's all about.

The pain involved as we begin our conscious descent into the body via such modes as body work can, for most, be too much to bear. But if we are to be more compassionate human beings, we must integrate the light and the dark, the 'higher' spiritually-oriented realms (*albedo*) with the 'lower' soul-oriented realms (*rubedo*).

I have little interest in listening to spiritual types who aren't in their bodies. Top-heavy (as in 'heady'), I find they lack depth and roots. Their bodies usually betray them before they even open their mouths as they often lack passion, juice, and vitality. Their fear somatised, they come across as dry, flaky, rigid and/or frigid, or stiff and/or uptight. Condescending, you also get the feeling they're looking down on you – and they usually are. There's a poem by William Butler Yeats called *Crazy Jane Talks with the Bishop* which highlights this spirit/soul split:

I met the Bishop on the road
And much said he and I.
'Those breasts are flat and fallen now,
Those veins must soon be dry;
Live in a heavenly mansion,
Not in some foul sty.'
'Fair and foul are near of kin,
And fair needs foul,' I cried.
'My friends are gone, but that's a truth
Nor grave nor bed denied,
Learned in bodily lowliness
And in the heart's pride.
A woman can be proud and stiff
When on love intent;
But Love has pitched his mansion in
The place of excrement;
For nothing can be sole or whole
That has not been rent.'

In this poem, Crazy Jane speaks for the 'bodily lowliness' of soul, and the Bishop, for the 'heavenly mansion' of spirit. But as Crazy Jane smartly concludes in a deft anti-Puritanism statement, 'nothing can be sole or whole that has not been rent.' The light can only get in and out of what has cracked up – including us. From the soul's perspective, perfection matters not. Wholeness is perfectly flawed.

So acquire knowledge, hang out in spirit by all means. After the darkness of the *nigredo* it often comes as a welcome relief. But then all that lofty learning must be incorporated, grounded down in the 'place of excrement,' here on earth. This is how we bring consciousness to matter so that, as Wikman says, 'what is matter and earthy is redeemed, is raised up into the spiritual realms and seen for its value, and what is spiritual comes down to earth.'

But there was something else bugging me about this issue of descending and I spent most of the workshop pondering it. If we hadn't have physically descended into a basement, I doubt I'd have caught the symbolism at all. Anyway, it was this: we went *voluntarily*. And to hammer the message home, the workshop was called Women's Invitation. We were *invited*. We weren't dragged, weren't forced. We went consciously and of our own accord knowing that, whatever we faced down there, it might potentially involve us being stripped bare and forced back on ourselves, as Marion Woodman says here:

A life truly lived constantly burns away veils of illusion, opening our eyes to our uniqueness.

A life truly lived burns away what is no longer relevant, gradually reveals our essence until, at last, we are strong enough to stand in our own naked truth.

– *Coming Home to Myself*

So why did this bug me? Because, despite descending into the Underworld, it didn't chime with Persephone's myth: she was dragged. We weren't. Up until this point I'd spent most of my time studying the Greek god and goddess archetypes. But there was one myth I hadn't spent a great deal of time with: The Descent of Inanna/Ishtar.

In this magnificent myth – which is, by the way, the oldest recorded myth, predating Christ, Odin, and the many other heroes who have since sacrificed themselves in one way or another in order to redeem us or atone for our 'sins' – Inanna (her Sumerian name; Ishtar being her Akkadian name) voluntarily descends into the Underworld to visit her sister, the Dark Goddess Ereshkigal – 'great lady under earth.' As Diane Wolkstein tell us:

From the Great Above she opened her ear to the Great Below.

From the Great Above the goddess opened her ear to the Great Below.

From the Great Above Inanna opened her ear to the Great Below.

– *Inanna*

109

Although Inanna is Queen of Heaven and Earth, she knows nothing of the Underworld and all it entails – namely, death and rebirth (better known collectively as Resurrection). Now, I don't know about you, but you've got to give credit to anyone who wakes up one day and thinks, 'You know, it's occurred to me I know nothing of the mysteries of death and rebirth. Hmmm, what to do, what to do... I know! I'll go visit my sister, the Dark Goddess Ereshkigal – she who rules all those things I've so far neglected and is everything I'm not. Though, with her dark and dreary disposition, I can't imagine she'll be best pleased to see me. In which case, I'd better make plans to ensure my return in case she keeps me hanging around. Where's my trusted minister and servant, Ninshubur? Think I'm gonna need her help for this one.'

You're damn right she'll need her help – especially when you read Sylvia Brinton Perera's description of Ereshkigal:

Ereshkigal defies differentiated consciousness. She is paradoxical: both the vessel and the stake. She is the root of all, where energy is inert and consciousness coiled asleep. She is the place where potential life lies motionless – but in the pangs of birth; beneath all language and its distinction, yet judging and acting. She is energy banishing itself into the underworld, too awesome to behold – like primal childhood experiences and the darkness of the moon, places of oblivion that are the perilous ground on which daylight consciousness treads, the primal matrix. And she holds the wisdom of that isolation and bitterness. She is receiver of all, yet adversary and death-dealing inevitable victor.

And if that's not enough to whet your appetite, she goes on to say:

She is full of fury, greed, the fear of loss, and even of self-spite. She symbolises raw instinctuality split off from consciousness – need and aggression in the underworld.

– Descent to the Goddess

She sounds like fun, doesn't she? As far as I'm concerned, there's looking for trouble and there's *looking for trouble*. Thanks to my mythic imagination, my penchant for symbolic thinking, and where I was in my own Great Round of Transformation, I knew there was more to come. I also knew it wouldn't be a barrel of laughs. But neither had I stopped to consider what I was about to let myself in for – not

110

consciously. Because if someone had taken me by the shoulders, looked me in the eye, and said: 'Thea, where you're going you're not coming back from. Even if you do, you'll never be the same. You're right those three marathons were a walk in the park. Even writing a book was a breeze compared to what you're about to experience. I'm telling you, bright eyes, that batshit crazy bitch is gonna open you up, expose your innermost fears and insecurities, rip you from limb to limb and hang you out to dry. We're talking resurrection, baby. And you know what that means? It means death. It means you're gonna *die*. After all, after *coagulatio* there inevitably follows a *mortificatio*,' I doubt I'd have ever emailed Shakti Tantra.

Speaking of the Resurrection stage, Christopher Vogler says:

> **Why do so many stories seem to have two climaxes or death-and-rebirth ordeals, one near the middle and another just near the end of the story? The college semester metaphor suggests the reason. The central crisis or Supreme Ordeal is like a mid-term exam; the Resurrection is the final exam. Heroes must be tested one last time to see if they retained the learning from the Supreme Ordeal of Act Two.**
>
> **To learn something in a Special World is one thing; to bring the knowledge home as applied wisdom is quite another. Students can cram for a test but the Resurrection stage represents a field trial of a hero's new skills, in the real world. It's both a reminder of death and a test of the hero's learning. Was the hero sincere about change? Will she backslide or fail, be defeated by neuroses or a Shadow at the eleventh hour?**

> **– The Writer's Journey**

He isn't kidding. Though at the time I set out to do this workshop, it was born out of an acknowledgement that I had to consciously face and submit to my body's wisdom and not because I wanted to 'die' in any sense of the word. I knew full well it was time to climb down from the high horse of my mind and get down and dirty in the Underworld. I also wanted to get down and dirty on the sexual front and reclaim those aspects of myself I'd repressed and ignored, and of which I was ashamed – the Dark Goddess.

Up until that point I'd spent years studying, reading, learning. Self-taught, I'd proved myself to myself countless times over, grappling with obscure texts, writing a book. Like Inanna, I now knew I was 'bright.' But I was never going to learn about the 'dark wisdom' of my body from books. No. To learn about my body's mysteries required conscious experience.

But like Inanna who makes arrangements with her executive, Ninshubur, before she makes her descent, I'd also made arrangements to ensure my return – only, I didn't know it. Thanks to my studies and a mythic mind, by the time I reached the Athens Marathon I was able to consciously approach it as a ritual.

So as soon as I descended into the basement in Liverpool that Friday night in February 2011, my imagination sparked to life as my soul aligned with an ancient knowing. The room hummed with it. If I wasn't familiar with the archetypes at play, it could have just been a group of women gathered to do body work, but it wasn't. Something deeper was at play and I could feel it. This energy was like nothing I'd ever experienced before. But the deal was done when I finally clapped eyes on my teacher, Hilly, with her fabulous shock of silver grey hair – Hecate/Yaga was in the house.

THE BINDING OF ISAAC

I liked Hilly right from the start. With the sex appeal of actress Helen Mirren and the *je ne regrette rien* of Brigitte Bardot, she reminded me of my aunt with her innate sense of self-confidence and ability to cut to the chase. Besides my aunt, she's only the second woman I've ever met with a Hecate/Yaga vibe. As we were in a Tantra setting you could say it was a Kali-like energy – and in a way it was. After all, I'd looked that energy straight in the eye in India and was all too familiar with it. But at the time I did this workshop I was more familiar with Hecate/Yaga, so it was those two who coloured my perspective of her.

One of the things I appreciate about such energy is its ability to contain. If you're in the presence of an initiated, bona fide Crone, her presence acts as a tuning fork: it resonates throughout the room, sets the tone for the space. My aunt does this with our family – contains it. It's not spoken. She doesn't need to *do* anything to contain it – her presence, her *beingness* is enough. That's natural authority.

When a space is contained, you feel safe to let go and be yourself because you know someone else is holding it. On entering the workshop I was immediately on the lookout for this. I don't care how much someone professes to know, how many qualifications they may or may not have: I was there to do body work and if I didn't feel safe enough to relax and let go, forget it.

Sat in a circle with a group of other women I felt this containing energy and I knew it was coming from Hilly. But it also made me smile – smile, because our culture isn't familiar with this energy and, so, it can bring out all sorts of strange reactions in people, particularly women.

I'd read about the dynamics of group psychology and heard Marion Woodman speak about her experiences of running women's BodySoul workshops. As such, I was aware the group itself can act as the archetypal Mother as it collectively holds and nurtures individuals who may not have had positive experiences of being mothered as children. For some, this may be the first time they've been seen and accepted for who they really are. This was what I meant when I said the archetype of Mother takes many forms and isn't just confined to biological mothers.

But although the group was collectively acting as Mother and Hilly, herself, is a personal mother (and grandmother), Hecate/Yaga was present. And, as previously mentioned, not only does this archetype wield a sharp discerning sword, it isn't sentimental either. She won't molly-coddle you. So when, as in the story of Vasilisa, the Baba Yaga asks you what you're doing here, don't try and suck up to her. And don't bother with the nicey-nicey act either. The Yaga can see straight through it.

Not that I'm saying that this is what Hilly's like – this is just my perspective of the energy I felt was present in the room. But I had heard, from others, that she had little patience for those who attempt to cling to her teats for acceptance or approval; those who start up with the attention-playing games; those women who storm out the room and refuse to return because they want her (mummy) to run after them with a reassuring, 'There, there.' Forget it. She has assistants – Demeters among them – for that.

In my experience of growing up with this archetype, that doesn't stop people from desperately trying to impress her, to seek her approval, to want her to like them. But the point of this work, near as I can tell, is you're there to be initiated into the fullness of your womanhood. As such, a severing of your old infantile ways is necessary and it *will* hurt. The Crone knows this. But this is not the place for namby-pambying, for wrapping you in cotton wool. She isn't standing by watching as you're dragged off into the Underworld to be ravished – she's holding the door open, pointing the way and, if necessary, kicking you down the damned stairs.

Though don't let me give the impression she's a cruel, callous old cow – far from it. If you're being true to yourself and are committed to coming to consciousness, her respect, support, and love for you is fierce. Just don't bother with the game-playing, attention-seeking nonsense. She has neither the time nor the wherewithal. There's work to be done. So get to it.

But what really nailed it for me, was something Hilly said towards the end of the first exercise she'd asked us to do. It was this: *Can you smell the sweetness in the room?* On hearing this I sat bolt upright in a move Lazarus would have been proud of. As soon as she said it I knew I was *absolutely* in the right place. The sweetness she spoke of was the same sweetness Woodman talks about which is naturally inherent in the body. The exercise she'd asked us to do had encouraged this sweetness. In fact, by the time we'd finished the exercise it was so tangible, you could taste it.

I'm not sharing what went on in, what we did in the workshop. The thing with this work is you have to be there. After all, the whole point of body work is that it's experiential. Besides, the work we did is in the spirit of women's mysteries which is why you're asked not to speak about what goes on to anyone outside. To do so is to profane the work and rob others of the unique opportunity to experience it for themselves. Not that *that* stops women blabbing. While you're in the workshop you're an initiate in a *temenos*, a sacred space, with Hilly and her ever-watchful assistants acting as temple priestesses, you might say.

In fact, they *are* acting as temple priestesses. They're acting as temple priestesses on behalf of Inanna/Ishtar and of all those goddesses of love, sexuality, and harlots who followed her including Cybele, Isis, and Aphrodite/Venus. This is why, despite being in a Tantra setting, the exercises and rituals we did felt to me like something straight out of ancient times. Sat in that basement I knew, beyond all shadow of doubt that, despite a 'lack of concrete evidence,' there *had* been such individuals as sacred prostitutes – they'd just gone underground.

Quashed by patriarchy and the rise of the Fathers in their attempt to control matter (including bodies, women, and the earth), the Dark Feminine had gone into hiding. But her soul hadn't died as I discovered much to my delight. She'd just become a subterranean renegade. And, as they say in Tantra, Shakti's rising.

So it's pointless telling anyone who hasn't been initiated into such mysteries what goes on in these sacred spaces. This work can't be understood nor comprehended from a cool, uninitiated distance. The only way to experience it is to surrender to it – to leave your rational, logical head at the door and surrender to the body's wisdom. Because it has a wisdom, believe you me.

For me, the essence of this first workshop entailed being turned back on yourself, being reintroduced to your body. And for many, this is where the fun begins – I was no exception. Prior to this workshop, getting my estranged head and body into the same room to talk terms, had been nigh-on impossible. Disconnected from the neck down, I did *not* want to know what went on down there (meaning anything below the neck).

Despite my reservations regards my bodily fears and insecurities, I had been 'prepared,' you might say, by means of four separate events in the years leading up to the workshop. And if I could survive them, I could survive anything Shakti Tantra threw at me.

The first event took place in late 2005. My Reiki teacher, Suriyah, offered me a full body massage in her new home. I knew she offered massages but I'd never had one. As she prepared the room and kindled the fire, she told me to get undressed. But as I approached the couch with my underwear on and towel wrapped around me, she looked at me and said, 'No, Thea – everything.'

'What, *everything* everything?' I said.

'Everything off,' she said. 'This is a full body massage. And you need to be naked.'

Though I may have attempted to be all cool and calm about it, inside

I freaked out. I was *mortified* about being seen naked – mortified and ashamed. To openly display my body was akin to bearing my soul's weeping wounds. The only reason I went along with it was because she was my friend and teacher and I trusted her... just.

Although Suriyah hasn't done any Tantra training she has an undeniable gift when it comes to massage and body work. Intuitive, her hands emit something that can't be taught – love. She loves bodies. She doesn't care about their shape or size: she loves them all unconditionally, exactly as they are. And I mean *loves* them.

It's not anything she says; rather, you feel it in the way she touches you. I've met many technically proficient masseurs, but none of them have ever come anywhere near her. She doesn't try and pummel your body into submission, iron out its kinks and knots with a forceful hand. She tends to it, cares for it, and sensually soothes it. Her philosophy is simple: she touches others in the same way she likes to be touched.

And so, on that cold November night by a roaring fire, she took me in her loving hands and gently coaxed my uptight body into a meditative state of bliss. My body felt like a baby's who was being celebrated and cherished. But even this upset me. Not because she'd done anything wrong, but because I felt she loved my body more than I did. If anything, this threw into even sharper relief the contempt I'd long harboured towards myself and made me feel even more ashamed. Still, despite my hang-ups, it was one of the most exquisite experiences I'd ever had.

The second event took place three years later after I picked up an injury at the Rome Marathon. When I realised the injury wasn't going to go away on its own and with the Athens Marathon looming on the horizon, I knew I had to seek help. But the thought of this (seeking help) terrified me.

Despite having lost a ton of weight and generally feeling sexier when it came to my physical appearance, I hadn't dealt with the underlying issues when it came to my psychological insecurities. The only reason I'd let go with Suriyah was because she was a woman and my friend. So when I eventually found a sports therapist, I was beyond horrified when he looked at me somewhat quizzically and said, 'Erm, you're going to have to take your pants off.'

We've since laughed about it ('How the hell did you think I was going to massage you if you didn't take your pants off?'), but at the time it was no laughing matter. For most of my life my thighs have been a source of shame and have held an inordinate amount of tension thanks, in large part, to my uptight attitudes surrounding sex. So to let a stranger – a man at that – see them in broad daylight? Are you kidding me? I would later learn, from Shakti Tantra, that the thighs form part of what are known as the 'shame muscles' for the same reasons I've just mentioned. But by surrendering to his healing hands I'd taken another small step at bridging the gap between mind and matter.

The next event took place a couple of years later in spring 2010 – this time at the Esalen Institute, Big Sur, California. Now this place was a treat. I was in the States for a Michael Meade workshop which was being held in the Santa Cruz Mountains and, later, to film an interview in New York about my recently released book. (You remember that one, right? The bestseller?)

Anyway, my friend Caitlin, who I was staying with in Santa Cruz, took me on a road trip along the breathtaking Pacific Coast Highway (the 'Amalfi Coast on steroids,' as I described it). Along the way we stopped by the Henry Miller Library where we had a picnic before later spending the afternoon at Esalen's cliff-side hot springs (also known as 'the baths') where my friend had booked us in for one of their famous massages.

What I didn't know, until we parked up, was this place was clothing optional. As I grabbed my bag with my swimwear, Caitlin looked at me and said, 'You won't be needing those.'

'What do you mean?' I asked.

'Everyone here goes naked. You're more likely to stand out if you're the only one who's wearing something.'

As the blood pooled from my face, my ghostly white expression must have said it all. Caitlin laughed at me. If I'd have known beforehand what I was about to let myself in for, I doubt I'd have gone. I mean, seriously, since when have the Americans done the whole naked in public thing? The Americans don't do naturism, do they? I'd always thought they were as uptight as us Brits. Well, apparently not.

Shuffling down the cliff-side slope from the main grounds to the cliff-side springs felt like the walk to hell. Though it was the image I was greeted with on arrival at the baths which has been forever etched, nay, *seared*, into my mind's eye. As we ascended the steps, I looked up to see an Adonis of a naked man saunter past with the most magnificent, most luscious lingam (another Sanskrit term for penis) I had ever seen. My mouth gaped open in awe. In retrospect this probably wasn't the best moment for such open-mouthed appreciation, but I couldn't help it. *Wow. This place really is all about the whole public-naked thing.* But the fun wasn't over.

Walking out onto the Oceanside veranda where all the hot-tubs are, I pretended I was okay about exposing my pasty, dimpled British backside to all these buff, bronzed Californian men and women (who, by the way, weren't – though my preconception was all Californians have beach perfect bodies). But it was my woeful attempt at climbing into one of the hot-tubs which really did it.

I was trying to be all ladylike about it, pressing my thighs together so

I could swing them over in one deft move, but it wasn't happening. Three men in a nearby hot-tub were watching me – probably bemused. After a couple of pathetic attempts, there was only one thing for it: unceremoniously, I flung one leg over opening my legs so wide apart they probably saw all the way up to my tonsils. And with that, I sank straight to the bottom of the tub in the vain hopes that, when I came up for air, everyone would have magically disappeared.

But Esalen still wasn't done with me. Oh no. Caitlin had booked us in for one of their famous namesake massages. Soon, it was my turn. *I bet I get a man.* And I was right. When he called my name, I stood up, stark bollocky buff, from my hot-tub and calmly followed him into the treatment area while still pretending I was okay with this being naked in public thing.

Once on the massage table he covered me with a teensy-weensy towel to protect my modesty. In the distance I could hear the waves of the Pacific crashing against the bluff below. As settings go, this has to be one of the most beautiful in the world in which to receive a massage. But at the time I was so busy being horrified I just couldn't appreciate it. So I decided there was only one thing for it – play possum.

As he began my treatment I lay there, deadweight. He'd told me beforehand I wouldn't have to move a muscle, that he'd manoeuvre my body into the necessary positions. He wasn't wrong. Doing my finest impersonation of a corpse about to undergo an autopsy, I feigned sleep as he made origami out of me, folding me this way and that. Any minute now he'd turn me into a plane and send me gliding out across the ocean. Not.

So it was towards the end of the treatment, while performing one of his more dexterous moves, that I think we were both glad I was 'asleep' when – and there's no other way to put this – the towel got wedged in the crack of my arse. I had to stifle my laughter as he discreetly tried pulling it out. Oh my goodness, the horror I felt. Not only was I the pasty Brit, I was now the pasty Brit with the towel devouring backside. Soon it would be on the rampage. Naked, screaming Californians, running for cover, diving into the Pacific to escape my Venus Flytrap towel-chomping cheeks.

Afterwards, Caitlin asked how my treatment was. I told her about the towel-wedgie moment. 'Yes,' I said, 'today will go down in my personal history as *The Day My Ass Ate a Towel at Esalen.*'

The fourth preparatory event – as if the others weren't enough – happened during a press trip in December 2011. It was my first press trip and I'd been sent to cover the opening of a new hotel complex in Taba, Egypt. During my flying visit I was offered a spa treatment. I opted for a rejuvenating scrub massage. What I didn't know, until I rocked up at my appointment, was only men worked in the spa (women were forbidden to under sharia law).

As he set about massaging my face, neck, and breasts, I recalled my previous experiences, gave up, and just let go. I lay there thinking how far I'd come with regards exposing my body to strangers these past years. Striding along the beach in India, my labia minora operation, naked massages, and bum wedgies. There was little point in getting all uptight about being seen naked anymore. My insecurities, although they hadn't gone away, had been massaged and trimmed to a weary pulp. Resistance was futile.

But though I didn't particularly care what this first workshop threw at me, doesn't mean to say I was happy about it. After we'd finished on the first evening, I didn't stay over (accommodation was optional). Instead, I jumped in my car and drove home; partly because I was so skint and couldn't afford it. But also because, deep down, I could only stand being turned back on myself to a certain point.

Depending on your relationship, or lack of, with your body, it can get pretty intense as you set about rebuilding bridges between mind and matter. It's not something that happens overnight, that's for sure. For several women, things got pretty hairy. So on the Friday and Saturday night, after we were done, I did the 60-mile round trip home and back again.

To be honest, I was glad to get out as it gave me the opportunity to reflect on what I'd experienced. Conscious reflection is my modus operandi. This work was new and I needed some time to myself to think and to see how I really felt away from everyone, even if it was only time spent alone in a car.

What I did notice, almost immediately, was just how angry I was – angry with myself for letting my unhappy situation with Finn drag on as long as it had and angry with him for being impatient, for expecting me to save him from the unhappiness he felt in his job and for turning against me when it (change) didn't happen fast enough. Then there was the anger I couldn't put my finger on. During the workshop there had been plenty of opportunities to share what the various exercises and structures had brought up for each of us. Although I didn't stop yapping, I didn't let on about the anger I could feel building. But on my drives back and forth, I could feel it brewing beneath the surface and it was *volcanic*.

Lay in bed next to him each night I barely slept. My mind was whirring, processing, assimilating all I'd experienced. There'd been a lot of talk of self-worth, of putting one's self first – the latter of which, it seemed, most women struggled with for fear of being called selfish.

My aunt had always told me to put myself first. 'That's where your foundations are,' she'd say. 'Otherwise, you're like ever shifting sands with no centre, trying to please everyone else and never pleasing yourself. It all starts with you. Because if you don't like or respect yourself, how can you ever expect anyone else to? And why should they if you don't? Your self-respect is a message to the world of your self-worth. And if they don't like you, fuck 'em. You're not here to be liked – you're here to be true to yourself. Always remember that.'

Now, in the workshop, Hilly was at it too. But not only was she encouraging us to put self first, she was telling us to be self full. She explained how most people go through the world with a begging bowl hoping others will fill it for them – sexually, emotionally, financially, creatively – rather than attempting to fill it for themselves; half-folks looking to be completed by other half-folks. 'Two people who, when they're together, barely make one person,' she said. In short, she was encouraging us to be one-in-ourselves – which, psychologically speaking, is the self-fructifying, self-fulfilling virgin archetype.

I knew she was right. Thomas Moore echoes this sentiment when he says:

> In sex we are also called upon to be generous, to be extraordinarily giving of our bodies and emotions. It's a simple thing, this virtue of generosity, and yet we might easily overlook its importance when we become entangled in the complexities of interpersonal relationship. In matters of the heart and the sexual body generosity is one of the central virtues, because sex usually requires the sensation of abundance – full presence, overflowing love, extraordinary attention, and volumes of pleasure. Two people give themselves to each other, and each hopes that the other has something to give and is free to give it abundantly.

> – *The Soul of Sex*

Osho also speaks to this overflowing self-abundance when he says:

> What ordinarily happens in the world is this: You don't have love; the person you think you love has no love in his being, either, and both are asking for love from each other. Two beggars begging each other! Hence, the fight, the conflict, the continuous quarrel between the lovers – over trivia, over immaterial things, over stupid things! – but they go on quarrelling.

> When you are in a state of overflowing joy, then you can share. The word selfish has taken on a very condemnatory association because all the religions have condemned it. They want you to be unselfish. People are told to help others, and

they are empty within themselves. They are being told to love others – love your neighbours, love your enemies – and they are never told to love themselves. The basic thing is to love yourself so totally that the love overflows you and reaches to others.

– Intimacy

I knew my aunt was right, too. But it can be tough putting yourself first, especially when your own mother has, in the past, accused you of being selfish; an accusation for which my aunt had leapt to my defence. 'She's right to be selfish,' she'd said. 'If she doesn't learn to put herself first, everyone will walk all over her.' But my mum is strongly identified with the Demeter (mother) archetype, whereas my aunt is Artemis/Hecate – one-in-herself.

Being among this self-affirming energy was fast filling my bowl. My body was greeted and accepted positively. Shame was being flung at walls, devils shook off, long-held rage roared. Though each of us had our own agendas we were united in our support of one another to be all we could be. In the outside world it's all about competition, about getting one up on others, pulling one another down, holding one another back. Not here. In this workshop it was about witnessing and supporting one another.

It felt like a long time since I'd been with other women in an environment like that, an environment in which I was mirrored, seen, and heard. By nature, I'm an introverted soul preferring to keep myself to myself. So I didn't realise what a relief it was to finally talk about some of the more personal issues I'd been hauling around with me – intimate issues such as my operation.

Sharing my experiences with others and hearing the feedback from Hilly, Sarah, and the other assistants, made me wish I'd been exposed to attitudes and opinions like theirs back in secondary school. There was no shame here, no rigid, frigid, morally uptight attitudes about sex, women, and their bodies. If every girl in our culture had done a workshop such as this in their teens, our culture would be nothing like it currently is with its high teenage pregnancies and body dysmorphic disorders.

But the overriding message I took away was I deserved better. Don't get me wrong, Finn wasn't a bad person – not at all. The pieces between us just didn't fit any more. Perhaps they never did. But in his cooling off and backing away, I'd come to realise what was important to me. It was time to stop pretending I didn't want someone to grab me by the hand, to complement me on my appearance, to love *and* lust after me. To buy me flowers – not because they *think* they should, but just because they can't help themselves and because they also know how much they make my heart sing.

Oh heaven help me, I'm such a romantic. I crave the beautiful and the mythical. A self-confessed aesthete, I love the finer things in life. And even when I don't have a pot to squat in doesn't mean I forego beauty. Art galleries and museums are free. Being out in nature and watching shooting stars costs nothing. A bon vivant, I appreciate and savour fine food and wine. I love to smell good and feel good.

In fact, while I'm on the subject of self-care, on the Sunday morning before returning to the workshop I'd showered using some organic products a company had sent me to trial. It was a luscious, pomegranate shower cream (what better for a trip to the Underworld?). While showering I consciously contemplated how I related to my body. Rather than mindlessly slathering it on while thinking about the day ahead, I slowed down and turned it into an opportunity to meditate on myself. Later, at the workshop, one of the girls commented on how wonderful I smelt, before going on to remark on my 'beautiful hair' – something on which several other women had also commented.

When she said that, I had to stop myself from crying. Aside from my family, I couldn't remember the last time someone had said something complimentary to me about any aspect of my appearance. Her comment wasn't in the least bit contrived either. For so long, I'd pretended being physically appreciated didn't matter. But you know what? It did. And you know what else? It felt damn good.

By the time I left the workshop on the Sunday afternoon I'd made up my mind to end my relationship with Finn. Enough was enough. We couldn't go on like this any longer. He was clearly unhappy and so was I. On the drive home I ran through everything I wanted to say to him. After that, I'd move my belongings back to my parents' house. But one thing was for certain – I no longer wanted to stay.

What I now find funny was, although fuming, during that drive home I listened to an album by Bliss called *A Hundred Thousand Angels* which is all New Age and, well, *angelic*. The contrast between my bad mood and the *Om Shantis* and *Shiv Shaktis* enveloping me couldn't have been starker if they'd tried.

But I wasn't the only one in a bad mood. Finn had obviously been mulling things over and was clearly unhappy too. No sooner had I walked through the door when a red mist descended and it all came out. Although Finn wasn't a shouter (not Apollo's style), the fact I was earning no money, had failed in my promise to have him out of his job by the Christmas just gone, and had now gone off to a Tantra workshop, well, let's just say he wasn't best pleased about it.

This, however, was the moment I discovered something about myself which could only ever have happened if my back had been firmly up against the wall. Listening to him talk I felt myself siding with an inner presence. What this inner presence was, I couldn't have told you. All I knew was, if I had to make a choice between Finn and this inner presence, however tenuous it may have been, I'd choose the latter.

The only thing that mattered was honouring this presence. I'd come too far to give up on it now. And if defending this presence meant losing everything and everyone, so be it. If defending this presence meant sacrificing everything, so be it. But I would *not* be moved. Even though I didn't have a damned clue where this was all heading, I'd sacrificed too much, come too far to give up now. In that moment I realised, soul through bone, for the first time in my life that I believed in something – my Self.

When we failed to reach a compromise, when I told him point blank that there was no Plan B, there was only one thing left to do – end things and move out. I packed up as many of my belongings as I could and threw them in the car. When I turned up at my parents with half my belongings on their doorstep and a face like thunder, they knew this was not the time for twenty questions. They quickly helped me unload so I could go back and collect the rest.

In the time it took to drive to my parents' place and back, Finn had obviously had time to cool down and think, because it was a very different man who greeted me on my return. Apologetic, he told me he didn't want me to leave. As he spoke, I stood in silence, listening. But I had nothing more to say.

Today, if I'm being honest, I knew then our relationship was dead in the water. Broken beyond all repair, the gulf between us was just too wide to reach across to one another. But as I listened to him share his feelings I also recognised, in myself, that the workshop had released raw, instinctual archetypal energies. In other words, if I left now, it would have been solely from anger – Ares being the Greek god of war (and whom the Romans called Mars). Of this archetype, Jean Shinoda Bolen says:

This is a reactive, here-and-now archetype ... when rage and anger arise he reacts instinctively and often gets into situations that are detrimental to him and damaging to others. In either case, not considering to whom he is responding, and what the consequences will be, leads to trouble.

– *Gods in Everyman*

Though not an angry person, I don't suffer fools gladly and, if provoked, my temper can be epic. I'm strongly streaked with Ares who, in astrology, is associated with the red planet, Mars (in my birth chart, I have Mars in Leo). The irony is I don't like being around violent, hostile, or uncouth people and yet, in contrast to my beauty-loving, somewhat sybaritic ways, I have a coarse underbelly that can be fiercely aggressive and can pour forth words that can peel the paint off walls. For someone who believed themselves a genteel, flower-like Kore, it's been challenging to acknowledge and integrate this raw, instinctual shadow-side of my nature.

Though I hadn't shouted and argued with Finn, I still recognised this anger as it surged through my body filling me with a false confidence and indignation at the wrongs I'd believed he'd inflicted on me. But I also knew, from reading Jung et al that when powerful new energy is released from the unconscious – whether through body work or therapy – the ego can temporarily identify with it and, if it's not careful, be overthrown. To identify with this energy is akin to identifying with the gods themselves – a state also known as *inflation*.

Right now I was feeling very inflated, all puffed up in a state of self-righteous anger. But what would happen once that anger passed and I resumed my normal human-sized shape again? I'd flounced out of one too many relationships in my life, flared up in moments I'd later come to regret. But I knew better now. In fact, there's a short story about a noble samurai warrior who, after his master is murdered, seeks to avenge his death. After many years he finally tracked down and caught the assassin. But as the samurai drew his sword to kill the murderer the man spat in his face. With that, the samurai sheathed his sword and walked away.

When the man spat at the samurai he made him angry. But the moment it became personal, the samurai knew that, had he killed the man, he would have no longer been upholding the samurai's conduct of honour or justice. To have killed the man under such circumstances would have been to go against the samurai's principles as he would have identified with the anger instead.

There was also another reason I chose not to leave even though I had serious misgivings about our future together. In alchemy, there's an idea I'd heard mentioned but, until that point, had never really understood. Michael Meade discusses it on one of his talks and it had always stayed with me. He put it like this: *Stay in the tension and the glue will be produced.*

When he says 'stay in the tension,' he's not saying to stay in an abusive or dangerous situation; rather, he's saying that, whenever we find ourselves torn between two opposing poles, caught between this and that, to hold off making an immediate decision. The idea is if you don't attempt to make a gut- or head-based decision, you make space for a heart-based decision to arise naturally of its own accord instead. And as we all know, the heart has reasons reason cannot know.

Author, Catherine MacCoun relates this idea to the alchemical stage of conjunction (*coniunctio*). She puts it this way:

... two is also the number of irresolvable conflict: the standoff, the stalemate, the obstinate stupidity of either/or. Where only two are gathered, there is nobody to break the tie. In its own way, two can be static as one, only this time the stasis is painful. Another being is present, yet we are isolated in our separateness, the conflict that establishes the two. If we could just become one, this painful tension would end. Hence the attraction of any religious idea or experience that promises to return us to the cosy cocoon of unity.

Neither one nor two is entirely satisfactory. Might there be a better number?

In alchemy, that number is three. As two is the principle of separation, three is the number of conjunction. Three is the dynamic form of one.

Of what does this three consist? If I am one and you make two, who or what is three?

Three is our between.

– On Becoming an Alchemist

Ah, the archetypal third. With regards this *threeness*, the Taoists and medieval alchemists share a similar precept. Whereas the alchemists say: 'One becomes two, two becomes three, and out of the third comes the one as the fourth,' the Taoists say: 'The Tao produced One; One produced Two; Two produced Three; Three produced All things.' Three is the number of mounting momentum, of change. From the third something new is created, a new situation arises.

If a situation between two people is stagnant – say they're stuck in a painful stasis – whether this is acknowledged or not, you can pretty much guarantee a situation will eventually arise so things can be loosened to enable things to flow again (solution related to the alchemical stage of *solutio/dissolutio*, remember?). After all, the one constant in life is change. And how does this loosening of the heart happen? Eros. Welcome on stage the magnetic, the alchemical goddess of love triangles, threesomes, and creation herself – Aphrodite.

Whenever I hear that someone in a marriage or committed relationship is having an affair or finds themselves as the outside *other* who has come between a couple, rather than judging the person/situation, condemning it as wrong, I now recognise something new may be trying to arise, something new created, new life brought forth. So instead of getting all moralistic about it, I'm more likely to ask, 'What has become stuck here?' 'What new situation seeks to be created or resolved?' 'What is trying to move here?' Of this Aphroditic archetype, Bolen says:

Aphrodite is a tremendous force for change. Through her flow attraction, union, fertilisation, incubation, and birth of new life. When this process happens on a purely physical plane between a man and a woman, a baby is conceived. And the sequence is the same in all other creative processes as well: attraction, union, fertilisation, incubation, a new creation. The creative product can be abstract as an inspired union of two ideas that eventually gives birth to new theory.

– Goddesses in Everywoman

As much as we like to think we spend our lives *doing*, we forget how much we're *done to*, acted upon by external forces – these forces being archetypal. These transpersonal forces (as represented by the gods and goddesses in Greek mythology) are more powerful and lie way beyond the scope of our human egos. 'I don't know what came over me,' we'll say. 'I was consumed with desire.' Well, *duh* – of course you were. I mean, seriously, since when did anyone wake up in the morning and decide they were going to fall in love with a specific someone of their own accord? Not only that, but make the person love them back? (Not that this stops certain naïve, disillusioned people from having a bloody good go as they set about focusing all their attention on another in an attempt to *make* them love them.)

What we often fail to realise is we don't generate love; rather, it comes at us out of leftfield. In other words, we're *hit* by it like a bolt from the blue (remember Eros, son of Aphrodite, and his arrows causing havoc left, right, and centre?). That's what it means to be love-struck. You walk into a bar when – BAM – you find yourself completely and utterly smitten with a stranger across the room. Or you suddenly find yourself attracted to a work colleague you'd previously considered a friend. That warm, gooey feeling in your heart? That spontaneous secretion of sticky stuff in your knickers/underpants? That's the fallout of Aphrodite – the archetypal minx of melting and merging. That's eros, *solutio* – the great alchemical loosener.

Now I'm not saying I condone affairs of the heart, but neither am I so quick to condemn them. We are, after all, mortal human beings whose lives are at the whim of forces far greater than we'll ever be able to comprehend. To believe ourselves capable of generating such transpersonal forces is akin to believing we are the gods themselves; an attitude which – like me momentarily aligning myself with Ares – is tantamount to hubris. What we should remember is we're mortal souls doing the best we can. To consciously accept this would allow us more compassion for the human condition.

Stood facing Finn I wasn't sure how my heart felt. My anger was fogging everything. My gut wanted out and my head wasn't far behind it.

But, like I said, I've been hasty before and have later come to regret it. I'd always been one to flit from relationship to relationship and I didn't want to do that anymore either. Relationships take work, they're not all plain sailing – I knew this now. So although I didn't necessarily believe the words he was telling me I decided to hold the conflict in my heart, stay in the tension, and see what 'glue,' if any, would be produced. After all, I had no better ideas. If it was really over I trusted the Fates would show me the way.

C IS FOR CURIOUSER AND...

The morning after the tumultuous night before I was still at sixes and sevens. My body was humming, pulsating from my experience at the workshop. My belongings were strewn up the walls with half of them still over at my parents' place. But though my anger had subsided, my head was still befuddled. When I feel like that I can't write no matter how hard I try and I had to write my piece about the workshop while it was still fresh in my mind's eye. *A workshop which caused holy hell*, I thought, as I banged away at the keyboard.

So to sit down and write an article straight out, especially under stressful circumstances, was unusual for me. Normally, I need time to reflect on whatever experience it is I'm writing about, tease out a thread of story – but not this time. In fact, it wasn't until I watched the words spill out across the screen that I realised the passionate extent of my feelings for the body work I'd just done. I felt this work was important, relevant, and much needed in our culture and I wanted to tell the world about it. Here's the article I wrote:

WOMEN'S INVITATION: WORKSHOP REVIEW

If there's one thing that tires (read: bores) me more than anything, it's the press's mind-numbingly predictable, tittilatingly-sensationalised coverage of all things Tantra related. The words 'Sting' and 'go at it for hours' spring to mind.

When it comes to sex and sensuality we're a prudish lot. Although we like to think we're sexually liberated and laid-back, we're mostly fearful, uptight, and embarrassed when it comes to sexual matters.

We're also terrified of intimacy. Speaking from my own experience, it never fails to surprise me how insecure and inhibited men also are once they're undressed and in a sexual situation. I've seen penises retreat so far inside bodies I'm surprised they've not popped out the other side. Men, it seems, carry as many sexual hang-ups and bodily insecurities as women despite their bravado to the contrary.

You see, no-one teaches us about sex. In fact, no-one even teaches us about our bodies and the intricacies of our intimacies. And so we stumble and fumble in the darkness beneath the duvet or in candlelight (if we're feeling adventurous). Although men regularly handle their vajras when they pee, and women may entertain their yonis with a vibrator or, horror of horrors, their fingers if they dare touch themselves 'down there,' the potentialities of our sexual centres remain a relative mystery.

My interest in Tantra stretches back five years. In fact it probably reaches all the way back to my early twenties (albeit unconsciously) when Sex and the City first ever aired in the UK. I watched the girls' every move, eavesdropped on their conversations in an attempt to learn all they knew about sex. Why? Because I already knew something was amiss in my own sex life – I either wasn't consciously connecting with partners, or was going through well-rehearsed techniques and rote routine. Whatever, sex was a tense, orgasm-focussed, BANG-BANG-BANG event rather than a juicy, sensually erotic opportunity to enjoy the experience in and of itself.

But with sex education limited to a half-arsed book and a biology class on the reproductive system, I was pretty much left to my own devices. And so it continued until early 2008 when a friend emailed me details of a talk being given to a group of women about Tantra by an organisation called Shakti Tantra. Intrigued, I went along. Although my curiosity was piqued it would be another three years before I finally wound up on one of their Women's Invitation weekend-long courses – last weekend to be exact.

I signed up for the course at the end of January somewhat absent-mindedly. I knew I wanted to do it but as I was busy elsewhere I didn't pause to consciously consider what the workshop might entail. 'It's with a load of other women,' I thought. 'It'll be fine.' Hmmm...

To say the workshop was life-changing would be an understatement. One of my very first thoughts was if every eleven-year-old girl did this workshop in secondary school our culture would be transformed overnight, pregnancy rates would drop, and the number of sexually transmitted infections would fall as young women's relationships with their bodies were given a solid, confident foundation from which to grow.

Contrary to the British media's parochial fixation about Tantra solely enabling folk to have sex for hours on end while withholding orgasm and/or ejaculation, it's actually about far more than that. It's about healing broken relationships with the body by consciously reconnecting with oneself from the neck down at a physical and emotional level. It's about carving away the many layers of long-held, mostly unconscious fear and bullshit, and coming into one's true essence.

For reasons of confidentiality I can't reveal specifics of what took place; suffice to say the women I attended the workshop with were among *the most courageous, most supportive, most inspiring individuals I've ever had the pleasure of meeting. Like me, these were women who were tired of trying to be something they weren't or no longer wanted to be. These were women who wanted to drop the guilt, shame, and fear and face all future sexual interactions with every single cell in their body consciously engaged and with an open heart and generosity of spirit. These were women with whom I laughed and cried and am now proud to call my friends.*

To be clear, none of the workshops Shakti Tantra run are for the faint of heart; rather, they're for those who are ready to drop the crap and connect with themselves and others at the deepest, most profound level possible. Let me put it like this: Hilly, originator of Shakti Tantra and our workshop leader, had more presence and sexual magnetism in her little finger than many so-called glamour models have in the whole of their silicone-pumped, surgically-enhanced bodies – one seriously sexy dame. Her assistants, also, were bottomless wells of support and compassion guiding us through all the exercises with the utmost tenderness.

And the food? Did I mention the food? I don't think I've ever seen such an erotic looking spread. It was the sort of stuff you want to lay all over someone and lick and pick off them at leisure. Everything about the overall experience was class. Nothing seedy or cheap. The venue, the food, the accommodation, and the teachings were all top drawer.

They also run couple's and mixed workshops. Whether you go alone or with your partner; whether you're single or in a long-established relationship, please – do yourself the biggest and best favour and book on one of their workshops. I guarantee it will change your life.

* * *

Later that week, after the article had been published, Hilly rang me for a chat. It seemed she'd enjoyed my piece.

'Right then,' she said, 'what are we doing about you and this work?'

'What do you mean, what are we doing?'

'Well, you're doing the women's programme of which there are four more levels,' she told me.

Was I? This was news to me. I mean, it's not that I didn't want to do it but as I wasn't earning any money how was I supposed to pay for all these workshops? Although I'd scanned through Shakti Tantra's website, I hadn't consciously registered what the whole of the programme entailed. I knew I could maybe negotiate the first workshop but after that I'd let go of any idea about doing any more. But Hilly wasn't having it.

That she was insistent I do them all – straight through to level five – intrigued me. As I've never been one to actively pursue a spiritual path

130

(besides reading books), my attention is always piqued whenever I find myself in front of someone who tells me, point blank, that I'm ready to do whatever it is they're proposing and that I *will* be doing it. Whenever I have one of these moments I feel like Luke Skywalker in *Star Wars* who's just been cornered by Obi Wan Kenobi. My first spiritual teacher, Barbara, had acted in a similar manner when she summoned me for my Reiki initiation.

Although I had no qualms about continuing the work I explained my only stumbling block was finances. I still had an apprenticeship to serve, a craft to hone. I was stumbling around in the shit of humility after having had my wings clipped by my high-flying, bestselling ideals. Four more workshops over the next two years (or however long it would take) would be a massive commitment both in terms of time and money. But in many ways it felt reminiscent of my eighteen month-long marathoning pilgrimage. And if there's one thing I like, it's a challenge.

So, off we went back down to the marketplace to negotiate and exchange sacks of rice and sell buffalos. What I've noticed about Hilly is she spends a lot of time at the marketplace, hustling, bartering. 'You soon learn how to hustle when you have six children to raise,' she later told me. 'Besides, I enjoy it.' And you can tell – the woman's a shrewd, persuasive, and savvy negotiator.

Though she's widely regarded as the teacher's teacher – the Grand Dame of UK Tantra – her organisation doesn't have the highest of profiles compared to other Tantra schools. I think her commitment to substance over style may have gone against her in an age when branding and spin is everything. During Women's Invitation, when asked why she'd never written a book she replied, 'Because it would be the shortest book in the world: *do the work.*' And that was the end of that.

But what I've noticed down the years is how, thanks to fortuitous turns, I've always wound up in front of great teachers. Not just great, but generous and down-to-earth. If there's one thing I can't stand it's flaky, airy-fairy, kaftan-wafting 'gurus.' As such, I have little tolerance for anyone who doesn't shoot from the hip and give it to me straight. For me, substance matters much more than style.

By the time I did Women's Invitation I'd been studying depth-related subjects for more than four years. I'd spent obscene amounts of time listening to lectures and reading books by such luminaries as Joseph Campbell, Carl Jung, Michael Meade, Marion Woodman, James Hillman, Robert Bly, Alan Watts, Marie-Louise von Franz, Mircea Eliade, Thomas Moore, Stephen Aizenstat, and countless others. Not that I'm suggesting that makes me an expert or authority in any way because it absolutely doesn't. But when you've spent time hanging out with voices like that, your tolerance for bullshit is significantly lessened.

So when I arrived at Invitation, though Hilly may have had a suspicious eye on me – understandable, considering the mainstream media's attitude towards Tantra – I was watching her and her assistants just as closely. So when every fibre of my being said *yes* to the work she was doing; when I felt my soul align with what I'd spent years studying and knew, beyond all doubt, that this was the school for me, I was more than happy to climb onto the nearest rooftop and shout about their work. Not that she ever asked me to (write about her organisation), because she didn't. I found this curious at first. But, that's the thing about the Yaga – she's not exactly renowned for public relations. Her attitude is that those who need to find her hut surrounded by its skull-topped picket fence, will.

Though the organisation is called Shakti Tantra my perspective of the work is that it's an amalgam of ancient occidental women's mysteries and shamanistic practices and ceremonies, peppered with teachings and rituals drawn from Tantra. So far as their work respects and elevates the status and roles of women; that their teachings can only be transmitted from teacher to student experientially; that they encourage a revaluation of negative states; that there's a revaluation of the body; and they encourage what might be deemed as transgressive acts then yes, that falls in line with several scholarly definitions of Tantra.

Because of my prior immersion in occidental mythology, however, I immediately felt the work to be more Aphroditic than Tantric – a sentiment echoed by Ginette Paris when she says:

> **The recent craze for Tantrism, or rather Neo-Tantrism, in which the role of women is seen in a different and more positive way, reveals the need for the spiritualisation of sexuality. This fad reintroduces an extreme spiritualisation of the sexual experience, since the original goal of Tantric sexual meditation was neither pleasure, nor emotion, nor psychological knowledge of the partner. As opposed to that, in Aphrodite's myth great importance is given to bodily pleasure and to the partner's personality, and there is not the ideal of control and detachment which Tantrism upholds. Aphrodite's cult valued the initiation of women from a physical, psychological, and religious point of view, while Tantrism, at least in its original version, was primarily a means of spiritual development for the man. In this regard, awakening Aphrodite might be more suitable to occidental women than borrowing Tantrism from the Orient.**

> **– *Pagan Meditations***

I agree with her when it comes to awakening Aphrodite and how it may be more suitable for occidental women than borrowing Tantra. But I think the key lies in the word itself. 'Tantra' carries an undeniable charge particularly in the West where it's largely become synonymous with sex. Thanks to the mainstream media that was my first association of the word too. David Gordon White, however, offers the following working definition of Tantra:

> **Tantra is that Asian body of beliefs and practices which, working from the principle that the universe we experience is nothing other than the concrete manifestation of the divine energy of the godhead that creates and maintains that universe, seeks to ritually appropriate and channel that energy, within the human microcosm, in creative and emancipatory ways.**
>
> *– Tantra in Practice*

What I draw from this definition is the world we see around us is the divine manifest as matter. Through Tantric rituals and practices we may come to know, experientially, the divine and/or our divine nature. This idea – of the material world as the divine manifest – is reminiscent of Sophia (Holy Wisdom) in Gnosticism: the feminine face of god who is also analogous with the soul.

In that tradition, Sophia fell from grace and has been trying ever since – along with her offspring (i.e. everything manifest) – to return to the holy heights of heaven. In other words, Sophia is the concrete, feminine, immanent face of divinity (soul), as opposed to the abstract, masculine, transcendent face of divinity (spirit). In the West, thanks to our monotheistic religions, we tend to think only that which is transcendent (spirit) is divine. In Gnosticism and Tantra that which is immanent (soul) is also considered divine – this includes our bodies.

Through the redemption and elevation of matter we may come to know God and/or be enlightened, hence the elevated state of females in Tantra and rituals and practices which involve the body. But as far as I understand it Tantrikas are *not* seeking sexual pleasure in and of itself; rather, men approached it as a form of spiritual development for which women, as per Paris's comments, largely served as a means to an end.

In several of the stories I've mentioned so far you may have noticed a recurring theme when it comes to the females: that is, they're all 'down here' or 'down there.' Kore is dragged into Hades from which she eventually re-emerges as Persephone, Queen of the Underworld. In Apuleius's tale of *Psyche and Eros*, Psyche's final task, as set by Aphrodite, entails a descent to Hades to fetch a box of beauty ointment from Persephone after which she's elevated to Olympus and granted divine status.

As mentioned earlier, Ereshkigal, Inanna's dark underworld sister, is described by Sylvia Brinton Perera as 'the root of all, where energy is inert and consciousness coiled asleep.' In Hindu hatha yoga and Tantra, *kundalini* means 'she who is coiled.' David Gordon White describes her as 'the female energy that lies coiled at the base of the yogic body. Through combined yogic techniques, the kundalini is "awakened" and made to rise through the cakras to the cranial vault.' In Gnosticism, Sophia is said to have fallen from grace. And in Tantra you often hear of Shakti rising.

Even my own reasons for embarking on a Tantric path entailed the redemption of my 'down below' (i.e. my body and my sex). In our culture when it comes to women's bodies what is above the hips generally tends to be associated with nourishing, nurturing qualities (breasts, the swollen round of a pregnant belly). Everything below the hips, however, is split off and disregarded as 'dirty,' as something to be ashamed of (the vagina and anus). Having said that, there are many – men and women – who feel cut off from the neck down, never mind the hips. But as someone who now knew she was 'bright' – much like our bright goddess, Inanna – I recognised it was time to 'open my ear to the Great Below' about which I knew nothing and reconnect with the body/Dark Goddess and her attendant lustful desires.

So though I was originally drawn to Tantra by the idea of having better, more pleasurable, more conscious sex, on reflection I don't think that was necessarily a bad thing. Because once I got through Shakti Tantra's door, I immediately felt Aphrodite's alchemical, transforming presence. Of Aphrodite, Bolen says:

> **Whomever or whatever Aphrodite imbues with beauty is irresistible. A magnetic attraction results, 'chemistry' happens between the two, and they desire union above all else. They feel a powerful urge to get closer, to have intercourse, to consummate – or 'know' the other, which was the biblical term. While this drive may be purely sexual, the impulse is often deeper, representing an urge that is both psychological and spiritual.**

> **– Goddesses in Everywoman**

The deeper impulse she speaks to is the 'something more' I'd long sought from sex. I realised early on that it wasn't about just having lots of sex with anyone and everyone. I didn't have to study Tantra to learn how to do that. No, I always felt there was something missing and I couldn't quite put my finger on what that something might be. As Thomas Moore says here:

> **Given our obsession with sex, we need to get more of it, not in quantity but in quality. It's like a person addicted to junk food.**

134

He eats as much as he can because there is nothing there. If he were to eat real food – unprocessed, close to its earth origins, wonderfully prepared – he might leave the addiction behind. We need more sex, not less, but we need *sex with soul*. [Italics mine.]

– The Soul of Sex

I longed so much to fully surrender, to yield to another – something of which I knew I was afraid. But what I now realise is I sought to surrender to – and be penetrated by – the other: that other being the divine Other. To put a mythic spin on it, I wanted to surrender my soul so that I might 'know' and be penetrated by spirit. Of course when you put it like that it seems pretty abstract and, in and of itself, doesn't really mean anything. But as I continue with my story I'll explain how this came to play out in my own life.

In fact there's a magnificent statue I've seen several times called the *Ecstasy of St Theresa* by Bernini which provides a powerful visual of the rapture I longed to experience both sexually and spiritually. The sculpture is based on a passage from Teresa of Ávila's autobiography in which she writes:

In his hands I saw a great golden spear, and at the iron tip there appeared to be a point of fire. This he plunged into my heart several times so that it penetrated to my entrails. When he pulled it out, I felt that he took them with it, and left me utterly consumed by the great love of God. The pain was so severe that it made me utter several moans. The sweetness caused by this intense pain is so extreme that one cannot possibly wish it to cease, nor is one's soul then content with anything but God. This is not a physical, but a spiritual pain, though the body has some share in it – even a considerable share. So gentle is this wooing which takes place between God and the soul that if anyone thinks I am lying, I pray God, in His Goodness, to grant him some experience of it.

– The Life of Saint Teresa of Ávila by Herself

If you have the good fortune to see this sculpture in person or even if you just see a photo of it, you'll notice Teresa swooning as she's about to be pierced in the heart by an angel holding a spear. It's one of the most spiritually erotic statues I've ever seen and I never fail to be impressed by the visceral intensity of the rapture St Teresa so obviously feels as she wholeheartedly and ecstatically yields to the penetration of the divine

Other. I remember the first time I saw it, gawping up in awe and thinking, 'Yep, I'll have some of that, thank you very much.'

Should you harbour a desire to experience something more, such as, for example, that sexual-spiritual rapture which so obviously has Teresa of Ávila all het up, where in our modern western culture do you go? For many seekers (myself included), the first port of call may be a Tantra organisation/practitioner or a copy of the Kama Sutra.

Aphrodite may indeed be more appropriate but, for me, the word Tantra is imbued with a mantra-like charge which the word Aphrodite simply isn't. Problem is, this leaves the door open to many individuals and organisations whose practices have little, if anything, to do with Tantra of which White quite rightly says:

> **Then there are Western dilettantes, the self-proclaimed Tantric entrepreneurs, who have hitched their elephant-wagons to the New Age star to peddle a dubious product called Tantric sex, which they (and their clientele) assume to be all there ever was to Tantra ... the for-profit purveyors of Tantric sex, who have no compunctions about appropriating a misguided nineteenth-century polemic to peddle their shoddy wares.**

– Tantra in Practice

I felt Shakti Tantra's approach with their focus on celebrating the body, increasing sensuality, and the promotion of pleasure borrowed heavily from the Aphroditic end of the spectrum. That's not to say the Tantric thread wasn't there (the word Tantra itself deriving from the Sanskrit for *loom* or a device for weaving; the underlying *essence*). It absolutely was – *if* you were willing to do the extra work. As with any spiritual or religious practice you get out of it what you put into it.

This is why Shakti Tantra encouraged participants, should they be inclined, to further their knowledge of Tantra in their own time. To help us on our way, they provided a comprehensive reading list which Ms Bookish, here, seized upon with relish. However, as mentioned in the preface, it was not my intention, with this book, to provide a detailed exegesis on Tantra. I don't claim to be an expert on the subject and I never have. My focus is on how Shakti Tantra's work changed me experientially. If you wish to further your own personal understanding of Tantra or of any of the other subjects covered within these pages, I've listed several publications at the back of this book to assist you. Because if there's one thing I feel strongly about, it's encouraging people to read more.

... CORRUPTED

Aphrodite is a lot of fun to hang out with.

When your life has been devoid of tenderness, of romantic gestures, of juiciness, of pleasure, of frisky frivolities, of playfulness, to invite Aphrodite over for tea and sympathy, well, let's just say she knows how to help cheer you up.

Not that I'm going to lay the blame for this sensual shortage solely at Finn's feet. It's like my teacher, Hilly, says – you're responsible for filling your own cup. So if you feel there's something missing in your life, rather than blaming others for your perceived lack, demanding they make you happy, nagging them to bring you what it is you long for, make like the Handless Maiden, get a grip and take matters into your own hands – which is exactly what I did. Ladies and gentleman, you're about to discover the lengths someone will go to in pursuit of great sex – with or without a lover.

Which is why I'll begin by saying navel-gazing is *so* last year. This year, naked dancing is where it's at. Moreover, naked dancing to a specially compiled Aphroditic soundtrack when no-one's home. Of all the nutty things I've done in my life, this has to rank right up there. But I tell you what, it sure beats pounding the pavements in preparation for a marathon.

The thing with the marathon and all it entailed was its focus on cultivating discipline and focus. It imbued me with tremendous determination to go the distance where I would have previously got bored and wandered off. But it was also *dry*. By dry I mean it was all about the heat as it fired me in its forge, burned away what no longer served me physically and psychologically. In spiritual alchemy this hot, fiery stage is called *calcinatio* – the substance (i.e. whatever issue it is you're working on) is burned until nothing remains but ashes.

During that period I voluntarily razed my life to the ground. My mantra might as well have been, 'Burn baby, burn.' I let go of everything (house, belongings, job) and set about heating the situation up, increasing the tension by running, training for the marathons, and studying psychology/working with my dreams so I could burn through the illusions that had long held me back.

As I write, my friend, Grace – who I met at Women's Invitation – is undergoing a similar process. She's enrolled on a several month-long Bikram yoga course – an intense form of hot yoga. She's also working closely with her dreams which have, in a nutshell, demanded she get bigger and stop being quite so sweet. As a result, she's eliminated sugar from her diet and is now co-organising the UK's Erotic Awards (nice work if you can get it). Compared with the woman I first met I can see how *calcinatio* is refining her, burning away the dross. Physically, she's lost weight. Psychologically, she has more fire about her. She's getting a grip on her life and has much more focus.

This is why *calcinatio* is often considered the first stage of personal/alchemical transformation. But now I'd cultivated self-confidence by setting and successfully completing several gargantuan goals (at least, that's how they felt to me) and stopped blaming others for what I believed was wrong with my life, I felt devoid of something I couldn't put my finger on. This is why *calcinatio* (fire) is often followed by a stage called *solutio/dissolutio* (water). With regards *solutio* the alchemists say: *The ashes are dissolved in water.*

Author, Catherine MacCoun says some of the symptoms involved with this stage are: yearnings, horniness, irritability, and disappointment. To those I'd add melting, intoxication, Dionysus, Aphrodite, orgy, communion, love, bliss, and rebirth. Here, MacCoun says the *prima materia* (base matter) you're working with is *desire* which, with work, can be transformed into *devotion*.

You may remember Tapan Goswami, the Indian priest I mentioned in the chapter, *The Goddess of Discord* who said 'One cannot really get close to the Goddess without devotional love. *Only bhakti justifies Tantra.*' Bhakti, in Hinduism and Buddhism, is a religious form of devotion to a personal god. One of the defining features of Tantra is visualisation and self-identification with a deity. For the priest, Kali was that deity. For me, it was Aphrodite.

As for what I desired? Well that was easy – better sex. As mentioned in the previous chapter that may sound shallow but, as we can see from the lengths I was prepared to go to in pursuit of it, I obviously wanted it badly or else I wouldn't go to all this effort. As MacCoun says:

In the beginning, selfish aims are also more likely to meet with success, because they draw on the bodily energy of the will. Altruistic desires might be entirely sincere, but they lack a certain volitional oomph. In trying to decide which desires are worthy of pursuit, the most productive question to ask is not whether a desire is selfish or unselfish, but whether it is authentic. An authentic desire arises from within you. False desires are a response to outside stimuli.

– On Becoming an Alchemist

When I signed up for the New York City Marathon I'd been motivated by envy and pride. As *prima materia* goes I couldn't have picked better issues to work with because, by the time I crossed the finish line in Athens, my seemingly irrational and petty reasons for signing up had, along the way, been transmuted. And in being transmuted they'd changed me for the better. That's alchemy in action – transforming a base matter (the lead of the psyche) into something of more value (gold). That's what my Dreaming Psyche meant when it said, 'You've got gold.'

Of course it wasn't a conscious decision. I didn't sit down and say, 'Ah yes, I think it's time I worked on transmuting pride and envy. Now, how to do that...' Although I've since read that's recommended (identifying and writing down the *base matter* you wish to work with), at the time this was happening I was flying by the seat of my Wonder Woman underpants. It's only now as I write and reflect, I can see what was going on. Hindsight – gotta love it.

When I set about frolicking with Aphrodite I didn't consciously realise I was working with a base matter (sex) in an attempt to transmute it into something of more value (devotion). But by devoting myself to Aphrodite, I was on the right track. As Jung says, 'The road is the goal.' And the lack I perceived, the yearning for something more, provided me with the 'volitional oomph,' the fervent desire I needed to bridge the gap and go the distance. After all, it's not without good reason they call it the 'sex drive.'

So after cultivating the disciplined, goal-oriented focus of Artemis – which had left me feeling somewhat detached, dry, and a bit too self-contained for my own liking – it was time to make way for the honey-toned, golden goddess. She's described as the alchemical goddess as through her love and attention the base material of everyday life is transmuted and made golden. Everything she touches is imbued with beauty, perfumed with sensuality, charged with eroticism. When you dance with her you make love your life. To be devoted to Aphrodite is to cultivate the art of everyday ecstasy. In fact, Jill Scott's song, *Golden* could easily be an ode to Aphroditic living.

Music featured heavily at Women's Invitation (I'd have been disappointed had it not). So, after the workshop, I continued this theme by compiling a playlist of the sexiest, smoochiest songs I had on my iPod. I wanted a soundtrack to keep me company, put me 'in the mood' as I went about my daily business. Though there are countless such ready-made compilations available, the songs I chose had to make me feel sexy – with the emphasis on *feel*.

This focus on what felt good to me would, over the coming weeks and months, be my guiding principle. Once I turned my attention to all things Aphroditic, what I noticed is how our culture continually attempts to define sexy and sensual for us. But as far as I was concerned it consisted of one cheesy, eye-rolling cliché after another. So, as I rifled through my music collection, I listened into my body to see how songs made me feel.

What this did was allow me to reconnect with *my* innate sexuality. Again, not what I *thought* was sexy; rather, what *felt* sexy. I wasn't trying to impress anyone, put on an act, or be deliberately provocative – I was feeling into my body for sexuality the way one might bore deep into the earth in search of oil. Whenever I hit on a song that made me feel good I knew I'd hit upon another aspect of inherent sexual gold. Thomas Moore amplifies this idea when he says:

> **Aphrodite emerges fresh and noble from the sea in one famous pose, as in Botticelli's well-known painting The Birth of Venus. Anadyomene means 'rising up after having been submerged.' This mysterious appearance out of the vast sea shows sexual feeling, sensation, and awareness coming into consciousness from a deep source that we may locate within us or at least in some reservoir of life possibility. In the spare and punning words of the Gloucester poet Charles Olson, 'she rose from the genital wave.' Sexual awareness and sensation do not appear from thin air; they rise dripping from whatever primeval element is their natural home.**

> *– The Soul of Sex*

This was such a joyful, simple exercise. It didn't cost me anything, didn't require I down tools and jet across the world in search of pleasure. Neither did I need anyone's permission. I never told Finn what I was up to. In fact *no-one* knew what I was up to because no-one needed to know. It wasn't anyone's business. I was nurturing my seedling sexuality and it was too early to expose it to the harsh, damning elements of the outside world.

What I discovered was the countless variations and subtle intonations of my sensual self. Sometimes it's big and bold, spills out all over; other times it gets down low, writhes on the floor. But the one thing it isn't is static – it's multifaceted, vibrant, and iridescent. In fact this is where the dancing came in. Because once I'd successfully hit upon my inner reserves of sexuality via music, it burst forth and moved me. And that's one of the many ways you know you've reconnected with Aphrodite – when she *moves you*. They say you can't keep a good woman down. For the record, once you welcome her into your life, you can't keep a goddess down either.

So though I felt completely stupid when I first started prancing about the house, when I stayed with it, once I pushed through my self-conscious, I-must-look-like-a-complete-and-utter-prat barrier, the happiness and sheer unadulterated joy I felt was indescribable. Before I knew it, I was gleefully ripping my clothes off, throwing them across the room as I stopped caring what I looked like, got down and dirty with my bare-naked self, and just let go.

After all, how could I ever expect to let go with another if I couldn't do it alone? As far as I'm concerned letting go starts at home. And I wanted so much to release the rigidity which had held me back in sexual encounters, stopped me surrendering to another in a moment of complete and utter abandonment. I wanted to share my innate joy, celebrate myself with another. Bollocks to being cool and restrained. I wanted unrestrained, I wanted authenticity. No more barriers. No acting. No trying to make the right noises, no trying to please another so they'd like me, attempting to make the right moves – just complete and utter sweet and sweaty abandonment. Just let *go*.

As the weeks rolled on and I let go more and more, I discovered a vibrancy about myself I'd never felt before; or, at least, not since childhood. For the record I've never been one to sit down and meditate – I'm far too fiery for that. But this daily dancing *was* a meditation because when I was doing it I didn't think about anything. When I danced I was totally and utterly present. I wasn't brooding over what Finn was or wasn't doing, I wasn't feeling sorry for myself or thinking about what chores needed doing, I was total, in the moment. A one woman party, I rediscovered an innate, joyful cornucopia of abundance which spilled out all over. God, did it make me feel good. But the dancing was just the beginning.

As mentioned earlier I've self-pleasured since I was eleven when, in the bath one night, the water from the shower head brushed over my clitoris. The onset of my periods may have robbed my childhood from clean under me but as conciliatory payoffs go, this discovery more than made up for it. Which is why I was devastated when the shower packed up and was replaced with one which just didn't hit the mark. That has to be one of the most frustrating moments of my life. After all, I could hardly march up to my parents and demand a more orgasm-friendly shower head.

Suffice to say I'm a determined bugger and I eventually found a way for the new one to work – but it was never quite the same. Due to my reliance on an external aid to help me orgasm, I'd never bothered learning a more manual approach (hands only). So, years later, when a friend bought me a Rampant Rabbit, made famous by the TV series *Sex and the City*, I was happy to discover the Rabbit's clitoral stimulant more than made up for my water-fuelled loss.

When I sold my house and got rid of most of my belongings, I was faced with a dilemma regards my large, pink, rabbit-shaped vibrator. I had visions of being detained by Homeland Security while an officer rifled through my luggage. I could just imagine him (because you can guarantee it would be a man) discovering said Rabbit while waving it in my face and asking, 'And what's *this?*' Oh, the humiliation. So I threw it out and decided to learn how to use my hands. Before you knew it I was an anytime, anywhere, O and Go gal.

But despite having always self-pleasured, since my operation I hadn't reacquainted myself with the rest of my yoni – not really. I'd always focused on my clitoris. But one of the books Shakti Tantra recommended was Betty Dodson's, *Sex for One: The Joy of Selfloving* (which I, too, highly recommend). As homework goes, I can think of worse things to practise than self-pleasuring. And seeing as nothing had changed on the intimacy front between Finn and I, sex for one seemed the only way to go.

In a section called *Making Love Alone*, Dodson opens with the following paragraph:

> **Since most of us struggle with periods of self-hatred, bad body images, shame and confusion over sex and pleasure, I recommend having a hot love affair with yourself. Sexual healing begins by learning how to turn yourself on, discovering your sexual fantasies, and giving yourself an abundance of selflove and orgasms.**

> *– Sex for One*

In this chapter one of several things she recommends you do is spend time looking at your vulva (I told you – navel-gazing is *so* passé). And I'm not talking a quick glance in the mirror, either. I'm talking a good hour or so to really examine it all. (By the way, the book is for men *and* women, so there are recommendations and exercises for both.)

This was when I discovered just how brilliant a surgeon I'd had for my labia minora reduction. But it's also when I got angry about cosmetic surgeons who offer labiaplasty (or vaginal 'rejuvenation' or vagioplasty) without warning women of the dangers they face and the irreversible loss of sensation they may experience. Though I may have joked about having had my 'bits trimmed,' that wasn't what I'd had done at all. (If you're squeamish, I recommend you skip the next paragraph.)

What my surgeon had done was remove a central section of tissue from the left side of my labia, then stitched the upper and lower edges of the excision together to create a smaller labia. As it wasn't cosmetic surgery her aim wasn't to make it 'look better' or 'tidy' it up. Her sole aim was to reduce the size of the side which had previously caused me problems. She hadn't touched the right side as I'd never had any problems with that.

That she'd left the outer edges of my labia alone was, as I was about to discover, an absolute *blessing*. What I didn't realise until I began exploring myself was just how much pleasure there is to be had by ever-so-gently stroking along the outer edges of the labia. For me it's beyond toe-curlingly exquisite. On the day I discovered this, mirror propped between my legs, I cried tears of joy and gratitude – gratitude that I hadn't had my beautiful vulva butchered, and joy that it was still sensitive to the touch and I could derive so much pleasure from it. If only women knew the nuanced pleasure buried between their legs they might think twice before having their labia lopped off.

To regularly take the time to look at and enjoy my sex, and feel the shame I'd long felt towards it gradually ebb away, is one of the greatest gifts I've ever given myself as a woman. It was also deeply meditative and unexpectedly calming. That intensive period of time spent reconnecting with my Underworld self was a pivotal moment in my initiation into conscious womanhood.

Like the dancing once I broke through the self-conscious, isn't-this-all-a-bit-self-indulgent barrier, I felt myself relaxing into the lower half of my body as never before. I also felt more rooted. The deep-rootedness I felt in myself is subtle and only something one can understand experientially. In other words you have to be willing to descend into your own personal Underworld and be with – without judgement, without shame – all you may have ignored and rejected. This exercise is the experiential counterpart of psychological shadow work.

Another of the exercises she recommends is called *Loving Yourself*. In this exercise she encourages you to 'look into the mirror and say to yourself out loud, "I love you." Smile, say "I love you," and add your name. It may seem strange, even make you feel embarrassed or foolish, but do it!' Well, I tried this but I just didn't *feel* it. I realised I must be more kinaesthetically-inclined as I seemed to gain more from the hands-on rituals such as, for example, one she calls the *Sensuous Bath*.

I adapted this exercise and combined it with one from Margot Anand's book, *The Art of Everyday Ecstasy*. I later shared my experience in an article I wrote for the online magazine, *Body*, an excerpt of which I share below:

Just last Saturday night I inadvertently ended up doing a ritual which turned out to be quite profound. With my boyfriend out for the night I turned our bathroom into a temple fit for a modern-day goddess. With dozens of fragrant candles dotted about the place, I scattered the entire bathroom floor with hot-pink rose petals, filled the bath with fragrant rose oil, and put some relaxing music on. I then spent the next few hours mindfully caring for and befriending my body. But it's what happened at the end which most surprised me.

*After drying off I slowly began massaging my favourite oil into my
calves and thighs, while saying the following which is adapted from an
exercise in Margot Anand's brilliant book,* The Art of Everyday
Ecstasy – The Seven Tantric Keys for Bringing Passion, Spirit, and
Joy into Every Part of Your Life:

**Thank you (legs) for carrying my weight in the world and
supporting my life. Thank you (knees) for your unique
mobility. Without you I could not walk, run, dance, do Pilates
or Yin yoga, and a thousand other joys. Thank you (thighs) for
your strength, for your willingness to be pillars of support to
connect my pelvis to my legs. You are of great help to me. I'm
sorry I've beat up on you every day with scorn and self-loathing
because I didn't believe you were sylph-like and slinky enough...**

*I then spent the next ten or fifteen minutes, quietly, tenderly massaging
the oil into my thighs. As I massaged they began to feel sore and somewhat
bruised – as though they were releasing long repressed pain and ancient
hurt. If a body part could cry – and I believe they do – then my thighs
did just that. As they did, I soothed and smoothed them lovingly as though
holding a child or loved one who was in pain. For the first time in my
life I held and stroked them with love – unconditional love and absolute
acceptance for how they were right now; not how they could be sometime
in the future but right now, in this moment. I told them it was okay, that
they could now let go of the hurt they'd held on to for goodness knows
how long; that I loved them.*

*Each night since, I've continued this practice – quietly, tenderly
soothing my legs – and ever since my entire body has been aching as
though it's detoxing. And to think that, up until this point, I only ever
thought a detox consisted of eliminating certain toxic food and drinks. I
never considered detoxing might also entail the release of long-held toxic
thoughts and feelings towards oneself which would result in a similar
'healing crisis' to what one might experience during the first few days of
a dietary detox.*

*We spend a lot of time in our heads, particularly those on a spiritual
path – abstracting, meditating, theorising, praying, analysing – but not
so much time consciously connected to our bodies, reconnecting with our
own flesh and bones. We think we do – but therein lies the problem. And
a mindless, routine yoga class won't cut it either. Our bodies carry so
much grief, so much unexpressed sadness and repressed hurt and anger,
I'm not surprised people turn to alcohol, for example, night after night
in order to numb themselves, anaesthetise the pain they've long buried;
overeat in order to swallow their anxiety, self-loathing, and shame; seek*

cake-fuelled sugar-rushes in order to counter their unconscious feelings of not feeling sweet enough. The list is endless.

But we're of no help to the outer environment (earth, nature) if we don't first consciously and compassionately reconnect with ourselves. Charity begins at home. Many a spiritual teacher has said, 'You must know and love yourself before you can truly love another.'

One final thing: this morning, while lay in bed, somewhere between sleep and waking, I felt my partner reach over and softly stroke my forearm before taking it in his embrace, kissing it, and holding it by his face. He's never done that before. I guess when you truly begin to love yourself, treat yourself with tenderness and compassion, others follow suit. Put another way, when you change, others around you change. The best bit is, he has no idea of half the Aphroditic/Tantric rituals and exercises I practise – and this is only the beginning.

Finn never made a tender or affectionate move towards me again.

A Series of
Unexpected Events

With Shakti Tantra's women's programme it's not just about what happens at the workshops (though they are, of course, undeniably powerful), as what happens in between. Each workshop acts like a time-release vitamin bringing much needed healing and nourishment to mind, body, and soul. The flip side, however, is it also brings the issues in the tissues to conscious awareness which, as with any detox, can spark something of a healing crisis.

So perhaps I shouldn't have been surprised when a series of weird and wonderful events unfolded between the end of February and the middle of June which was when the next workshop, Women's Celebration, was due to take place.

The first event happened the weekend following Women's Invitation. Finn and I were walking to the coffee shop on the Sunday morning when, suddenly, I felt my chest constrict and my heart rate start up. It was a tachycardia attack. I'd not had one since late 2008, just before the Athens Marathon.

What I hate about these attacks is the panic they're likely to induce in those around you if they suddenly find you doubled over and gasping for breath while clutching your chest. So what I've always tried to do is keep calm and carry on. But this one was *ferocious* – so much so I told Finn as I was afraid I'd pass out.

To his credit he didn't panic. Instead, he stayed with me while I bent over and breathed through it. But when he put his hand to my chest even he was surprised at how fast my heart was beating. Although my initial light-headedness soon passed and we continued on to the coffee shop, my heart rate would not calm down. It beat away at a rate of knots for almost an hour. As attacks go it was one of my scariest.

Because of its severity I finally decided it was time I seek professional help and so, the following week, I went to see my doctor. He immediately arranged a series of tests, including an ECG (electrocardiogram). To my relief all the results came back clear. There was, however, a blood test which returned something unexpected – apparently I was anaemic.

Due to the large amount of blood I lose each month during my periods, my iron levels were languishing at incredibly low levels. This explained the ongoing lethargy and tiredness I felt. When my doctor talked me through ways I might deal with this he casually presented my options which ranged from taking iron tablets, through a series of minor surgical procedures, culminating in a hysterectomy. Suffice to say I opted for the iron tablets. Once I started taking them the difference it made to my energy levels was akin to Popeye swallowing a can of spinach. Almost immediately I felt livelier. I couldn't believe I'd functioned on such paltry reserves for so long.

In another corner of my life a more positive development was the ongoing benefits brought about by writing for *Body*. As previously mentioned I'd originally been commissioned to write about cocktails in the city but, as I've also said, I wanted to write about spiritual alchemy in its abstract form (personal transformation). But this would entail a coming out of sorts. By 'coming out' I mean I'd be exposing my more spiritually-oriented side to a larger audience. So far I'd only ever shared that aspect of myself on the safety of my blog and with friends. So to share it with the kind of mainstream audience who read the online magazine would mean opening up and coming out about the fact I cared about issues regarding spirit and soul – a prospect which left me feeling pretty nervous.

After all what would people think? One minute I'm a girl about town writing about something considered cool on which everyone seemed to have an opinion (i.e. cocktails); the next, I'm cosying up with spiritual teachers talking about the meaning of life – because that's exactly what I did.

My first interview was with Marianne Williamson, author of the international bestseller, *A Return to Love: Reflections on the Principles of a 'Course in Miracles'* from which the following is taken:

Our deepest fear is not that we are inadequate. Our deepest fear is that we are powerful beyond measure. It is our light, not our darkness that most frightens us. We ask ourselves, 'Who am I to be brilliant, gorgeous, talented, fabulous?' Actually, who are you not to be? You are a child of God. Your playing small does not serve the world. There is nothing enlightened about shrinking so that other people won't feel insecure around you. We are all meant to shine, as children do. We were born to make manifest the glory of God that is within us. It's not just in some of us; it's in everyone. And as we let our own light

shine, we unconsciously give other people permission to do the same. As we are liberated from our own fear, our presence automatically liberates others.

This famous quote has often been erroneously attributed to Nelson Mandela who used it in his 1994 inaugural speech. When I read Williamson's book many years ago, my soul rose diaphanous when I came to this passage so I'm not surprised it's since taken on a life of its own.

When I found out she was due to speak at an event in Manchester I was beyond excited. An accomplished and eloquent public speaker, I'd long admired her oratory skills. Now I was writing for *Body* and, as such, covering issues of a more spiritual nature, I arranged an interview with her ahead of her visit – not that you could call it an interview.

I don't know if it was because I finally had an opportunity to geek out with a like-mind who'd made this field her life's work, but we seemed to spend our allotted time yip-yapping about everything other than the questions I had lined up. Warm and generous, I could have easily talked with her all night.

Next I arranged an interview with film director, David Lynch about his work with Transcendental Meditation (TM) – well, *almost*. After much toing and froing with his people (Marianne had people too – you can tell you've hit the big time when you need a wall of people to beat back your adoring public), I was put off interviewing him by an acquaintance who cast a downer on TM telling me it was considered a cult and had been banned in several schools in California.

This was one of those times I wish I'd taken no notice and gone ahead with the interview. But her comments cast such a dark cloud over proceedings it wiped out my enthusiasm in one fell swoop. I learnt an important lesson that day – some things are better kept close to your chest. Oh, and if you don't have anything positive to say, don't say anything at all. Anyway I still hope to interview him one day.

Though I did have more luck with another British spiritual teacher – Barefoot Doctor. You may remember I went to see his Travelling Medicine Show back in early 2006? What struck me about that experience was how I felt I knew him. I'm sure many people have had similar such experiences on meeting public figures, especially if they've read their books and, as such, feel intimately acquainted with them. But I seriously felt I knew this guy – I mean *really* knew him.

So when I interviewed him I wasn't the least bit surprised when we hit it straight off. As I've said, it's not often I open up and reveal my more esoteric side so when I do it all comes gushing out. In fact, we got along so well he came to visit and spend the weekend with me at Finn's.

I'd like to say this was surreal but it actually wasn't. It all felt quite normal. It wasn't to my friend, Bing, who couldn't believe the man who is perhaps the UK's most famous spiritual teacher was spending the Royal Wedding weekend at her friend's place. She was a giddy ball of excitement. 'You'd better introduce me,' she'd demanded (which I did, in case you're wondering – we met up with her for afternoon tea).

Finn, on the other hand, had no idea who Barefoot was. In one way this was a blessing as he, too, acted normal towards him. But once he arrived I felt awkward – awkward because, like I said, Finn had few, if any, interests outside of the supermarket. Most of our conversations consisted of him talking shop and little else. And despite his saying he didn't want me to leave nothing had changed between us.

Having said that, while Barefoot was there he suddenly turned on the PDAs (public displays of affection) – something I felt was infuriatingly false of him. I felt he was 'spraying his territory,' but what I didn't want to do was start a fight in front of our guest. Although he said nothing I'm sure he picked up on the underlying tension between us.

What I did notice about myself that weekend, perhaps for the first time, was how much smaller I felt with Finn. My usual enthusiastic exuberance was tempered with him around. Let me put it like this: if you have someone coming to stay who's led as interesting and varied a life as Barefoot, wouldn't you want to hang out with him, strike up conversation over a meal at the very least? Wouldn't you be just a wee bit curious to learn a little more about a man whose books adorn the shelves in your house? Granted, Finn was at work during the daytime but when he got home he turned on the TV, opened a bottle of wine, and that was that.

I just wanted to pack up and leave. Despite our previous conversation he was still as physically and emotionally distant as ever. It was only Barefoot's impending visit which got me through as I decorated the spare bedroom in preparation for his arrival. Texting Bing as I painted the walls, I told her how desperately unhappy and alone I felt. Like me, she knew the end was coming – it was just a matter of how and when.

In fact, the weekend before Barefoot arrived, Finn and I had another argument during which he accused me of being 'deep,' said that I 'read too much into everything,' and asked 'Why can't sex just be organic?' I wrote this straight into my diary as it captured the essence of the tension between us.

These accusations of being 'deep' and 'reading too much into everything' are, I now realise, archetypal responses of an Apollonian identified man as Jean Shinoda Bolen reminds us:

Apollo men are rejected by women who want a deeper bond, with more intensity and emotional expressiveness, than he can provide. The integrity in which an Apollo man may live out his

precepts or live up to his agreements draw admiration and respect, rather than love or passion. Women who are aware of these priorities will not choose him to begin with, or, on discovering what is lacking, may reject him as a lover later.

– Gods in Everyman

Finn had known me since I was a teenager. My interest in body language and psychology were hardly new to him. He even had a copy of a book on body language I'd lent him back from when we first ever dated. Unlike Adrian who I met in Goa, who also described me as 'deep,' Finn knew me better. If I'd developed a spontaneous, overnight interest in depth psychology I may have agreed. But I hadn't.

This is pure conjecture and I may be *way* off the mark, but I felt he was uncomfortable with my insistence on probing the depths and people watching. The person I watch closest is myself. It's only if something smells distinctly 'off' that I may turn my attention more closely to another and/or others or if someone asks for my perspective on their life or dreams. But yes, on the whole, I am deep and inclined towards symbolic thinking (I'm often described as 'intense' and 'analytical'). Psychologically speaking that's just the way I'm shaped – always have been, always will be. If you don't like my apparent probing intensity, however, please don't ask me to spend time with you, let alone date you.

In my journal underneath his comment asking, 'Why can't sex just be organic?' I wrote, 'What, you mean *unconscious?*' Again, I've noticed it's Apollonian men who have made similar such comments since I started down this Aphroditic/Tantric path. They'll say to me that it (sex) is 'just something that happens.' 'Why do you need to practise it?' they'll say. 'It should be natural, in the moment.' They seem to have some warped idea that, because I 'study sex,' as they put it, I plan the minutiae of the act down to the last detail. This couldn't be further from the truth.

This detail reminds me of the instruction Eros gave Psyche once they were married. 'Don't ever look upon me at night,' he said to her. Well, we all know how that one's going to turn out. If there's one thing we can count on throughout the stories and myths of all time, it's this: you tell a woman not to do something – don't open that box, Pandora; don't open that box, Psyche; don't look back, Lot's wife; don't bite the apple, Eve – and you can guarantee she'll do it. This deliberate transgression is called a *felix culpa*.

A *felix culpa* is a fortunate fail (in the Catholic tradition) – a double-edged event that initially looks like a fault but often turns out to be a blessing (if Eve, for example, hadn't eaten the apple and got thrown out of the Garden of Eden along with Adam, Christ would never have incarnated and redeemed us all of our 'original sin'). So when Psyche shines the light of consciousness on Eros, though he flies away and she has to submit to a series of tasks at the hand of her mother-in-law, Aphrodite, she is eventually reunited with Eros and elevated to the divine heights of Olympus where she's granted immortal status. If she hadn't disobeyed Eros, she would have likely remained in the dark forever. But her disobedience ultimately led to an increased level of consciousness as psychologist Erich Neumann reminds us here:

> And, we must not forget, Eros himself did not want such a Psyche! He threatened her, he fervently implored her to remain in the paradise-darkness, he warned her that she would lose him forever by her act. The unconscious tendency toward consciousness (here toward consciousness in the love relationship) was stronger in Psyche than everything else, even than her love for Eros – or so, at least, the masculine Eros would have said. But wrongly so, for though the Psyche of paradisiacal state was subservient to Eros, though she had yielded to him in the darkness, she had not loved him. It is in the light of knowledge, her knowledge of Eros, that she begins to love.

> – *Amor and Psyche*

It was when Finn said to me, 'Why can't sex just be organic?' that I first felt the myth of Psyche and Eros rear its head in our relationship. Modern-day folk think myths are a load of hooey – that they're twee old tales that have no bearing on our lives today – but they're absolutely not: they're alive and kicking in many a modern psyche. Because we've lost touch with them we don't see the patterns when they rise to the surface and shape our lives.

Don't think that because Psyche is a female this story relates only to women in relation to their male (or female) partner, either – it's equally possible that when a man shines the 'light of knowledge' on eros, it could cause problems in his relationship with his female (or male) partner. Psyche and Eros, remember, are personifications of psychic energies.

For anyone seeking to increase their knowledge of eros, I believe this is an important story with which to be acquainted as it flags up issues which may potentially arise in a relationship. As Neumann says, 'though she had yielded to him in the darkness, she had not loved him.' That was how I felt with Finn – I didn't feel like I really 'knew' him. Like Apollo, he'd kept me at a distance.

At the beginning of our relationship sex had always been a lights out, underneath the covers affair. So long as I'd been solely identified with the archetype of Artemis, Apollo's twin sister, who can be as aloof and detached as him, there'd been no problems between us – after all, I was as distant as him. But once I started hanging out with Aphrodite and decided I wanted to 'know' the other, started probing deeper, Apollo, threatened by the emotional intensity of this melting, merging archetype, turned on me as Walter F. Otto says here:

> **Apollo rejects whatever is too near – entanglement in things, the melting gaze, and equally, soulful merging, mystical inebriation and its ecstatic vision.**
>
> **– *The Homeric Gods***

It's at this point I'd like to say something about the ambiguity of the Self. When I first started working with dreams I naively assumed the Self (God, the Dreaming Psyche – whatever you want to call it) was good, that its advice and guidance was benevolent. After all, I figured, if consciousness is trying to become conscious of itself isn't it in its best interests to help me? What I didn't realise is the Self transcends duality and is beyond such concepts as good and bad. Let me give you an example.

Despite wondering, when I went to the supermarket with mum, if I might see Finn again, I felt ambivalent about going on a date with him. I hadn't experienced any of those stoned in love feelings one has when you first fall in love. You know those gooey, intoxicated feelings you have when it's all romantic and all you do is stare into one another's eyes? Well I'd felt none of that. It's like he fixed his arrow on me from afar and would not give up until he hit his target. But there were never any of the mushy, melting feelings, no sticky knicker moments which are the hallmark of Aphrodite.

What changed my mind about dating him was a dream I had: the one mentioned in *Running into Myself*, in which we were naked and locked in embrace, chest-to-chest, face-to-face, with our legs wrapped around one another in the Tantric yab-yum position – the one in which our union was 'wildly ecstatic.'

When I had that dream I was consciously heeding the Self's wisdom, integrating it into my waking reality. So when it sensed I wasn't sure about Finn and knew that, had I been left to my own devices I would have likely spurned his advances, it dangled a rather alluring, carrot-shaped dream in front of me in the promise of Tantric, sexual bliss with him. The Self, after all, knows me better than I know myself.

Like Vasilisa and her intuitive doll I was more likely, back then, to pay attention to my Dreaming Psyche than to what someone may have been telling me. So if the Self hadn't have intervened with that dream I doubt Finn could have got me to go out with him as there just wasn't enough of Aphrodite's magnetic pull. So it was only the dream's potential promise of sexual ecstasy that made me change my mind. I figured the Self knew something I didn't – that it was showing me something yet to pass. Well it was and it wasn't because, as you've read, it turned out my relationship with Finn *would* lead me to Tantra: but not *with* him; rather, *because* of him. In light of this I have two words to sum up the Self – *cunning swine.*

On realising this – the ambiguity of the Self – I immediately removed my rose-tinted specs. Should you choose to follow a spiritually-oriented path don't for a minute think that all things spiritual are good or nice; that nothing bad will happen to you because you're heeding the wisdom of 'higher powers' – the totality of the Self contains both light and dark; its nature, beyond opposites. To further illustrate this point, I'd like to share an excerpt from one of my favourite books by Edward Edinger in which he discusses Job's ordeal from the *Book of Job*:

> Since Yahweh and Satan are working together, they can be considered as two aspects of the same thing, i.e. the Self. Satan provides the initiative and dynamism to set up Job's ordeal and hence represents the urge to individuation which must break up the psychological status quo in order to bring about a new level of development. The serpent played the same role for Adam and Eve in the Garden of Eden. Also similar to Eden is the fact that Job's ordeal is designed as a temptation. He is to be tempted to curse God. This would mean psychologically that the ego is being tempted to inflation, to set itself above the purposes of God, i.e., to identify with the Self.
>
> Why should all this be necessary? Evidently Job still has some tendency to inflation. In spite of his blameless reputation, or perhaps because of it, there is some question whether or not he knows decisively the difference between the ego and the Self. Therefore the program is arranged to test the ego in the fire of tribulation and out of that ordeal comes Job's full encounter with the reality of God. If prior purposes can be discerned on the basis of effects we can say that it was God's purpose to make Job aware of Him. Apparently the Self needs conscious realisation and is obliged by the individuation urge to tempt and test the ego in order to bring about full ego-awareness of the Self's existence.

> *– Ego and Archetype*

As I said – *cunning swine*. In fact, you might say that by following that dream, much like Alice following the White Rabbit down the hole into Wonderland, I committed something of a *felix culpa* – a fortunate fail. Granted, no-one told me *not* to heed the wisdom of the dream, but there was nothing to stop me weighing up the pros and cons, thinking it through and, from there, making a rational, ego-based decision. Especially as I've since been in situations where the Self – via dreams and intuitions – has said 'do it' or 'go there' and, after carefully examining all available information and considering the circumstances, I've ignored it.

The Self, after all, isn't running a day-care centre – it wants to know whether you have the common sense to figure things out for yourself without always turning to it for direction and guidance. Intuition is one side of the equation, yes, but logic and good old common sense are just as important. When both sides are working together that's when you might say you're 'firing on all cylinders,' with each side complementing the other. But it's equally important the self is able to stand up to the Self and say *no* from time to time. The ego's challenge is to learn to hold the tension of opposites between spirit and soul, between the manifest and unmanifest as Marie-Louise von Franz says here:

> **The ego of an individuated person, for instance, would be a manifestation of the Self, it would be open to the unconscious. Such an ego manifests the Self by having a double attitude towards – and being constantly, humbly, open to – the unconscious and thus offering a basis of realisation for the Self. God needs our poor heart, says Angelus Silesius, in order to be real.**
>
> **– Alchemy**

Speaking of being open to the unconscious, around this time my Dreaming Psyche really stepped things up a notch and began coming at me in surround sound.

To be clear, I always dream. There are periods when, depending on what's going on in my waking reality, my Dreaming Psyche draws back like the tide. But on occasion a Big Dream breaks through. Even those who are new to working with their dreams will tell me they know when they've had a Big Dream. There's just something about it that stands out and demands their attention. If they don't understand it, they'll ask me to help them make sense of it.

Big Dreams also prompt dream sceptics to contact me for my opinion on whatever it is that's pulled at their conscious attention. If, after talking

154

it through, they like what I have to say they may heed its wisdom. If, on the other hand they don't, they dismiss it as 'just a dream that doesn't mean anything.' What they fail to realise is most of the world they see around them originally existed in someone's imagination before it was brought forth and made manifest. Everything was, at some point, 'just a dream.' After all, culture entails the **cult**ivation of our inner na**ture**.

So in this Big Dream I met the keepers of the Firth of Forth Rail Bridge in Scotland which then transformed into the Golden Gate Bridge in San Francisco. I met all the men who slept on it, maintained it, and made it their home (the dream took place on the unseen, underside of the bridge). My guide was a scruffy looking man reminiscent of movie actor, Rhys Ifans. He shared his makeshift, homeless-style bed with me. I was more than happy to sleep on the floor with him. He was surprised by my willingness to hunker down and sleep rough with everyone and huddle together so we could keep one another warm. He was happy I was so down-to-earth. He liked me and acted kindly towards me. In fact, all the gatekeepers acted friendly towards me. Rhys's father and friends (all male) had maintained the bridge all their lives. At one point I was right in the middle of the bridge, sat perched at the very top, looking out towards the Pacific Ocean. It was a beautiful, sunny day. I felt the gatekeepers were looking after me and I, in turn, trusted them. Despite my fear of bridges I felt safe. In fact, my fear of bridges seemed to have disappeared. On waking I felt fabulous.

What immediately struck me about this dream was my own attitude – my humility, open-heartedness, my ease of trust, and my non-judgemental attitude towards what were, essentially, squalid living conditions. I'd never seen myself act like that before. It's not that I didn't believe I had those qualities in me but, on waking, I felt so proud of myself. With some dreams I feel you're given an objective insight into aspects of yourself you may ordinarily dismiss or overlook in your waking reality.

The other detail which struck me was how there were no women on the bridge. Not one. I spent the next several months mulling over this detail. It was only while ferreting about on a numerology website and working with Liz Greene's *Mythic Tarot* card deck that I discovered I was born in a Hierophant year (known as The Pope in traditional tarot). I should say that, in the spirit of Jung, I have my inquisitive fingers in many pies – from the I Ching to tarot to depth astrology, I leave no symbolic stone left unturned when it comes to exploring the unconscious.

The Pope is also known as the *pontiff* – a name which derives from the Latin, *pontifex*. Pontifex stems from the Latin words *pons* (bridge) and *facere* (to do, to make). In Roman antiquity the pontiffs were considered the most illustrious of the colleges of priests of the Roman Religion, The

155

College of Pontiffs and were also considered the 'bridge-builders.' In tarot, the Hierophant is a true pontiff as he builds the bridge between deity and humanity. But the College of Pontiffs consisted of men only and would explain why there were no women on the bridge except for me.

The other detail which struck me was how I no longer felt afraid of being on a bridge. At the time of this dream I still had something of a phobia of bridges. Running the New York City Marathon helped me 'get over' this fear somewhat, seeing as there were several of them along the route including the seemingly never-ending Verrazano-Narrows Bridge. During my time in New Mexico, Sam and I had also driven to the middle of the downright terrifying Rio Grande Gorge Bridge near Taos, where we stopped and got out so I could face my demons head-on. That he started jumping up and down did *not* help matters. And a year before this dream I finally fulfilled a lifelong wish to see, and cross, San Francisco's Golden Gate Bridge.

As a child I'd stare, transfixed, at a photo on my uncle's wall of the Golden Gate Bridge. It was the most beautiful thing I'd seen in my whole short life. There was something about it which lit me up from the inside out. Though it wasn't just the bridge – I wanted to visit San Francisco itself. There was something about the place which made my heart sing and was the one place I longed more than anywhere else in the world to see. I couldn't tell you exactly why I wanted to visit – I just knew I did. So when I finally did go, I insisted my friend drive us back and forth across the bridge while I soaked up my long-awaited moment. Small pleasures.

Seeing as we're in San Francisco let's stay there for a moment as I share the second Big Dream I had during this period – the day before Women's Celebration, in fact.

In this dream, a woman, Sophia (Holy Wisdom), was growing up out of the rocks outside of a cathedral in San Francisco. The rocks resembled the Giant's Causeway in Ireland and were a continuation of the cathedral itself – like a concrete skirt which overflowed and spilled out towards the water in the Bay. It was as if Sophia were a giant stalagmite who was being formed from the ground as the rain trickled down on her and nothing else.

Once again the Golden Gate Bridge featured but on waking I couldn't remember how they'd been connected. Elsewhere in the dream, down in a cavern-like space, a friend, Christopher, kissed me in celebration. I woke up from the dream singing R Kelly's, *The World's Greatest*.

'The image of rain in the mythologies of many peoples,' according to *The Book of Symbols*, 'represents the penetration of the earth below by descending celestial, fertilising powers and points to the sacred marriage of heaven and earth.' On account of the rain and the simultaneous appearance of Sophia, I named this dream The Precipitation of Wisdom.

From Edinger we learn that:

Jung interprets the descending dew as the water of divine Wisdom or 'Gideon's Dew,' a synonym for the aqua permanens. It 'is a sign of divine intervention, it is the moisture that heralds the return of the soul.' This corresponds to the recovery of feeling after succumbing to the deadly, barren state of intellectual abstraction ... As Jung tells us, 'The alchemists thought that the opus demanded not only laboratory work, the reading of books, meditation, and patience, but also love.'

– Anatomy of the Psyche

The imagery in the dream reminded me of the sacred marriage – the descent of spirit and the ascent of soul. In the dream, Sophia, the divine face of the feminine who has fallen to earth is seen 'rising' as she receives the celestial power of spirit as symbolised by the falling rain.

This sacred marriage, also known as the *hieros gamos*, is the yab-yum position assumed by the deity (Shiva) and his female consort (Shakti) in Tantra. In ancient Sumer it is said the High Priestess of Inanna (a sacred prostitute) engaged with the king in a sacred marriage. And in alchemy King Sol unites with Queen Luna.

Not only was this dream awesome to behold (downright numinous, in fact), it was also filled with promise. I knew my life was dry, that I'd neglected soul and the body at the expense of spirit (barren intellectualism). So this dream showed me all was not lost by heralding the 'return of the soul.' That I had this dream the night before Women's Celebration left me feeling I was on the right track.

The work I was doing with Shakti Tantra was concerned not only with strengthening the body so it might be strong enough to receive and be penetrated by a human other, but with strengthening the soul so it might fully open to spirit. Catherine MacCoun puts it this way:

Some describe the soul as a grail – a cup or chalice that the alchemist is preparing so that it will be worthy of holding the spirit. The myths of the quest for the Holy Grail are allegories for the process of transforming the soul. Others use the metaphor of a wedding. Soul and spirit are a couple who meet, woo, and win one another. During their courtship, they have to learn to love, respect, and accommodate the other.

– On Becoming an Alchemist

Where many people fall foul is by believing another person completes them – 'my other half,' they'll say. What you're ideally looking for is to become one-in-yourself. It isn't anyone else's responsibility to fill your bowl or complete you. So this sacred marriage isn't just something that may happen in a concrete, sexual sense – it's an ideal, inner state where masculine and feminine energies (spirit and soul) are joined together thus rendering you an individual in the true sense of the word (one and indivisible).

Sophia wasn't the only feminine deity who was keen to impress herself upon me. George emailed me asking if I'd like to go on a press trip to Brive-la-Gaillarde, France. It was only my second ever press trip – the first having been several months earlier when I was sent to Taba, Egypt.

Immediately before my Egypt junket I'd been holidaying in the Languedoc region in the South of France with my friend, Christian, which, in light of me being summoned to Egypt, we'd had to cut short. We'd gone so I could do his Reiki initiation and generally chill out (and if you're wondering how I managed to afford it – buffalo and sack of rice). On the way back we stopped to visit Chartres Cathedral near Paris. This was the first time I saw Chartres' famous Black Madonna (Our Lady of the Pillar) I'd read so much about. As religious idols go it left a profound and lasting effect on me. I'd never seen a black female deity elevated and venerated like that before. Though I'd met Kali on the streets of India, I'd never seen a statue of her so I spent some time stood before Our Lady of the Pillar in quiet, reverent contemplation.

It was during my short break with Christian that I also recall being woken from a dream as the name 'Cybele' was spoken loudly in my ear – nothing else, just 'Cybele.' It scared the bejesus out of me. Sat bolt upright in fear, I stared into the inky darkness to see where the voice had come from. There was something about the Languedoc region which felt particularly ancient and feminine. Powerful land, that.

Anyway, before we got to Chartres I'd spotted a sign on the motorway for a place called Rocamadour. I'd read Rocamadour also had a Black Madonna and dearly wanted to see it but there'd been warnings of heavy snow in the north so we couldn't risk stopping in case we missed our ferry and, in turn, my flight to Egypt.

Though always grateful for such free opportunities to travel I couldn't help feeling a tad disappointed by the fact that, once I got to Egypt, I was nowhere near sights such as the Valley of the Kings or the Giza Necropolis. I was, however, near St Catherine's Monastery, Mount Sinai, which I did visit.

Never one to miss the symbolic undercurrents of such unplanned events, I wondered if the site had any feminine significance other than being named after St Catherine – especially as I seemed to be on something of a serendipitous streak when it came to female deities. Much later I discovered that, indeed, it did have feminine undertones. Author, Lucia Birnbaum tells us that:

> ... in 40,000 BCE african migrants created the 'oldest sanctuary in the world.' Later, this african sanctuary became the site of Mount Sinai, foundation place of judaism, christianity, and islam. On migratory routes of paleolithic africans, then on the paths of neolithic west asian farmers, then on trade routes of semitic canaanites, people looked to a dark woman divinity, to whom they built, in the common epoch, sanctuaries of black madonnas.

– Dark Mother

So you can imagine my delight when I saw a guided tour of Rocamadour's seven churches and chapels was included on the itinerary for my press trip to Brive-la-Gaillarde in one of which was the Black Madonna I'd longed to see months earlier. I could have kissed George for putting me forward for that assignment. In fact, that whole trip felt tailor-made to my interests as it also included a guided tour of Gouffre de Padirac.

Gouffre de Padirac is a colossal natural limestone chasm with a diameter of 35 metres. Leaning over it I couldn't help thinking of Luke, Hans, and company being dangled over the Great Pit of Carkoon in *Return of the Jedi*. Two elevators lowered visitors 75 metres into the subterranean bowels of a watery netherworld that left my fertile imagination reeling. Once below, our visit included a short trip on a punt along a river (103 metres below ground-level), followed by a walking tour of the vast internal caverns (the second largest open to the public in Europe).

If descending a set of stairs into a basement in Liverpool had excited me, you can just imagine how this experience almost made Inanna, here, pee her panties. In a culture obsessed with scaling the heights and travelling into space, there was something particularly powerful about descending into the earth's depths. When I eventually ascended and stepped back out into the blinding afternoon sunshine I felt I'd undergone a bona fide Underworld initiation that would forever leave its mark on my psyche.

That this descent immediately followed my guided tour of Rocamadour felt even more poignant. In the morning I'm face-to-face with a beautiful, exalted Black Madonna to whom hundreds of thousands of people have, for centuries, made long and arduous pilgrimages; in the afternoon I'm descending deep into the watery womb of the Dark Mother herself (earth). And the best bit? I didn't plan any of it.

Even the fact that Rocamadour has seven churches and chapels excited me as, on her descent into the Underworld, Inanna has to pass through seven gates at each of which she must leave an item of clothing or regalia so that by the time she arrives in front of her sister, Ereshkigal, she is stark naked. But staying with the Black Madonna for a moment, Marion Woodman and Elinor Dickson tell us that:

> Literally hundreds of shrines to the Black Virgin sprang up throughout Europe in the twelfth and thirteenth centuries. One reason for the Black Virgin's great popularity during this period was the growing adoration of the chaste Virgin Mary. Courtly love, the legend of the Holy Grail, the veneration of the Virgin, the ascendency of the idealised woman, were balanced by the compensating adoration of the Black Virgin. She was an underground figure; much of her so-called paganism still adhered to her (fertility, nature, earth). She was revered in an underground way – the blessing of the crops in the field, the blessing of pregnancy and childbirth, the dark excesses of sexuality and delight in the mysteries of the body, and the wisdom that can be experienced in lovemaking. She it was who in the most intimate experience possible to the soul, opened herself to the Holy Spirit, was impregnated, and bore God a son. In her aloneness she was independent – a liberated image of the feminine.

> *– Dancing in the Flames*

Here again we get a sense of how the dark, chthonic, sexual face of the feminine was split off and went underground. Not that that stopped her being worshipped. Like I've said, all that seemed to happen was her followers – including such figures as the sacred prostitutes – formed an underground movement and became 'subterranean renegades,' if you will. To further amplify this point Birnbaum goes on to tell us that:

> In Italy, archaeological ruins of the many images of our ancient mother are often located underneath or near sanctuaries of black madonnas. In the common epoch these were places of religious heresy, persecution of witches, and sites of popular uprisings of dark others for justice. Images of black madonnas, and of other dark woman divinities, I came to realise, may be

considered signs of resistance to the dominant culture of church and state, as well as signs of the dark mother's values – justice with compassion and equality.

– Dark Mother

What's further interesting is how many of the Black Madonna shrines Woodman and Dickson speak of are concentrated in the South of France – like I said, powerful land. The San Francisco Bay area too is, I later discovered, also considered powerful land when it comes to associations with a woman divinity as Birnbaum says here:

> Interest in the woman divinity – whom 'new age' and other theorists call 'goddess,' third world scholars call 'mother,' and I call 'dark mother' – is particularly vibrant in the San Francisco Bay area. This is not to understate wide interest in this subject throughout the world, but to offer a specific case.

– Dark Mother

What strikes me as curious is how both of my Big Dreams during this period took place in the San Francisco Bay area. I came across Birnbaum's book more than eighteen months later, so at the time of my dreams I had no idea how prominent a role the Bay area played in the ongoing research of the dark woman divinity of prehistory.

So it was the Black Madonna who accompanied me and became my sacred symbol on my women's programme. During my trip to Chartres I bought several photos of Our Lady along with a candle with which I created a small altar back home. I felt a strong urge to feel her presence near me as I underwent my Tantric/Aphroditic Underworld initiation.

I arranged the photos and candle, together with fresh flowers and other meaningful, symbolic objects on the hearth in our bedroom to which I later added images of Rocamadour's Black Madonna. I liked having her there, watching over me as I began the slow and painful journey of reconnecting with and reintegrating my Underworld self. I felt reassured by her presence.

Following her thread felt right to me. It didn't feel forced as though I was picking up any old female deity just for the sake of it. There was something about this Black Virgin figure which resonated – especially in light of the old black woman I'd met in my dream a year earlier and the series of dreams and unexpected events I'd had since.

When I took up naked dancing in the bedroom and spent time

exploring the dark folds of my feminine I felt her queenly presence watching over me in approval, encouraging me. Unlike the chaste white Virgin Mary, I felt this Black Virgin was much more on my level – that I could relate to her down-to-earth nature. Despite my Aphroditic shenanigans I never felt judged by her. As a woman raised by two black mothers she also felt reassuringly comforting and familiar to me. The Dark Mother is all I've ever known. But it went even further than that.

Something told me, when I first stepped foot in Women's Invitation, that if I descended deep enough I'd end up in the realm of the ancestors – those ancestors being my Ghanaian ancestors. As with any intuition I'm not sure where it came from – it was just a vague, felt sense that, in going down, I'd somehow be going back.

Since my grandfather ran away from his tribe no-one in our family had been back to Ghana. But since meeting this Black Madonna in Chartres Cathedral and Rocamadour and embarking on my journey with Shakti Tantra, I'd felt the deep pull of long-lost roots calling across generations, calling me back home to the land of the original Dark Mother – *Africa*.

CELEBRATION

One of the many valuable lessons having no money has taught me is not to get too attached to anything – if I can't afford it, I can't have it. Hence, my attitude towards each workshop was if I'm meant to be there the money will be forthcoming; if I'm not, it won't. But I wouldn't force the issue. So when mum gave me money for my birthday a week before the workshop, followed by Finn, I knew I was absolutely meant to be there and, to be honest, heaved a huge sigh of relief. This workshop was called Women's Celebration which was described as follows:

> **This three-day residential workshop builds on the healing work of Women's Invitation and gives women permission to experience their erotic selves, celebrate their sexuality, and start to explore their pleasure. We work to identify sexual imprints and release tensions, which allows us to increase physical energy and to move into our orgasmic flow.**

Though that may sound fun (or not, depending on your personal issues), what bothered me was it was a residential workshop which meant I had nowhere to run. For the record, I'm an introverted soul who likes her own space and requires undisturbed sleep. So though I found Women's Invitation intense at least I was able to escape each night. God knows then, what this one would bring up for me penned into, as we were, a retreat atop a hill in Glastonbury.

As with the marathon I was well aware the demons we'd face on this programme would be ours – *uniquely* ours. That's why I'd never – nor could I ever – profess to say what this course is about as it raises different issues for every participant. All I could ever do is share what issues it raised for me.

My issues kicked in as soon as I had to make arrangements to travel. I need my space and like being independent, so this depending on others for a lift was already pushing my Artemisian buttons. Though don't let me give the impression I'm a hairy-arsed hermit who scowls at vistors and mutters only monosyllables – far from it. I'm happy to socialise and love meeting new people, hearing their stories, learning all about them. I'm also happy to attend parties alone, mingle with guests, and can chit-chat into the wee early hours – just so long as I have a bolthole to escape to at the end of the night. For me, solitude is golden. It's how I recharge after being around others. So to be locked in with a group of women for a long weekend would be something of a challenge for me.

Though this was nowhere near as worrisome as the issue I faced during the drive there – I got my period. Of all the things that could go wrong, this was it. The dread with which I was consumed as I felt my moon trickle into my underwear was just about the worst thing that could happen, *ever*. I felt the world had been pulled out from under me.

Although I had no idea what they had in store for us, it was a safe bet the body work we'd face would only get deeper and more intense. So when I got my period I knew from its 'divine timing' I'd be facing old, old issues – issues reaching all the way back to my first year in secondary school when, on telling my tutor I needed to be excused from class more frequently during menses, I was told I was overreacting: it just seemed a lot because it was new and that I was *average*.

You have *no* idea how angry this makes me. In fact it fucking *infuriates* me. How a woman can turn around to a young girl, entrusted to her care, and dismiss her concerns regards her burgeoning body. Do people have any idea how damaging an off-the-cuff comment like that can be to a girl stood at the threshold of womanhood?

I've since met many women who dismiss menarche as something you 'just deal with.' Many of these women, I've noticed, are strongly identified with the Athena archetype, the father's daughter. Athenas are cool, calculating customers who tend to be all up in their head. I know when I'm in the presence of a woman strongly identified with Athena when her icy comments leave me feeling cold as stone (the shadow side of Athena is the Medusa whose gaze turned those who looked at her to stone). Their lack of connection with their bodies, their unfeeling nature is palpable – at least to me.

Anyway, that comment drove an unconscious wedge between my body and I – a wedge which was never reconciled. Rather than growing closer to my body, I grew away from it, tried to gain control over it – mind *over* matter. On some level I felt I'd done something wrong; that I was overreacting. I didn't think I was but on some unacknowledged level I was unsure – as if adolescents don't already have enough uncertainty to contend with.

All through secondary school I envied, what appeared like, every other girl who seemed to handle her periods with ease. I, on the other hand, would sit in class trying not to cry while I felt blood seeping through my knickers, through my underskirt, and onto my clothes. I walked home on many occasions with a jumper or coat wrapped around my waist to cover blood stains.

One teacher dismissing my concerns regards my periods was bad enough, but she wasn't the only one. On another occasion a P.E. (physical education) teacher fired a similar such statement at me, accusing me of trying to make my periods an excuse to get out of lessons: until she saw me climb off the trampoline with my bottom covered in blood. Despite apologising it was too late – the damage was done. Yet another woman had dismissed both me and my bodily anxieties.

When I came off the contraceptive pill and started using a Mooncup (a reusable, silicon-shaped cup you place inside yourself and empty out), not only did I begin the process of consciously reconnecting with my blood – which, at first, I admit I found horrifying – but I also discovered, by being able to measure how much blood I lost, that I wasn't 'average' and, finally, felt vindicated in my adolescent protests. So when I felt my periods welling in my underwear on my way to the workshop I knew I'd be facing the shame I'd long harboured and, on some level, likely somatised.

I'm not saying what we did. All I will say is, yes, I did face my worst fears in the most intense way imaginable (at least, that's how it felt to me). The first forty-eight hours of my period are usually the heaviest so it was never going to be the most pleasant of experiences. But once I surrendered and let go it ended up being one of the most liberating, most healing experiences I'd ever had. Permission to gush (no pun intended).

I realised, in this workshop, just how necessary the work these women do is needed in our culture. Beneath the surface, behind the scenes, these priestesses are quietly, stealthily, putting broken women back together again, initiating girls into conscious womanhood, before releasing them back into the world so they can fly, soar, as they were always meant to.

That's how it felt for me. I felt they held me, supported me while I birthed a woman from the girl who had, for so long, teetered at the threshold of womanhood, unsure of how to cross over. As the weekend wore on I felt shame and guilt and a whole host of issues, conscious and unconscious, gradually ebb away. But not only did they birth me, more importantly they cherished me. They cherished my body and reaffirmed all that being a woman entails with a resounding yes. There was no 'issue' with my bleeding. To them my blood was gold – yet another aspect of womanhood to be openly and unashamedly celebrated. With these women I could just be.

This was the finishing school I'd unconsciously yearned for since they fucked it all up back in secondary school. For twenty-four years I'd felt lost, unable to bridge a gap I hadn't even been able to articulate. So this workshop showed me that it's never too late to go back and pick up the pieces, put them back together again in new and stronger ways. I'm just glad I had the courage to trust and surrender to their wisdom. But this wasn't the only gap to be bridged during this weekend.

As I'd spent the past several years engaged in intellectual pursuits it proved a challenge to switch my head off. By this I mean I didn't know when to shut up. I've already mentioned how I yakked on at Women's Invitation but I was doing it again at this workshop, giving rambling discourses rather than keeping my answers short and to the point.

I know why I was doing it: I was so excited to be in an environment I felt complemented my studies that I couldn't contain my enthusiasm. Whenever we had an opportunity to share, the words just kept on bubbling over. During one such tortuous treatise one of the assistants, Julie, a no-nonsense, straight-to-the-point woman clearly exasperated by me going on and on and *on* cut in and said, 'Thea, what do you feel? Not what do you think. The question was what do you *feel*.'

As soon as she said that I knew she was right. It took me straight back to something Sam always asked me: 'Thea, what's on your heart?' It was a question he'd ask in an attempt to bypass my head and cut straight to the heart of the matter. He was the first person who brought to my attention the tendency I have to answer questions with more questions and waffle on about what I *think* I feel, as opposed to sitting with the question for a moment and saying what's actually 'on my heart' – in other words, my *feelings*.

The truth was I didn't know how I felt. I was still out of touch with my body. This was, after all, only the second workshop. There was still much work ahead. I knew, when it came to the issues surrounding my periods, I was angry and ashamed and fearful about what had happened all those years before but I didn't come right out and say that. No. Instead, I launched into a meandering diatribe on what I thought *about* anger and shame and fear that would have made Plato proud, rather than just saying I was angry and ashamed and afraid – until Julie stepped in and stopped me dead in my philosophising tracks.

That I was willing to witter on, however, was progress for me. After coming out about my psychospiritual orientation on the online magazine, I was now coming out about my intellectuality. Prior to this workshop I would have held back and downplayed my knowledge so as not to stand out or potentially overshadow others. It was another fear carried over from secondary school – even if you know the subject standing on your head, don't come across as the class know-it-all. But I was done with playing down my talents lest others should feel intimidated or insecure. I was done apologising. This was me – a studious, self-taught, self-disciplined bookworm who does her homework. And then some.

Although not hiding my light under a bushel was a positive step for me, I later found out not everyone in the group saw it that way. The first morning while in the bedroom, a woman, Justine, flashed me such a dirty look I'm surprised she didn't burn me to a crisp. Thing is, I had no idea who she was as she'd arrived in the middle of the night so I couldn't think what I might have said or done to warrant such an ossifying glare.

So fast forward to the end of the workshop, during our last sharing, when I did something I'd never done before – I told two of the girls they got on my nerves (or words to that effect). I don't know who was more shocked at my outburst – them or me. I'd never been one to rock the boat, especially in public situations. After all I was a nice girl – *wasn't I?*

I wouldn't mind if I'd been thinking about it (what I said), but I hadn't – at least, not consciously. But here's the thing: up until this point I'd been peddling an idea of who I thought I was. But who I *thought* I was and who I actually *am* were, as I was now discovering, two very different people.

I'd got it into my head that I was a 'nice' girl. This was the persona I presented to the world. But in thinking I was 'nice,' I'd driven my more forthright, opinionated self underground and into my shadow. One of several reasons I'd done this, I think, was while growing up I'd seen the devastating trail of damage my Hecate-like aunt had left in her wake in the form of uncensored thoughts and opinions. When I say she didn't give a damn what anyone thought I mean she *didn't give a damn.*

But where she had no investment in being nice, I did. I was, after all, a good girl – the Kore – and I couldn't stand not being liked. I didn't want to appear as mean and as harsh as my aunt (which was how I perceived her treatment of others when I was younger). My trick, then, was to say the right thing, to people please, and to make everyone like me. So I would never, *ever* say anything, even if I was thinking it, which might make people not like me or go against this nice idea I had about myself – until now.

This was the first explicit experience I'd had where I felt betrayed by something 'other' within: that my ego wasn't the only psychic entity; that there were, in fact, others rattling around my psyche and that those others had voices of their own – especially if they felt they'd been pushed into a corner, overlooked, and ignored. If you've ever heard someone say, 'I don't know what came over me,' 'I don't know what got into me,' or 'She was like a woman possessed,' you'll know what I mean.

If I was to present this scenario to a dream tender they'd likely ask, 'Who is visiting now?' This question is as relevant to waking reality as it is the dreamtime (well technically it's all the dreamtime but to fully open up that concept lies beyond the scope of this book). So, in that moment, if we were to ask, 'Who is visiting now?' I tell you who was visiting – the Baba Yaga. I wouldn't have been surprised had I looked down and found a fiery skull atop a stick in my hand. I could feel her presence in me and around me. Frankly, I was shocked. But it was too late. The Yaga had spoken and she couldn't care less.

My comments, as you may imagine, shocked both women and ruffled the atmosphere in the room. Meantime, while I'm sat there trying to figure out where the hell this foreign tongue came from and furiously trying to backtrack, Justine, whose look had turned me to stone on the first morning – and who was sat between these two women – hit back with a sharp-edged comment.

My first thought was that her comment had nothing to do with what had just been said – that there was something else behind it. Turns out I was right. Months later, while hanging out with Justine, she opened up and told me her first impressions of me. She spoke of how she'd always been top of the class – until, that is, she met me. Here was someone (i.e. me), she said, who was intelligent and articulate and who had apparently done their homework – traits which left her feeling not quite so top of the class and may also explain the glare with which she fixed me at the workshop.

All credit to her for being honest with me, though. What she said wasn't prompted by anything we'd been discussing so she didn't have to tell me any of this. But as she opened up and shared her initial opinion of me, I felt I'd been punched square in the solar plexus. But, like I said, it also bridged another gap. If I was ever going to be more authentic, more true to myself and others, I had to stop worrying what others may or may not think about me and come clean about who I am, right now, in this moment – no apologies. If who I am doesn't make me popular, so be it. But at least I'm being true to myself and that's all that matters to me.

I also share this because, back at the workshop, after we'd finished and were packing up to go home, Esther, one of the two women I'd pointed my fiery skull at approached me to tell me how my comments had upset her which, under the circumstances, I could fully understand. But then she said something which knocked me for six and was along the lines of me giving off the impression that I thought I was the group's queen bee. I had to stop myself guffawing out loud. *Me? Think I'm the group's queen bee? Are you kidding me?*

If there's one thing I always do, however, it's reflect. So though I could have dismissed her comments as hogwash I realised I must have done *something* to give off this queen bee impression – especially when it was later compounded by Justine's 'top of the class' insight.

Looking back I'm glad the Yaga 'spoke me' otherwise Esther and Justine may have never shared their impressions of me, with me. In the immediate aftermath of my outburst, however, I felt the Self had betrayed me by putting me in a situation which it could walk away from unseen and unscathed. *It's alright for you*, I later scrawled in my journal, *but it's me out here who has to deal with it*. So when the Self hit back with: *It was the truth wasn't it? That's how you felt?* I was stopped in my tracks. (I often employ a stream of consciousness style of writing when dialoguing with the Self – a technique I recommend.) *And another thing*, it went on, *stop denying your leadership qualities otherwise they'll come back to bite you on the arse. Why do you think you always bitch about those you believe have more power than you? Why do you think they irritate you? And don't pretend they don't because I know they do. It's because you're denying your own power, that's why. You're denying your queenly qualities. You know full well you want to be in charge. Well it's high time you looked at that, lady.*

Wow. Was I denying my queenly qualities? Was I denying my power? The more I reflected on this the more I realised it was true. Then I remembered that this attempt to keep up nicey-nicey appearances is one of the shadow sides of the Kore. Kores, you see, don't do anger and have a tendency to deny their power and live vicariously through others.

I'd spent my life relinquishing my power, handing it over to others I perceived more powerful than me, hiding behind them, courting their good graces while all the time resenting them for it. But my Kore-like persona was now cracking and slipping. So long as I continued to deny my true nature it would only cause me further problems.

But you know what? My queen-like tendencies have always been there. In my first year of secondary school I decided that when I got to fifth year, I was going to be Head Girl. It didn't matter that I was never the most popular of girls or part of the in-crowd – I was going to be Head Girl and that was that. (A position I eventually attained.)

Then there was a comment Barefoot made when he'd visited. He'd asked about my ancestry. I explained my grandfather was supposed to be the next chief but decided he was having none of it and ran away – abdicated, you might say.

'So you're a princess?' Barefoot asked, perfectly serious.

'Er, *what*? It was just a tribe in Ghana,' I replied.

'No,' he went on, 'had your grandfather stayed with his people, he would have been chief. You're descended from royalty. It doesn't matter if you dismiss it as 'just a tribe.' Being a chief is serious business. You only have to look at this weekend (Royal Wedding) to see how seriously we take it over here.'

I looked at him incredulous and left the conversation there. But there was something in the metaphor – after all my grandfather *had* ran away from his responsibility, relinquished his power. Years later (late 1940s), his family sailed to the UK, en masse, to demand he return and assume his duties: a fact which, my Ghanaian-descended friend, Kwasi, said, proved my ancestors had money and plenty of it. Was I trying to relinquish my innate power like my grandfather before me? Were these leadership/queen-like tendencies part of a greater ancestral myth?

The more I thought about it, the more I remembered numerous comments and situations made down the years which all tied in with what Esther, Justine, and others had remarked on regards my demeanour ('powerful,' was how another woman described it) and the air I gave off. It was this revelation – about what was apparently 'written all over me' – which led me back to a story I first heard told by Joseph Campbell, of which my telling is a slight variation.

In the story a lion cub finds himself alone and abandoned after his mother dies while giving birth to him. He's later adopted by a flock of sheep who take him in and raise him as one of their own. And so he grows up eating grass and making meek meow-like noises in his attempt to 'baa' like the other sheep. As the lion is a natural carnivore the grass doesn't agree with his digestive system. By the time he grows up he looks like a pretty pathetic specimen of his species.

One day a magnificent male lion penetrates the sheep's territory on the prowl for fresh meat. As he pounces, the sheep scatter – all, that is, except the young lion who just stands there looking at him. Appalled at the appearance of this paltry excuse for a lion who's bleating and eating grass, the big fellow marches up to him and asks him what he's playing at.

The young lion, who has no idea what this big beast's on about, replies with one of his meow-like noises. After clubbing him round the head a few times with his giant paws, the beast drags the young one off to a pool of still water and demands he look into it.

'What do you see?' asks the big fellow who's also looking into the water's reflection. 'You've the face of a lion. You see that? You're like me. *So be like me.*' At this point, the young lion's beginning to get the message. But the big guy isn't done yet. Next, he drags the lion back to his den where there are the remains of a slaughtered wildebeest. The big fellow tears a hunk of flesh off the carcass and demands the young lion open his mouth but the young one backs away in an 'I'm a vegetarian way.'

The older one, having none of this, gets hold of him and shoves it down his throat. The young one gags on it – after all, the truth can be hard to swallow. Despite gagging on it, as it's his proper food it activates his nervous system and jolts him into life. With that, he lets out a little lion roar. 'Now you're getting it,' says the big one, 'now you'll eat lion food and become fully who you are – a lion, King of Beasts.'

The moral of the story is we are all lions living as sheep. As Campbell says, commenting on his version of the story (called *The Tiger and the Goat*), 'The function of sociology and most of our religious education is to teach us to be goats. But the function of the proper interpretation of mythological symbols and meditation discipline is to introduce you to your tiger face. Then comes the problem. You've found your tiger face but you're still living here with these goats. How are you going to do that?' Indeed. This is the task, this is the toil.

After all, just because we're shaped a certain way – that we have certain qualities written all over us – doesn't necessarily mean we'll fulfil our potential, as author Liz Greene says here:

> The operative word here is 'potential.' It's potential in the same way that an apple seed will potentially produce an apple tree. It contains the entire cycle inside it: seed, young plant, tree, flower, fruit, seed. But if you hold it in your hand, it's still only a seed. A lot can happen to a seed. Nurtured, fertilised, watered and given sufficient sunshine, it will produce a splendid tree. Neglected, it will produce far short of its potential, or may not produce at all. We are given certain potentials. What we make of them is our own business. We have the option to become ourselves in full flower, or produce a stunted tree that bears no fruit. And the gardener isn't anyone but oneself.

> – *Astrology for Lovers*

My grandfather, once he arrived in the UK, continued to exude a regal air dressing in tailor-made suits, carrying a pocket watch. My aunt said he was a proud man, elegant in demeanour; that he exuded statesman-like qualities and commanded attention wherever he went, doffing his hat to folks on meeting them. So though he never fulfilled his potential of being his tribe's chief, his destiny – the person he was born to be – was still written all over him despite his absconding.

To put yet another spin on this, imagine for a moment you're a brown square. You, however, have decided that gold stars seem to have all the fun so you spend your life trying to be a gold star. Everything you do is focused to this end (becoming a gold star). Only problem is, you are a brown square. To deny the fact you're a brown square is to deny the fated qualities you were born with – those physical and psychological traits unique to you and you alone.

So long as you attempt to be a gold star you'll miss out on the opportunities which are only open to brown squares such as yourself – opportunities, which in turn, are not open to gold stars or red triangles for that matter. (I know this may sound silly, but stay with me.) Instead, you live in limbo: a No Shape's Land, if you will. Neither a brown square nor a gold star you spend your life drifting, betwixt and between, not

171

feeling as though you belong anywhere. Then you wonder why you're *de-pressed* – because you're not *ex-pressing* your true shape.

Though you might not think it's sexy or interesting to be a brown square, to quote Jung: 'The privilege of a lifetime is to become who you truly are.' Many associate being extraordinary with something larger than life. For me, though, to be extraordinary is to be exactly that: *extra ordinary* – to be all the *you* you can be.

For a brown square to follow the path of a gold star would be a sin (*sin* in ancient Greek meant 'to miss the mark'). In other words by following the wrong star home you'd be 'missing the point' that is *your* life – a life that is uniquely yours.

What generally ends up happening is brown squares want to be gold stars; red triangles want to be blue circles – everyone trying to be anyone other than themselves. But as Oscar Wilde said, 'Be yourself; everyone else is already taken.' If you are a brown square, there's a very good reason you're a brown square – it's because the world needs you to be a brown square to the utmost of your ability. To accept your brown squareness with a generosity of spirit is to say *yes* to life and when you say *yes* to life, again, to quote Campbell: 'Doors will open for you that wouldn't have opened for anyone else.'

In the story of the lion and the sheep, so long as the lion insists on being the wrong shape (i.e. a sheep), he denies the world of his innate, leonine nature and misses the mark that is his life. As everything is interconnected he, in turn, denies others of the opportunity to be fully who they are. To deny the fullness of your reality is to deny others the fullness of their reality.

To bring this back closer to my life, say I'm destined for a position of leadership and responsibility but insist, for whatever reasons (false modesty, insecurity, fear, unworthiness) on denying my destined shape. In denying the world of the unique qualities with which I was innately imbued, I leave a 'vacancy' which others will (wrongly) try to fill.

Take my grandfather. From what I've heard he sounds like he would have made a great chief – after all, he was born to do it. But when he ran away he left a vacancy – a chief-shaped hole. This created an imbalance, upset the status quo and my ancestors, who were *not* happy, came after him to try and restore balance.

This is what happens to all of us when we deny our fated qualities – it irritates others around us, upsets the psychological ecosystem, you might say. Others sense, or can see, that we have certain qualities written all over us so wonder, consciously or unconsciously, why we aren't living them out. Soon, the environment – Life – starts to rattle you. Keep this denial up and, sooner or later, the world will come after you. It may be in the form of a depression or a redundancy, a relationship breakup or a midlife crisis. In the Hero's Journey, this is the Call to Adventure – except when it's calling it doesn't necessarily feel like an 'adventure.' What's happening is you're being called to your potential which, when it comes rapping at your door issuing its demands, may feel nothing short of terrifying.

To say *yes* to your life – to accept with grace, dignity, and a generosity of spirit the *extra ordinary* human being you are, right now and to be who you truly are – that is the Hero's Journey we each face. To say *yes* to the Hero's Journey is to stop trying to be something or someone you're not and start being yourself, without apology – no more, no less. Because, despite what we may have heard, this world owes us nothing. We, however, owe it to the world to be ourselves – wholly, uniquely ourselves.

Accepting your destined shape carries just as many challenges as trying to fit into another's shape as I discovered when I came out, first with my spiritual tendencies and, later, with my bookish qualities. But the relief I finally felt inside far outweighed anything anyone could have ever said to me about what they thought of me. After all, it's me who has to live with myself.

Of course, you can always say no – that is, after all, what free will is all about. My grandfather said no. Nothing is absolute or set in stone. We can accept The Call or we can hang up. Doesn't mean to say Life will stop rapping at our door, calling us to be ourselves. You can remain forever a seed, full of potential, 'always gonna, but never do,' as my aunt says. Or you can choose to come clean with yourself, begin to own up to who you are, drop the act, and bridge the gap. It's not necessarily easier but at least it's authentic and promises integrity.

It was thanks to this workshop that I realised, big time, I may have been missing the mark. For whatever reasons I'd put my queen-like tendencies 'in the bag.' But, despite what I thought, I wasn't fooling anyone. What, then, was life calling me to do? In what way was I supposed to fulfil my potential? What was I not seeing in myself that others saw written all over me? What qualities had I disowned, forgotten, or lost along the way?

My life was being rattled, I could feel it. I'd unleashed the geek within – not easy, but I'd done it. I'd also faced long-standing bodily insecurities around my periods. Again, it wasn't easy, but I'd done it. So what else was I afraid of? What was holding me back? Or, rather, what was I holding back?

In a corner of my mind I had an idea what part of the answer may be: I was afraid of myself – I was afraid of how big I might be. I was afraid if I filled out to the size I felt capable of, I'd take over the joint. I was afraid to roar because, if I roared, people might look – and I wasn't sure how I felt about that. I was afraid of my voice. In short, I was afraid of being myself.

But inside I was simmering, bubbling. Though I wasn't entirely sure what was causing it I could feel the pressure building. Something was trying to get out. My Yagaian outburst was an early warning sign, a volcanic tremor. I knew it was only a matter of time before the plug blew.

On my return I wrote a piece for my blog about my experience of the workshop which I share here:

WOMEN'S CELEBRATION:
WORKSHOP REVIEW

'The feminine has slower rhythms, meanders, moves in spirals, turns back on herself, finds what is meaningful to her, and plays.'

– Marion Woodman

So my Tantra journey continues with level two of Shakti Tantra's women's programme, Women's Celebration. After doing level one (Women's Invitation) I was surprised to discover there were four more levels. 'How much deeper can the work go?' I thought. Turns out deeper. Much deeper.

This work reminds me of Russian dolls: you crack open one to find another woman nesting within. Each doll represents a deeper, more authentic, more passionate, juicy, and vital self you'd have never discovered had you not done this work.

You could spend years talking through your issues with a counsellor, analyst, or therapist and you'd make progress for sure. Alternatively, you could work through your issues in what I consider to be one of the most powerful experiential settings available in the UK today, with the most courageous, supportive, and inspiring women you're ever likely to meet.

As a staunch believer of the dictum 'Talking is fun, but doing gets done,' I know the value of consciously including the body when it comes to facing and tackling deep-held conscious/unconscious issues. Talking will carry you so far, but when it comes to certain psychological issues there are times when you just have to bypass the rational logical mind and approach it physically.

I've seen countless folk talk themselves out of relationship with their bodies, terrified of feeling, terrified of being fully present in the skin they're in. I know because I was one of them. They retreat up into the safety of the head and stay there. Meanwhile, the body becomes nothing more than an unconscious stick used to prop up the head, a mass of unconscious flesh. Thing is, the mind isn't located in the brain: the mind is located in every single cell of the body. That's where this work comes into its own.

If you don't consciously know what the issue is – what's holding you back, restricting you, inhibiting you – it doesn't matter. This work goes straight to the heart of the matter – that matter being your body. And remember, the word 'matter' shares its roots with 'mater' which means mother. This, therefore, is healing at the deepest, most profound level imaginable.

I love this work because it cuts to the chase and releases you from any false illusions you may have had about yourself, leaving the mind reeling in its wake. That doesn't mean you can't consciously reflect on what you experienced afterwards and draw your necessary lessons etc. My point is once you do this work your relationship with your Self and your body is changed forever and will never be the same.

Bring on level three.

WATCH THE THRONE

The week after Women's Celebration I began taking Spanish lessons. Having enjoyed a torrid tryst with Italy for several years I wanted to explore another country and, with it, another aspect of my personality. Italy gave me permission to explore and express my more glamorous side as it's one of the few countries in which, as far as I'm concerned, you can never be too overdressed or overdramatic. Compared with the stiff, British reserve it was a breath of fresh air.

Not wishing to impose or reinforce cultural stereotypes I'd always thought of Spain as impassioned, intense, and fiery. Perhaps it had something to do with their bullfights and head-held-high flamenco stamping señoritas, but something in me was stirring and I felt the urge to visit. So, off I went to the marketplace to negotiate a summer holiday at an eco-retreat in the south-east of Spain for Finn and I. As I didn't speak a word of Spanish (neither did Finn), I also enlisted on an evening course to brush up on the basics.

What struck me, during my first lesson, was my inability to open my mouth and speak – I was *terrified*. I hadn't felt so afraid since the threat of learning French loomed over me in my final year of primary school (French was compulsory in secondary school), the thought of which had consumed me with dread.

For the first few lessons I left nursing a shocking headache and feeling like an all-round failure. I wanted to open my mouth, speak loud and with confidence. Instead, all I could manage were pathetic, meek meow-like noises. Whatever, it was obviously poking at insecurities as it left me feeling vulnerable and, oftentimes, on the verge of tears.

In another corner of my life, meanwhile, I decided it was time to further expand on my solo Aphroditic shenanigans. I'm glad to report this was much more fun. With my leftover birthday money I bought myself a couple of crotchless thongs. I bought them for my pleasure and my pleasure alone as I was trying to figure out and feel my way around what felt sexy to me.

Though they looked interesting on the website – and even more curious on arrival – it was only during a trip to buy paint from the DIY store that they really came into their own.

I'd discovered a track hidden in the recesses of my iPod by Herbaliser called *The Sensual Woman* which I found playfully rude and sexy as hell – talk about a tune to put a wiggle in your walk. In the spirit of making love my life rather than narrowing it down and compartmentalising it, I slithered into my crotchless panties. Over them I threw on a pair of jeans and a plain top. My aim, after all, wasn't to look sexy but, rather, to *feel sensual*. With that I set off to the store.

I've done some things which have made even me giggle, but this had to be one of the most fun. Slinking up and down the aisles it was all I could do not to laugh out loud at what I was up to. I don't know why I'd never done it before. I'd probably only ever done something like that if I was trying to impress a partner. But as an act of self-pleasure to make me feel good? No, never.

But do you know, I actually felt like I was conducting a clandestine love affair with all this sneaking about which, technically, I was – with myself. Finn knew nothing of what I was up to (he never seemed that way inclined to begin with – into me dressing up in sexy lingerie etc.). Neither did anyone else for that matter. I never discussed it with anyone. Actually, I tell a lie – Bing knew I'd been 'experimenting' and that I'd bought a couple pairs of easy access knick-knacks, but I don't think I ever told her about my secret store-strutting escapades.

Though I did tell her about something else I got up to. You may remember me mentioning I'd been left with two tiny holes in my labia after my operation? Well, by this time, I'd spent so much time inspecting her (yoni), I decided it was time to treat her, zhuzh her up a bit. So I decided to invest in a little intimate jewellery. After much research I finally settled on a titanium ball closure ring in a pretty, iridescent colour. Slippery sucker to fit but once it was in it didn't half put a smile on my lips. Hers, too.

'You've bought what!' Bing said, when I told her about my latest investment.

'You know that MTV show, *Pimp My Ride?*' I replied. 'The one where they take an old car and restore and customise it? Well, think of this as *Pimp My Punani.*'

'You've blinged your minge, that's what you've done!'

At the time Bing had earned herself a new nickname – Slinky – largely on account on the amount of weight she'd lost during her stressful divorce. She was already a slip of a thing, so when she dropped even more weight I took to calling her Slinky or Slinky Bing – which is what made her next comment all the more funny.

'We're a right pair aren't we, eh?' She said, pausing. 'I don't know – from Slinky Bing to Blingy Minge.'

177

I wouldn't mind but it bloody well stuck (the nickname that is, not the jewellery). Bing took great delight in calling me Blingy knowing full well no-one knew what she meant.

Joking aside, no longer ashamed or embarrassed, I enjoyed wearing a pretty piece of intimate jewellery as it kept me in constant contact with my Underworld self. I don't think I'd have had the guts to have it pierced but, as I already had the holes, I figured I may as well make the most of them.

Months later I took it out – simply because I got bored of it. But, on reflection, it proved to be a powerful, healing exercise in exorcising any remaining negative feelings I may have harboured towards my sex. Whenever I see it in my jewellery box it always makes me smile.

I knew the work I was doing, both at the workshops and on my own, was having a healing effect on my body and soul largely on account of the dreams I had. The day after Women's Celebration, for example, I had a simple dream which clearly summed up what was going on at the level of the subtle body.

In the dream I was in a hospital basement with a woman I'd been paired with during the workshop. My first thought on waking was that healing was happening in my root chakra. That's one of the many gifts about working with your dreams while doing body work – you're given an insight into what's going on at the profoundest soul level.

Elsewhere, Aphrodite and I were playing with a whole host of decadent goodies I'd been sent to review. After an initial trickle of products I'd since been overwhelmed with boxes upon boxes of delicious smelling skincare, beautifully scented candles, and luxurious 'intimate lifestyle products' (read: posh sex toys). I may not have been paid for my articles but this more than made up for it simply because it helped make me feel good about myself again.

As a child I'd never been one to play with make-up or even dress up for that matter. So it felt wonderful to give myself permission to adorn myself with fragrant fripperies, indulge my body, and have a good old play. After years spent buried in books this world still seemed foreign to me. In particular, I'd admired the way Sally, the Tough Nun, seemed to enjoy herself. Although beautiful, she's not full of herself. In fact on first meeting her she can seem aloof, though she later told me she's actually quite shy.

We've since joked about how she's always camera ready, striking a pose as soon as a lens is turned her way. I'd always felt too shy and inhibited to act like that. So it was a joy to watch not only how she did it, but how she also seemed to enjoy herself in the process. I wished I could loosen up and be more like her.

But my single, biggest self-revelation during the period between

Women's Celebration and our third workshop, Women Behaving Badly was something I said to myself one day. I'd like to hide behind the excuse I'm a writer to justify the fact I frequently talk to myself or put it down to being an only child. But the truth is I often waffle on and on and *on*, out loud, to myself.

So I'm stood in the kitchen, one day, preparing dinner and having a proper good chinwag with myself, when I'm shocked to the core at the following words which tumbled out of my mouth before I'd had a chance to stop them: 'Yeah, but you don't deserve it.'

Those words stopped me dead in my tracks simply because I couldn't quite remember what I'd been saying to myself in the run up to this comment.

'I don't deserve it? Don't deserve what?'

Nothing.

'What don't I deserve?'

Still nothing.

I felt sick to the stomach – sick because I knew I'd unearthed a long hidden belief which had finally risen, after being buried for goodness knows how long, to the surface level of consciousness. I felt sad and awful and confused. I couldn't believe I'd said that to myself; that I didn't deserve. But *what* didn't I believe I deserved?

One of the best pieces of advice I've ever been given was something Sam once said to me: *Stay in the question.* Rather than look for meaning or look for an answer, stay curious and open to the fact that you don't know, and continue exploring and asking questions. It's a humble approach which I also apply to dreamwork. So, I did the same with this unbidden statement which had gushed forth from the unconscious by pondering, mulling, and reflecting on it.

As the summer wore on I gradually discovered many things I didn't believe I deserved or was worthy of: I didn't deserve to be loved; I didn't deserve a life of beauty; I didn't deserve tenderness; I didn't deserve being paid compliments; I didn't deserve happiness; I didn't deserve to be with someone who was kind and generous and considerate; I didn't deserve to be bought flowers; I didn't deserve pleasure; I didn't deserve nourishing, nurturing sex with someone I loved and who loved me; I didn't deserve to be cherished; I didn't deserve to be wined and dined; I didn't deserve to be with someone I found handsome and fancied the frickin' pants off; I didn't deserve to be paid well for the work I did; I didn't deserve respect; I didn't deserve the life I'd envisioned for myself; I didn't deserve, I didn't deserve, I didn't deserve.

These were not easy admissions to make, even to myself, because the truth was so long as I didn't believe I deserved, I'd only continue to settle for less. After all, beggars can't be choosers. Although I'd been nurturing abundance by bartering my writing skills down at the marketplace I now realised that, in other areas of my life, I was still very much like the sister in the story – selling myself cheap because, deep down, I didn't believe I deserved.

The longer you stay in a question like this (What don't I believe I deserve?) the more painful the discoveries can be – especially once you cast a ruthlessly honest eye over all areas of your life and start to see the many ways you've settled for less and sold yourself cheap out of fear that this might be as good as it gets. But what if it isn't, I thought? What if I do deserve? What if, for once in my life, just once – like the sister in the story – I waited for the pearls?

Until I addressed this deep-rooted belief I obviously harboured nothing would ever change. It wouldn't matter what positive intentions or ambitious goals I set myself; if, at the most fundamental level I didn't believe I deserved what made my heart sing out with gladness and joy and gratitude, I'd only ever continue to sabotage myself, back away from what my heart truly desired, and settle for less.

The upshot of this discovery, though, was now I was aware of it I could do something about it. After all, better out than in. It also allowed me to hold a new thought at the forefront of my mind – namely, 'I *do* deserve it.' Whenever I found myself teetering on the edge of not believing I deserved something I'd stop myself, pause, and say to myself, 'Actually, I *do* deserve it.'

There was one area in particular which this revelation highlighted – my relationship with Finn. I now realised that, like Sam before him, he wasn't the man with the pearls – at least, not for me. He was a good man, dedicated to his work. But the more I reflected on this 'I don't deserve' issue, the more I realised there was something important missing, something which mattered very much to me: he lacked, what I call, the Blush Factor.

When it comes to men I've never had a 'type.' If you were to line up all my ex-boyfriends they'd look like the police line-up from the movie poster for *The Usual Suspects*. So I always know when I'm in the presence of someone I *really* like when they make me blush. Looking back, I've only ever had two boyfriends who have made me blush.

The first was a typically tempestuous teenage relationship. You know the one when it's all slamming doors, storming out, and making up every other week. The other was with a guy who only ever threw me a few scraps (not much of a relationship, then). But never have I had a mature relationship with someone who made me blush. I realised that's what I wanted more than anything – to be with someone who I respected, admired, and to whom I was so deeply attracted that he made me blush before I had a chance to stop myself.

Though that may sound silly and a bit girly, it's my truth and it's what mattered to me. But if I was ever going to have that it would inevitably mean letting go of my relationship with Finn – something which was now beginning to happen.

If you want to know the true state of your relationship, whisk it away to a secluded spot for a lengthy break – that'll cut through the crap and reveal the reality of what's going on (or not). Which is why, when we arrived at our hotel in Spain, I knew we were really over by way of four separate events.

The first involved the card game he'd taught me during our previous short break in Scotland – a game at which he'd thrashed me. I wasn't particularly bothered by this as, when I was a kid, mum regularly took great satisfaction in beating me at various board and card games. But to me, win or lose, it's about having fun.

When I found myself on a winning streak, it was what it was – a game. But not to Finn. My winning seemed to annoy him. He really seemed to take the hump with me. So when I beat him he turned to me, quite serious, and said my win had nothing to do with skill, but, rather, luck. When he'd first explained the game he said it was a combination of skill and luck, of 'making the most of the cards you've been dealt' – something I'd been busy practising in other areas of my life since our last holiday and, judging from this outcome, something I'd obviously gotten good at.

The next event was a dream he had. I knew something was up when he'd barely spoken two words to me all morning. It was only as we drove to lunch that he opened up and told me what was going on. In his dream he was in a library waiting for me. I was off somewhere else, researching, when a librarian asked him what he was doing. He told her he was with me. 'Oh, that's okay then,' she said, her attitude towards him softening. Her reaction, however, seemed to have irritated him. Owing to the already tetchy atmosphere I left both the conversation and the dream, there.

The third event came by means of a canyoning (also known as canyoneering) excursion. This was another experience I doubt I'd have committed to had I known, beforehand, what it entailed. I thought the marathon was tough but it was a veritable stroll compared to this.

Fitted with wetsuits we donned helmets and, over the course of several challenging hours, swam along the river at the bottom of a canyon, scrambled over rocks, jumped off countless umpteen-feet high drops into the icy depths below, abseiled down claustrophobia-inducing crevices, and had the time of our lives. The invigorating escapade reminded me that I'm made of tough, brave stuff that I often forget when shuffling somnambulantly through the concrete jungle of daily life.

But close to the end, while swimming the last stretch, it suddenly got tough – *really* tough. I felt I had a ball and chain holding me back as it seemed to take every last ounce of effort to push through the river's oncoming current. When I looked back I saw Finn had hold of my ankle. He's admitted he's not the best of swimmers but it was all I could do to haul my own weary arse to the end, let alone drag someone else along.

I initially felt flattered he considered me strong enough to pull him along too. Later on, though, when I'd had chance to recover, the metaphor hit me – I was being held back. I realised I had tremendous endurance and courage and determination and strength to go the distance despite the odds and despite overwhelming obstacles. What I didn't need was to convince someone else about why I was making the decisions I was – decisions I'd made long before that person came along. I was tired of explaining myself, justifying my actions as though I'd done something wrong.

I also realised that it didn't matter how little money I had, as money can't buy you any of those things (courage, determination, endurance etc.). Neither can it buy you self-belief. It's who you are and the decisions you make when you have no money and few resources that matter more and reflect the kind of person you really are.

I also got the feeling he wasn't happy about playing second fiddle to me in any way, shape, or form. I'm not saying that's the truth because, ultimately, I don't know. But he was a man who liked to be in charge. Often described as a maverick at work, he didn't like being told what to do. But what if, I wondered, my profile was set to take off? What then?

Though we'd spoken, back at the beginning of the relationship, of me supporting him down the line, I wasn't so sure, now, whether he really wanted that. It takes great strength to be vulnerable, to follow your dreams. It also takes great strength to be vulnerable enough to allow someone else to support you while you do that – something I had first-hand experience of. You have to trust that the other isn't going to take advantage of the situation and start power-tripping you because they have what they consider to be the upper hand.

Power dynamics – this got me thinking. When we first met I was in a self-confessed position of vulnerability. After all, I had nothing (or so I thought). But now I'd learnt to make the most of the cards I'd been dealt things were shifting between us. No longer so reliant on him I was making moves of my own. But had I missed something in the dynamics of our relationship? Especially when I learnt that one of Apollo's precepts was, 'Keep the woman under rule' which, Bolen says, describes what this kind of man tends to do to his inner woman (in Jungian psychology, a man's inner feminine is known as the *anima* – soul).

As previously mentioned, he never said a single complimentary thing about me or of the work I did. He never read my articles, never asked about my studies, nothing. He did, however, always tell me about the women at work he'd helped mentor and who, as a result, had been promoted. He seemed to favour helping women more than men, always telling me about his latest protégé. So it always struck me as odd that he never said anything complimentary to me, his partner. I could have been paranoid but it felt like he was deliberately withholding praise from me.

What he didn't realise was ultimately, I answered to the Self. What mattered to me, more than anything else, was that I did, to the best of my ability, whatever the Self called me to do. That would always be my first priority. Whoever I was with would need to understand that about me.

But I don't think Finn did. As he'd never asked, I never told him just how deeply religious I was – not in the sense of being affiliated to any organised religion; rather, in being bound or wedded to the Other (Self, God, whatever). Though its origins are disputed, one of the etymological roots for the word *religion* means to 'reconnect to' or to 'bind fast.' So it would never matter how much he held back on praise or compliments – ultimately, I looked to something beyond him. But the thought still saddened me that he couldn't give praise where it may have genuinely been due.

The final nail in the proverbial coffin was when he made a move on me. His attempt at foreplay had been to hang his arm around my neck during a day out, lolling on me like a teenager. His actions hadn't been imbued with the slightest bit of warmth or genuine affection. I don't know if he just thought it (sexual intimacy) was a tap you could just turn on and off at will. For me it wasn't.

Back home after our holiday, after dropping Finn off on a night out, I sat surfing the web while waiting for an Amy Winehouse tribute to come on the TV when a piece of music on a programme in the background caught my ear. I stopped what I was doing and immediately turned it up. It was Gustavo Dudamel conducting the Simón Bolívar Symphony Orchestra for the BBC Proms. I had no idea what the piece was but it had me rapt. By the end of it I was in tears. It was only as the programme ended that I discovered what they'd been playing: Mahler's *Resurrection* symphony – a magnificent piece that transports its listeners from life through to death, before finally delivering them to eternal life. My heart sank. *Oh shit. Not resurrection. Please not resurrection.*

Never one to miss the symbolism in the dreamtime or in everyday situations I knew that, as soon as I heard that piece, trouble lay ahead. It would be easy, for the casual observer, to dismiss something like this or fail to see it altogether. The Australian aborigines, however, have a saying for this: *yorro yorro* – which means, 'everything standing up alive.' Because the majority of modern-day folk are metaphorically-challenged and mythologically disinclined, unfamiliar with coincidences and unversed in the language of the dreamtime, they fail to see the symbolism that bombards them day and night. They see corporate driven advertising, sure, but the whispers of the psyche they miss and, along with it, their lives.

If this resurrection theme had just been contained to this one appearance, I may have downgraded its importance – but it hadn't. While on holiday I'd been bombarded with peacock medicine. The damn things were coming at me from all angles. Whenever an animal seems to get in my face I look up its associated symbolism (known in shamanic traditions as animal medicine or animal totems) to see what it has to say. Oftentimes I find it ties into symbolism I may have encountered in the dreamtime. Other times I notice it shows up whenever an archetypal situation is constellating.

Perhaps I should explain more what I mean by this term, 'constellating'.

I've noticed that whenever an archetype is moving into consciousness it begins to activate by means of a series of related events. Taken alone they may not amount to much. But if you journal and keep track of dreams, animal medicine, synchronicities, coincidences, serendipitous encounters, you may notice how the events are connected, how they join up and form a picture – much like the stars in the night sky.

To the uninitiated the heavens may look like nothing more than a mass of stars dotted randomly about the place. But if someone versed with their background mythology (an astronomer or a constellation mythographer) were to help you join the dots, you'd suddenly see the many characters and stories which nightly revolve around us.

To those familiar with archetypal motifs and mythological symbols that's what life looks like. No longer a series of random, unconnected events, those with depth perspective see beyond the surface level of life to the underlying stories and motifs that are actually giving rise to the events themselves. We don't shape stories – we are shaped *by* stories just as we are shaped and directed by archetypal events. So though I was aware the archetype of the Hero's Journey was circumscribing my life, moving me, shaping me, doesn't mean I can control what happens and when.

From a symbolic perspective peacocks are associated with the phoenix – the mythical, solar bird which represents death and rebirth. 'The peacock,' says *The Book of Symbols*, 'signified rebirth and early Christian art adopted the image as a symbol of resurrection.' So when I found myself drawn to this Resurrection piece by Mahler – a synchronous event in itself considering I rarely watch TV – I knew something was constellating.

The thing with the resurrection stage of the Hero's Journey is it consists of two stages – death and rebirth. The only thing that gave me a vague (and I mean, *vague*) sense of hope, was an idea I'd heard shared at the mythology group I'd studied with while in Santa Fe which was this: *As soon as you're aware of the myth you're living, you're already onto the next.*

Life, you see, is a bit like looking in the rear view mirror of a car in the sense that what you're currently seeing is the outcome of decisions you've already made.

As Christopher Vogler says in *The Writer's Journey*, 'resurrection is the hero's final exam, her chance to show what she has learned. Heroes are totally purged by final sacrifice or deeper experience of the mysteries of life and death. Some don't make it past this dangerous point, but those who survive go on to close the circle of the Hero's Journey when they Return with the Elixir.'

The theme of 'closing circles' was further amplified by a series of dreams I had that same month. One dream consisted solely of circles divided into twelve segments and nothing else. Another dream said this: 'A circle has been closed, you can feel it.' But the most telling dream was one in which I was building a bath with the following dimensions: 60 x 60 (= 360). Followed by another bath with the dimensions, 30 x 30 (= 900). Talk about ram the message home. The dimensions of a circle followed immediately by the three trimesters of pregnancy all wrapped up with bath symbolism (water, *solutio*) – *rebirth*.

It may be tempting to say I was looking for such symbolism. What you have to bear in mind is I can't *make* dreams happen, just as I can't create synchronous events, drum them up at will. All I can ever do is remain alert to the symbolism as and when it arises. I should also say it's usually only after the event has happened that I'm able to get a clearer perspective of the situation – a process that may take several months, if not years, before I'm finally able to understand what's happened.

So when I had a dream, while house- and cat-sitting for Bing, that Finn was flirting with someone at work – a dream which seemed more vivid than usual – I immediately texted him to tell him about it and share my concerns. When I later asked why he hadn't replied he said because I hadn't asked him a question (I'd just shared a dream – what did I want him to say?) before going on to tell me how ridiculous it was (said the man who earlier refused to speak to me on account of a dream *he'd* had).

But I wasn't convinced. After all, he told me he liked me when we bumped into one another years before but because he was still in a relationship he didn't do anything about it. He 'just knew' it would eventually happen. Still, despite not immediately doing anything about it, long-sighted Apollo had already taken aim. In view of this I wondered if he had his eye on someone at work. He may not have done anything about it but that didn't mean to say the attraction wasn't already there.

I had another dream while at Bing's which also felt particularly important. (By the way, from here on out I'm going to switch to telling dreams in the present tense – it's a technique employed in Dream Tending which reminds us that, in the realm of the psyche, dreams are alive and always happening.)

I'm working on the checkout in the same supermarket where Finn also happens to be a manager. I'm processing a cheque presented to me by two Asian men which they're using to pay for their shopping. Behind them two other customers are sat down, patiently waiting for me to serve them. Finn is stood proudly in the background, watching me. When I finish we walk off together, laughing and joking. The feeling between us reminds me of the ease we had back when we first met. There is a closeness between us, an unspoken respect and understanding – an unbreakable bond.

'What if it means I'm checking out?' I asked my friend, Ellen, while out running together along the trail one night.

'Why would it mean that?' she asked.

'Because I can't get the words 'check out' out of my head,' I said. 'They're like vultures circling overhead. But you know what? It's more than that – it wasn't so much *what* happened as how I *felt* during the dream.'

'What do you mean?' she asked.

'It was the feeling we had towards one another when we walked off. One minute I'm talking to him. The next minute I'm behind, watching us walk along together. The only way I can describe what I felt would be to say that, whatever happens from here on out, underneath it all, that's how we truly feel about one another – that that's how we've always felt about one another and always will. That connection we had is our fundamental, base-level truth. The love between us transcended words. It's as if I was given an insight into the true nature of our relationship that I should hang onto regardless of whatever happens from here on out.'

Dreams aside, it was an event which happened towards the end of my week house-sitting at Bing's which most provoked my curiosity. I received an email from a man who'd come across my website and wanted to know more about the work I did. Soon, we were emailing back and forth as he asked me questions and shared with me the story of his life. Turns out he was a banker – or, rather, used to be.

Not any old banker, mind. Oh no. This guy was big – bigger than big: a fact that earned him the rather unoriginal nickname of 'Big'. For reasons of confidentiality I'm limited by the information I can share. Suffice to say this guy had scaled the dizzy heights of the international banking world (been there, got the T-shirt – next!) and was now eyeing a life imbued with soul.

This amused me no end. *Trust me to align myself with one of those who are being vehemently scapegoated by the masses.* But it's like Sam always said, 'Saints and sinners, they're all welcome here' – a philosophy I also share. Saint or sinner, I don't care – so long as someone's genuinely interested in personal transformation, I'm more than happy to lend a hand and share everything I know.

But personal mentoring wasn't something I advertised. Despite starting out as a life coach I soon realised not only did I have a lot to learn, but that I was better suited to working with groups. When not skulking about, hermiting, I have a fiery, larger-than-life personality which lends itself better to an audience than it does to working with individuals. If I'm not careful, my passionate intensity can be a bit too much for some people.

Not that any of that put this guy off. Though I tried my best to dissuade him, once he'd made his mind up that he wanted to work with me, that was that. All I had to do was tell him how much it'd cost and he'd transfer the money – bish, bash, bosh, deal done. I wasn't used to dealing with someone for whom money wasn't an issue and who, once they'd made their mind up, didn't mess about. I should have realised there was a good reason he'd been a banker and a successful one at that. After all, successful bankers know a good punt when they see one.

When I told Finn about my new client he was as surprised as me. 'Yeah, well, wait to see if you get paid first,' he said. 'People can be all talk.' So when he paid for a bulk of sessions up front, no hassle, I was stunned. *This guy's clearly not messing about – I like his style.* But it was what Finn said in response that stunned me even more: 'Why would anyone pay you that much?'

I swear to God, I was so shocked by this question, words failed me (I had to scribble it straight in my journal in case I later thought I'd imagined it). Pity I didn't share with him something Big later told me – namely, that he would have happily paid me five times the amount I'd asked for. Why? Because, he said, I was worth it.

Can you imagine how this made me feel? Especially after years of being devalued and mithered to get a job (any old job, at that)? *See, that's what happens when you wait for the pearls. That's what happens when you hold out for your true worth – along comes someone who reflects your inner sense of self-worth.* As the poet Rainer Maria Rilke says: 'What is within surrounds us.' In this case not only had Big reflected my sense of self-worth, he'd knocked it right out the ball park and into previously unimaginable realms.

But intuition told me there was more to this Big character than met the eye. Perhaps it was the timing of it but I sensed he had a larger yet unknown role to play in my life.

Anyway, I'd like to share two more Big Dreams from during this period (as if I hadn't had enough). In the first dream I am in Manhattan with my friend, a psychologist. I look up to see a plane fly into one of the Twin Towers, followed immediately by another plane. Unlike the tragic events of 9/11, however, the second plane flies into the same tower as the first, but at a vertical angle (the first had flown in horizontally) so that, together, they form the shape of a cross. Knowing what's about to happen next (tower collapse), I grab my friend and we run towards the Hudson River ('where the water is clear,' I wrote) to escape the dust cloud which is right behind us.

You may recall me mentioning Edward Edinger in his book on alchemical symbolism saying 'dreams of planes crashing or objects falling generally refer to *coagulatio*.' To amplify the point, he goes on to share the following analysand's dream:

I am in midtown Manhattan. Tall buildings are being razed. A huge boulder from the top of one of the buildings comes crashing to the ground, almost hitting me.

– Anatomy of the Psyche

Though I narrowly managed to escape the aftermath of the 'fallout' this time, I knew it was only a matter of time before everything collapsed and turned to a mass of confusion and rubble. Of this *coagulatio* stage, Catherine MacCoun says, 'subjectively, this stage is a lot more like falling apart than like falling together.' This is a stage which, once in motion, one can only surrender to. Once love breaks down there ain't a whole lot you can do about it.

The doubling motif (two planes and two towers) further reinforced the point that I ought to pay attention to events which were now unfolding. But it was the shape of the cross which most caught my eye. After all, what symbol most exemplifies Christ's death than the cross on which he was crucified? A crucifixion, lest we forget, which foreshadows his eventual resurrection. The airplanes, too, also resembled the shape of a cross while overhead.

The second Big Dream involved Prince William and his brother, Prince Harry (doubling motif again). By this point I'd had a series of dreams involving the Princes and Catherine, Duchess of Cambridge – too many to go into here. Suffice to say they'd been playing out for almost a year and were providing me with an illuminating and, at times, downright amusing insight into the dynamics playing out between my inner masculine and feminine energies.

In this dream I am stood waiting in the basement of Buckingham

Palace with the two Princes when William shows me a piece of paper with the following numbers written on it: '*1, 2, 2.5...*'

As soon as I woke up, I knew: momentum was mounting – the arrival of the archetypal third was nigh.

THE ILLUSTRATED MAN

I always knew I'd get a second tattoo – it was just a matter of when. I knew the design I wanted: a triple spiral (also known as a triskele) similar to the design found inside the Newgrange passage tomb, a Neolithic monument in County Meath, Ireland. It's a Celtic/pre-Celtic symbol found on several Irish Megalithic and Neolithic sites.

As I have a deep respect and affinity for symbols, what I won't do is have any old design inked willy-nilly on my body. I have to live with the thing for the rest of my life so it's never going to be a decision I'll rush. What I liked about the symbol I'd long eyed was how it complemented the one I already had. Whereas my fire dragon tattoo is a sharp and angular oriental sign, the triple spiral was a curved, flowing, occidental sign. I wanted it etched on my inner right hip to balance the dragon symbol already inked on my inner left hip. Like I've said, I think carefully about these things.

Finn had offered to pay for me to have it done on a couple of occasions but I told him it wasn't the right time. I was waiting for a sign, a prompt – when the time was right, I'd just know. Not only that but when I did eventually have it done I wanted to pay for it myself.

I'd had my first tattoo done at a time when I was taking back my life and my body on my terms, doing things my way. Whenever I look at it (tattoo) it reminds me of, what proved to be, a major turning point in my life – an initiation, if you will. I never doubted my next would be any different, which is why I wouldn't force the issue.

When two dreams (surprise!) arrived on two consecutive nights, a couple of weeks before my third workshop with Shakti Tantra, I knew the time had arrived. I wouldn't call them Big Dreams – these felt more like heralds.

In the first dream I'm having an affair with a banker who works in the Cooperative Bank. He's boyish looking, reminds me of Stuart (iPodge), Bing's ex-husband. He then resigns from the bank. We try to continue the affair and go back to his terraced house, but I discover he already has a girlfriend (the supermodel, Elle MacPherson) and three young sons. I'm not sure whether his sons are from his relationship with

Elle or from another relationship. He also has a decrepit-looking father who lives in another terraced house nearby. Elle goes to get him, brings him back to the house, and sits him down in the kitchen.

Prior to my arrival the sons had been upstairs, asleep. They then come downstairs for breakfast. One of them is called Lucius. One of them – I'm not sure which – then climbs on my back in a happy, playful way. In fact, they're all friendly towards me. In the final scene I'm stood talking with Elle in the kitchen. She's leant against the kitchen counter, smoking a cigarette.

With this dream it wasn't just what happened as how I felt while in it. There was so much going on at a feeling level that, in many ways, words fail it. And in case you're wondering, Big didn't work for the Cooperative Bank. Much later, though, he told me he often saw Elle MacPherson dropping her children off at the school across the road from where he lived – a curious detail in light of this dream. He'd also, later, prove to be a rather cooperative banker...

Lucius is derived from the Latin for 'light.' Here we have something of the light (spirit) descending. I don't wish to explore, in any great detail, the rest of this dream. Suffice it to say I was also intrigued by how the psyche used a 'supermodel' (archetype) called Elle (a name meaning 'she') who was also a mother. Taken together one of my associations was that this figure represented the archetypal Mother.

But it was something Edward Edinger said of the alchemical stage of *mortificatio* which caught my attention:

> **The infirm and weak old man represents a conscious dominant or spiritual principle that has lost its effectiveness. It has regressed to the level of the primordial psyche (dragon) and must therefore submit to transformation. The cave in which it is shut up is the alchemical vessel. The torture is the fiery ordeal that brings about transformation in order that 'out of the Three may come One'; that is, that body, soul, and spirit may be unified within an integrated personality.**

> *– Anatomy of the Psyche*

Though Edinger is writing about an alchemical text, I couldn't help noticing how much of the symbolism paralleled the imagery in my dream. Kitchens are often thought of as 'alchemical vessels.' After all, they're the room in which we take raw ingredients and cook them in a 'fiery ordeal' in order to bring about a transformation. In the dream the old man is seated in the kitchen.

Not only does it parallel my dream, it also references Michael Meade's earlier statement I shared regards *coniunctio* symbolism: *Stay in the tension and the glue will be produced* ('Out of the Three may come One'). Especially as Edinger goes on to say:

> The 'hero of peace whom the whole world shall behold' is the Philosopher's Stone, the reconciler of opposites, but this way of putting it implies that what is undergoing mortificatio and rejuvenation is nothing less than the collective God-image.

> *– Anatomy of the Psyche*

Putting his comments on the 'collective God-image' aside for the moment, the Philosopher's Stone, the 'reconciler of opposites' he's speaking of is, in essence, the human heart. But what we also have here is *mortificatio* – death. As if I hadn't already had enough death, rebirth symbolism to contend with, this dream alluded to heartbreak too. Oh joy.

If none of this makes sense it doesn't matter. I've been working with my dreams and alchemical imagery for some time so am able to draw subtle inferences which I'm all too aware can be lost in translation – especially when sharing them with others. I also have an eye for symbolism which would make author, Dan Brown blush. In essence, the feeling tone of this dream alerted me to the fact that something old and outworn was about to be transformed. That's all that matters.

The dream I had the following night was this: a frog hops past me, followed immediately by a much bigger one.

Here we have a doubling motif again (knock, knock – pay attention says the Dreaming Psyche). We also have an animal symbolic of the number three: egg, tadpole, frog. Frogs are a totem of transformation, of metamorphosis and, most interestingly, in early Christian symbolism, of resurrection. They're often considered to be tiny versions of dragons. From *The Book of Symbols* we learn that:

> In dreams and fairy tales the frog arrives, quite suddenly, out of water somewhere, just as an aspect (often princely) of self-substance emerges from the waters of the unconscious, but is not yet in fully conscious, recognisable form. In many such fairy tales, this fertile little being from the watery regions must be accepted and attended to in its frog form, however unattractive or odd it may seem, and inevitably it transforms into the soulful prince or princess.

Ted Andrews in his book, *Animal Wise* says, 'Whenever frog appears, we are entering a time of new beginnings. The creative energies are awakening, and it is time for new birth and fresh starts. The appearance of the frog is a reflection of the maturity from the polliwog stage. It is time to hop into new areas of endeavours. It is beneficial to accept invitations and offers.'

Taking both dreams together I read the signs as symbolic of transformation, transformation, transformation. Whether I liked it or not the cues and clues were coming at me thick and fast – initiation loomed. So with that, I scurried straight out the door in search of a tattoo studio. A woman on a mission I wanted my tattoo and I wanted it *now*.

'We've no appointments today,' said the young lad on reception. 'You'll have to come back on Friday.'

Four days? I have to wait four days? Dammit. For the record, once I've made my mind up about something I don't like hanging around – especially if it involves prompts from the psyche and permanent body markings.

Meantime, he took a deposit, looked up my design, and discussed my choice of colour with me. Like my previous tattoo I wanted it done in henna brown. The problem with this colour, though, is it doesn't make for as sharply defined a tattoo – an issue which can put some artists off doing it. Depending on skin tone henna brown can also bleed a lot thus requiring several touch ups. Again, this didn't bother me as I wanted something that looked more natural, as though it had been done by hand and not with the aid of modern technology.

On the Friday morning, after a trip to the Post Office to collect a parcel containing a delicious and rather wicked assortment of goodies for my escapades at my upcoming workshop, I arrived for my appointment. It turned out one of the owners, Tim, would be doing my tattoo: a dude of a guy plastered with tattoos some of which, frankly, scared the shit out of me.

But what intrigued me, once we settled down, was how warm and – dare I say it – *tender*, Tim was. His nature seemed so at odds with the scary-arse tattoos he was covered with. Years ago there were TV adverts in the UK which involved tattoo-toting motorcycle-riding men getting all soft and silly over kittens. That was what this guy reminded me of.

Having a tattoo done is an intimate experience at the best of times, but even more so if it means the artist is hovering around your crotch. Add to this the artist in question is – once I got over the initial shock of his scary tattoos – attractive, engaging, and funny and let's just say it threw me for a loop. As our conversation continued I felt myself softening. He made me feel much the same as when I first spoke with Sarah, the honey-voiced one.

Heading home I couldn't stop musing over my experience. Not only was I thrilled with my latest bodily addition but I couldn't stop thinking about this guy. It'd be no exaggeration to say he got under my skin and left his mark – because that's *exactly* what he'd done.

As the weekend wore on I couldn't stop thinking about Tim and his chocolate centre-filled eyes which had melted me, turned me into a pile of do-what-you-want-with-me putty on his treatment couch. Flames fanned, I could feel a pressure building – volcanic Venus was fuming, seething, demanding to be let out. Nancy Qualls-Corbett puts it this way:

> **Often the human man who appears is literally a stranger. There is no romance or overt intention on his part to save the woman from an empty existence. And there are no promises of an enduring relationship. Such a meeting cannot be planned, for that would be plotting, trying to manipulate fate ... The stranger's eyes penetrate the woman's inner being; his very presence awakens the dormant sacred prostitute and the sensuous feminine nature contained therein. She may hide behind conventional standards, denying her rightful, innate relationship to the goddess of love, but such a screen only delays or aborts her psychic development ... if he is not welcomed, the goddess too is slighted and turns her dark side toward the woman. The consequence is that the woman remains cut off from her spirituality, which would contain and enhance her sexual nature.**

> **– The Sacred Prostitute**

Then came the lurid, juicy, flesh-filled fantasies. Not that I needed encouraging, especially with my third workshop now only days away – a workshop which, by the way, was entitled Women Behaving Badly. But, oh – what I wouldn't give for a private appointment with Tim and his tattoo needle...

On the Sunday evening, now consumed by a dark and devilish Dionysian mood, I emailed Tim and asked him if I could interview him for an article when I was back from my workshop. Finn would be away on holiday for two weeks (he flew out the day my workshop finished). But as if to really drive the message home, I emailed him while sat in the same room as Finn.

What was peculiar about this turn of events has to do with a dream from five weeks earlier. In the dream I am sat in a bar in Manchester city centre with a gorgeous guy who is flirting with me. Although I know Finn is sat elsewhere in the bar, I ask this stranger for his number. As I leave, Finn joins me. Out on the street he asks me who the man is I've been talking to. I lie and tell him he's a work colleague.

I woke up from that dream feeling guilty as hell. Heavens above, it was all I could do not to tell Finn about it such was my guilty conscience. I'd never lied to him about anything. So I was surprised, in light of my actions, when I later flipped back through my journal and found this somewhat prescient insight.

But unlike the guilt I felt on waking from that dream a switch in me had finally flipped. Despite knowing I may be about to unleash hell, I went ahead and hit the 'send' key anyway.

BEHAVING BADLY

A few days later, after finishing up early for his holiday, Finn gave me the car and I bade him farewell for a little over two weeks and made my way to Women Behaving Badly – *alone.*

I had tunnel vision with this workshop: tunnel vision that demanded I be alone so I could gather my thoughts and focus on the weekend ahead. Not that I knew what lay in store. As with the previous two workshops I had very little idea. Here's Shakti Tanta's online blurb:

> **We provide this three-day residential workshop for all women who have completed the first two levels. This workshop gives women the opportunity to dance with the inner and outer expressions of the feminine; the goddess and the slut.**

Slut – now there's a word. A word often used in an attempt to denigrate women, keep them down, in their place, and out of sight. It's used in a derogatory manner towards a woman who has had sex with multiple partners; a woman who is sexually aggressive and/or unabashedly lays claim to her own sexuality; a woman who expresses her sexuality in such a way that does not conform with patriarchal attitudes; a woman who is openly sexual; a woman who wears 'provocative' clothing – clothes, for example, that are perceived as 'too tight,' 'too revealing.' (For a pithy introduction to the issue of 'slut-shaming,' I recommend an excellent online blog – *Finally Feminism 101* – from where much of this information was gleaned.)

Furthermore, from the online 1911 Encyclopedia Britannica's entry on *promiscuity* we learn that:

> **[Terms for women who 'sleep around' include] fast woman, hussy, doll, inamorata, siren, gypsy, minx, vamp, wench, trollop, coquette, bint, crumpet, floozy, scrubber, slag, groupie, nympho, and slut ... The comparatively small field devoted to male promiscuity reinforces the notion of the double standard alluded to previously. The tenor of the terms is also entirely**

different: Casanova, Romeo, Lothario, and Don Juan derive status from their literary and historical pedigrees, while ladies' man, lady-killer, gigolo, stud, and sugar daddy obviously do not have the same condemnatory overtones as most of the female terms. They embody machismo notions of power and conquest. The sole exception is roué. The invocation of great lovers of the past, real and fictional, serves to provide role models suggesting respectability.

In short, it's okay for a man to sleep around, brag about his sexual conquests but when a woman does it, she's considered inferior, lowly, a slut, a dirty bint. This perfectly exemplifies the virgin-whore split I spoke of earlier: the chaste Virgin Mary of a mother-mate and the chthonic, lustful whore-mistress with whom men tend to shack up when they have affairs.

What's further interesting to me, about this issue, are the many women I know who haven't told their current partner how many past lovers they've had for fear of being judged. When I ask them why they haven't said anything they say it's not relevant, that it's in the past, that it has nothing to do with their present relationship. Fair enough. But what if he asked? Would you tell the truth? No, many women have replied. These are well-educated women, many of whom consider themselves feminists. But when it comes to openly and unashamedly standing by their sexual pasts, they prefer to fiddle the numbers or just keep schtum.

I've never been called a slut. Though I've never been open about my sexuality (in light of this book that may yet change). I have been called a minx – a nickname my first Reiki teacher, Barbara, called me (she called me 'minxness'). She used it as a term of endearment but I do wonder if she saw something in me that, at the time, I didn't see in myself.

At the more subtle end of the sexually judgemental spectrum are those women who have, in the past, openly admitted to me that they were surprised by how intelligent I am. Why? Because on first meeting me they considered me beautiful. I couldn't possibly be beautiful *and* intelligent... could I? ('Damn you that you were!' said one woman, a self-professed feminist.) And that was before I threw my sexuality into the mix. This leaves me wondering if men and women could ever truly accept a woman who was openly and unashamedly sexual, intellectual, *and* spiritual. Or would such a thought be inconceivable?

As a young woman my aunt was slapped with various labels, from 'lesbian' to 'scrubber' (she's long collected paintings of female nudes; in her younger years had a string of close female friends, and was also sexually forthright). Mum tells me my aunt's attractiveness and self-confidence was renowned and lots of men were wild about her. Consequently, she would pick and choose who she wanted to be with. This attitude often caused women (and men) to say, 'Who does she think she is?' Confident and comfortable in her skin, that's what.

But like she said to me in a recent conversation, 'I didn't care what they called me. If you find the need to label me, try and do me down and put me in a box, it says more about you – your fears and insecurities – than it does about me. I did what I liked and I liked what I did. It was my business – no-one else's.' Let me tell you, when you grow up in the slutstream of a powerful, unapologetic woman, you learn a thing or two.

Which is why, as far as I'm concerned, slut-shaming women for being sexually 'out there' boils down to little more than a feeble attempt at control – the last vestige of patriarchy attempting to wield power, control *over* another (something from which women are not exempt – they can be just as bad, if not more so, than men). It also smacks of fear. Because, as I was about to discover, a woman in full, unapologetic possession of her slut energy is just about the most powerful thing you're ever likely to see. A woman connected to her vital wellspring of sexuality is an *awesome* sight to behold.

I had a clear intention for this workshop. What I wouldn't do is rock up unprepared. If the marathons had taught me anything it's that you get out of this process what you put into it. As such, I believe your preparation reflects your attitude towards yourself. Journaling, reflecting, and working with my dreams provided me with ample *prima materia*. What this allowed me to do was stay focused on myself, honour my truth, and not get too swallowed up by others' personal issues or group dynamics which inevitably arise in such situations.

After chewing over events from the previous workshops I had several issues I wished to work with. First and foremost was the opportunity to behave badly – *very* badly. For me, behaving badly entailed reclaiming the dark, wanton, lustful underbelly of my sexuality which I'd put 'in the bag' back when my mum slut-shamed me in my early twenties for taking sexually provocative photographs of myself in my office.

Curiously (or perhaps, serendipitously), a couple of weeks before the workshop I'd discovered a piece of stream-of-consciousness writing which had since been stored at my parents' place. It was a piece I'd originally written in July 2007 (proof of the fact I've been wrestling with these issues for years). When I discovered it I was astounded at its relevance particularly in light of the workshop I was about to embark upon. I asked Hilly if I could share it with the rest of the women during our opening circle. Here's the piece:

THE DANCE OF THE CHASTE AND THE CHTHONIC

There's a savage woman within me and she tears through flesh, rips off her clothes, orgasms, struts around naked, is a slut, revealing, busty, voluptuous, wet, sexual, provocative. I envy her, hate her, despise her, love her, want to sit with her, lay with her, let her caress me. It is her who seduces my lover, walks into a room, fills his being with her scent, intoxicates him, arouses him, and I hate her for it.

I want to kiss her.

She opens me, excites me. I watch her as she lays out, revealing all my insecurities to me – torsion, tension, pulled tight, frigid to the touch. There is nothing flaccid about her direction. She walks straight into the cave, the unknown, voracious appetite, carnivorous almost. She appears complete, total, whole, always able to surrender, expose herself, vulnerable to his whims.

He pulls her to him and I pull away. A blue light, fluorescent, cold, crude. She moves with candlelight, a hot wax that drips, sears, burns, melts. Agony and ecstasy, shame and pride slip away into something she runs with, opens up to. And I revere her.

La Dolce Vita. She parades, dances, flouts. He rains down on her and she is wet. Fountains, always fountains and street lamps at 4am. She eats breakfast while I still sleep; a subterranean world, shadows, exotic backdrops, she enthrals him, seduces him, leads him astray, opens her legs. And I lay asleep, curled up afraid, closed.

I watch her from rooftops, along streets. She fantastical, pouring all his wants, her desires, their ardour into the moment. He is drunk, swaying in her wake, licking the honey from her fingers over espresso and croissants. Warmed, sweet, fragrant. She delights, he devours and I dissolve, despair, despise.

She throws her head back, I hang my head. My gulps to her swallowing, tasting. She gently teases, chastises; I, religiously chastised, uptight; the Virgin Mary, undone, revealed, exposed; a statue cracks and falls apart. Too much tension.

Her heat warms, relaxes, wets, soothes. She purrs, responds. And I bolt like a dog. But still, I watch her with my lover, she watching me watching them writhe with pleasure, delight.

And I want them to make love to me.

That piece of writing set the tone for my personal workshop experience, framed it *perfectly*.

Next was my commitment to fulfil my innate potential. It was time for me to step up, step out, and get *bigger*. For years I'd been playing smaller than I knew I was capable of – but I'd fooled no-one. I knew I had a powerful, larger-than-life personality so I decided, beforehand, enough of the bullshit; enough worrying what others may or may not think, enough apologising for who *I am*. If who I am takes over the joint, so be it; if who I am is in your face, so be it; if who I am is flamboyant, dominates, and is a great big fucking show-off, so be it – but enough of the self-deception.

Another issue I wished to work with related to my recent self-discovery regards 'I don't deserve.' Though I didn't know what structures we'd be doing I suspected it would build on the work we'd done at the previous workshops around pleasure. Armed with my self-revelation, I decided my overriding mantra for this workshop would be 'I *do* deserve': I *do* deserve pleasure, I *do* deserve beauty, I *do* deserve to be loved, I *do* deserve to be treated with respect, I *do* deserve to be wined and dined, I *do* deserve to be listened to, I *do* deserve to be pampered and indulged and cherished, I *do* deserve abundance, I *do* deserve to be successful, I *do* deserve, I *do* deserve, I *do* deserve. But perhaps most important of all, 'I deserve to receive.' I am worthy and *I deserve to receive*. This, of course, would entail me staying present, facing my fears, fully opening, surrendering, being vulnerable, and saying *yes* with both feet and all of my heart. But I didn't care. I wanted it. *I deserved it.*

When you confront your issues, find your edges, and start to push through them, it's inevitable you'll push up against others' too – especially in an intimate, self-contained setting like this. But I couldn't worry about that. I wasn't there for anyone else, I was there for me. Other people's issues, other people's edges were exactly that – *their own*. I'd spent my entire adult life apologising for causing others upset, uneasiness, or embarrassment, real or perceived; for putting others' pleasure before mine; for worrying about what others may or not think of me when I voiced my wants, my pleasures, my desires. Well, enough. It was time to put me first, satisfy my innermost yearnings, and fulfil my fantasies.

What I discovered about myself, as the weekend wore on, was how inwardly wicked my long-repressed sexuality felt – wicked in a dark, deliciously Dionysian way. I'd already got a sense of this after being around Tim. But never before had I been given permission to explore it in such an overt way. Who in our culture, after all, encourages women to really let rip? But it wasn't just about permission – it was about being safely contained and feeling held and supported while we did so.

As always, Hecate Aphrodisias (aka Hilly, our teacher) kept a watchful eye over proceedings. As I've said, you know when you're in the presence of a fully initiated Crone when the energy doesn't spill over and the situation lose control which could so easily have been the case especially when you unleash the wild, dismembering Maenad within. This was, after all, a workshop of debauched Dionysian proportions. That's how it felt to me, anyway. The thing with Dionysus is, if you're not careful, it can explode into an ecstatic frenzy, especially as he's the god of the orgy, as Jean Shinoda Bolen reminds us here:

> The celebration of Dionysus was called the 'Orgia' of the god (from which the word orgy is derived). With wine or other sacramental intoxicants and with rhythmic dances accompanied by the frenzied music of reed pipes, drums, and cymbals, the celebrants entered into an ecstatic state and felt themselves 'one with' the god.

> *– Gods in Everyman*

Though there were no intoxicants (not necessary), let's just say I took full advantage of one particular structure to let go and let *rip*. I wouldn't so much say the lid came off – rather, it *blew off*. As eruptions go this was of supervolcanic proportions: mega-colossal. For months I'd felt the pressure building, my blood pounding, my sap rising. So when I finally got my chance I grabbed it. Like a one-woman geyser I sprayed black PVC up the walls, spewed out sluttiness, gushed forth fishnets, and sank my claws into both my teachers (Hilly and Sue). By the time I'd finished and been finished with, I was a dismembered woman, torn to pieces. Damn it felt good to let it all out, no holds barred. If you ever get the chance I highly recommend it.

It was only afterwards that I realised I'd been 'at one with' the god. For the first time in my life I'd been totally and utterly 'in the moment.' Total. I'd been total. I hadn't planned what I was going to do; rather, I'd been fully present, open to whatever wanted to arise and be released through me. In short, I *surrendered*. No wonder I couldn't stop shaking once I was done. I'd never felt an adrenaline rush like it.

Being aware of archetypes, as I am, I knew I'd surrendered to Dionysus as he thundered through me, filled me with his being. I knew I shouldn't *identify* with him, but, instead, *relate* to him but on this occasion I chose to ignore that advice and decided to remain in my inflated state. I knew it wasn't something I should do, but I didn't care. I wasn't done having fun.

The thing with this archetype is its tendency to swing between extreme states – from the ecstatic highs to the soul-sapping lows. Dionysus, after all, is the god of intoxicants such as wine – and we all know how too much of that can leave us feeling.

As much as I tried to ignore it I must have had a faint awareness of this at the back of my mind as, despite the ecstatic, pleasure-filled mood of the weekend, I couldn't help feeling an underlying sense of melancholy. Not that it got in the way of me enjoying myself or of my pleasure – it didn't. Not remotely. Still, I sensed it.

Part of this may have been due to the fact that, deep down, I felt ashamed of my sexless, loveless relationship but I just couldn't bring myself to say it out loud and share it with the group. I'd also got it into my head that all the other women were in happy, satisfying, sexually-fulfilling relationships or had gone off into the world after the first two workshops and were now having lots of sex (great sex, hot sex, passionate sex).

Meanwhile, Tess the Tantric Tortoise (aka, yours truly) was fumbling around, alone, because the man I was with didn't even want to hold my goddamn hand, let alone say one nice thing to me.

By the way, I know I keep prattling on about this lack of hand holding but, to my mind, it's the simplest form of affection a couple can share that says 'We're together.' I know it's not everyone's 'thing' and I don't mean to whine on and on about it but, as public displays of affection go, it's one that matters to me. What can I say? I'm a romantic with a soft underbelly. So sue me.

Anyway, by the end of this workshop I was well and truly *rinsed*. But I'd also had an epiphany. As epiphanies go, this has to be one of the biggest I've ever had – *ever*. It was this: *It takes great strength to receive.* One more time for the cheap seats:

It takes great strength to receive.

This was when the penny finally dropped and I understood, not theoretically but experientially, soul through bone, that in order to receive you first have to open. You have to open yourself so wide that it leaves you fully exposed and, most of all, *vulnerable*. This was what I'd long feared – opening myself and feeling vulnerable. When you open yourself to receive love it also means opening to loss and hurt, disappointment, sorrow, and heartbreak. But so long as you deny love – so long as you continue your attempts at control, of saying no, of curling up and closing off – you deny life itself. Put simply, to say yes to love is to say yes to life; to say no to love is to say no to life.

What I finally understood is there's nothing passive or weak or wimpy about receiving. And I'm not talking unconscious receiving; I'm talking *conscious* receiving – there's a big difference. For perhaps the first time in my life I understood that so long as I refused to receive, I would only continue to resist and block the flow in other areas of my life. After all, as much as we like to think we can, we cannot compartmentalise our lives. If I'm having difficulty receiving in one area – whether it be receiving

202

compliments or money or love or kind gestures – you can guarantee I'll be refusing it elsewhere, whether I mean to or not.

Take, for example, two people having a conversation. If the receiver (listener) isn't fully present and actively receiving what the speaker is saying, there's no conversation. In order for there to be a conversation, the listener has to be present and open to receiving the speaker's words. In a true conversation, the receiver plays as active a role as the giver. Otherwise it's just one person talking *at* another (which is mostly what happens).

So it's all well and good setting goals and intentions, saying, like me, that you do deserve; but unless you open yourself up and make yourself vulnerable, all the intentions in the world will amount to nothing if you can't consciously open yourself to receive. And, as I'd now discovered, it takes great strength to receive.

Sat rocking in the corner during our final sharing, I could barely see straight – *that's* how powerful this workshop was for me. In fact this was the first time I actually feared for my safety diving home as I'd been completely knocked for six and was struggling to focus. My body was vibrating, my mind whirring. Every fear, every issue I wanted to focus on and work with, I had.

As usual, on my return I wrote a blog about my workshop experience of which I share a modified version here:

WOMEN BEHAVING BADLY: WORKSHOP REVIEW

Women Behaving Badly is the third of five levels of the women-only courses Shakti Tantra offer and was the level I was most looking forward to even if I had no idea what it entailed. After all, who can resist a workshop entitled Women Behaving Badly?

You see, back in my early twenties I put my 'badly behaved' self in the proverbial bag. Over the years my bag has steadily grown into 'baggage'; or, to be more specific, into an innocuous looking hand-luggage set that had been stored at my parents' place since 2007. When my mum wheeled it into the centre of the bedroom she was redecorating (the irony of the symbolism isn't lost on me), it seemed like the right time to take it home, empty it out, and wash it off ahead of a new set of adventures. Though when I discovered a notepad in it with a piece of writing entitled The Dance of the Chaste and the Chthonic, *I was shocked to say the least. Seems it was really was time to get my issues out of the bag.*

The difficulty I face in writing about these workshops is that I can't disclose our exact shenanigans. This is, after all, a mystery school – a mystery school that helps you discover your inner mysteries; a mystery school that helps you unfold, blossom, be all you can be while surrounded by the love, care, tenderness, encouragement, and support of the most inspired, generous, and courageous women I've ever known.

I'm a heady person. But the thing about these workshops is they challenge you experientially. They draw you down from the lofty, abstracted, disassociated heights of your head and into – what is for most folk – the unknown quantity that is the body.

Many of us think we're consciously connected to our bodies. We may think we've got our bodies sussed, know what they're up to, what they like to eat, how they like to be exercised, are aware of the issues in the tissues. But once you're in a workshop like this, you fast realise you haven't got a clue about the shame, guilt, loathing, fear, [insert issue here], you've been lugging around for years, perhaps even decades. And the thing with issues is they stick. They stick to our bodies. They hurt. They also numb. And they eat away at us. They eat away at our relationships with others, too. Worst of all, they eat away at our authenticity. You want to get real with yourself and others? Do this work.

So what did I get out of this particular workshop? I tell you what I got – I got permission. I was celebrated. My fellow Shaktis and I got to be funny, powerful, deliciously wicked, curious, awesome, total, magnificent, playful, commanding, sexy, naughty, expressive, mischievous, magnetic, mothering, nurturing. We rocked it. We had presence, we were outrageous. Beneath the light of the (almost) full moon, we frickin' ripped it up.

Let me tell you something else: to witness a total, fully conscious, authentic woman at her most magnificent best is one of the most awe-inspiring spectacles one can ever hope to behold. I saw it again and again and again during our long-weekend together. And each time I was humbled to the core. These were women with the ovarios to stand, dance, and strut from the centre of their womanhood.

Yeah, we kicked ass.

Our culture has a lot to say about femininity, about women. However well-educated we think we are, however conscious and spiritually enlightened we may profess to be, many of us unquestioningly accept culture's definition of the 'slut' without ever stepping into the actual energy and trying it out for ourselves. Though once you're given permission to 'behave badly,' you discover a vital, dynamic wellspring of strength that's always been in you but has languished under millennia of scorn, judgement, disdain, fear, and control. You see, above all else, what I discovered during this weekend was, a woman in possession of her slut energy is a woman who is one-in-herself. She is who she is, because that is who she is. Her back is straight and she looks the world in the eye. She's the one-woman party where all the fun's at. Put another way, her cup runneth over.

Our patriarchal society knows all too well the immense power of slut energy and so, to keep it under control, has labelled and loaded the term itself with judgement, loathing, shame, and scorn. But the myopic, parochial label and the actual, physical reality couldn't be any more different if they tried.

So, during my weekend, I got the fragile bird that is my wanton, wayward slut back out of the bag. I told her I was sorry for ignoring her, for being ashamed of her, for listening to others' opinions first and misunderstanding her. Despite being repressed, shunned, and ignored for fifteen years, she told me she loved me and kissed me on the lips. Then, she took the steering wheel and drove me home.

We've not stopped dancing since.

THE FALLOUT

I started getting ready for my interview (interview – who am I kidding?) with Tim at lunchtime, drawing myself a long, hot fragrant bath in which I soaked for several hours. I wanted to savour this experience and take my time over every last detail.

As he was so different to me with his bazillion tattoos, his rebellious attitude, and his rock music, it meant I could try on an aspect of myself I'd never played with before. Saying that, I can't remember the last time I'd got dressed up to go out on a date, period. Finn and I never went anywhere together. We'd only been to the cinema twice in three years and even then I'd had to drag him.

Before I left for my workshop I'd ordered a make-up pencil that was supposed to make it easier to apply smoky, sexy eyes. As I was still somewhat inexperienced at this make-up malarkey I needed all the help I could get. I was going for the 'just got out of bed' look: big hair, bees-stung lips, smudged eyes. With Jack White's band *The Dead Weather* providing the rock-fuelled soundtrack to my transformation I couldn't help laughing at how much fun it was exploring the dark, previously hidden side of my sexuality – my Black Swan.

I loved how it flouted every rule of what a 'good girl' should be, how it laughed in the face of my mum's earlier, scornful slut-ridden comments, how it stuck a proverbial finger up at the culture with its moralistic judgements on how women should or shouldn't act and behave. I can't tell you how powerful I felt by the time I left the house. It wasn't so much how I dressed which – in and of itself – wasn't particularly sexy (jeans, t-shirt, heels). Rather, it was how I felt, how I moved. This power was deep-rooted, centred, focused.

As soon as I left the house and set off down the street I discovered just how strong you have to be to hold this energy. Men and women *will* look at you. If you haven't done the psychological groundwork and expose this aspect of your sexuality before it's had a chance to take root, there's every danger you'll be picked apart by someone's withering look or hateful comment. Be warned – your energy will arouse attention and/or be perceived as a threat.

That's why women often turn on women who carry this energy. Their belief is you'll either steal their man or you'll bag the man they want. Should you attract the attention of their heart's desire – whether deliberately or inadvertently – then watch out you frickin' tramp, slut, whore.

By the time I arrived at the bar where Tim was waiting for me I was a dark, brooding excess of wanton carnality. I wanted one thing – him. If that forthright sexual aggressiveness meant I was a slut, then I didn't give a damn. This last workshop had unleashed a woman who had been caged for far too long. There was no putting her back in the box now. Neither did I plan on trying to.

Turns out I wasn't forthright enough. Over several hours of conversation during which neither of us touched a drop of alcohol (he had a big job the following day for which he had to be fresh and I didn't want alcohol clouding my feelings), although I could tell he was attracted to me he didn't make a move. So when it got to closing time and we were being asked to leave, I realised it was now or never.

'So,' he said, lingering, 'you got everything you want?'

'No,' I said. I held his gaze.

'What else do you need, then?' he replied.

'Hmm... you really can't tell?' I said, *staring* at him.

I watched as the penny finally dropped.

'I like you,' I went on.

'Oh, for fuck's sake! Why didn't you just say then? You could have saved yourself several hours if you'd have just told me. Look how many hours we've wasted which could have been put to, well... *better use*.'

That's what I meant when I said I was trying this new aspect of myself out. That moment taught me a thing of two about cutting to the chase. Despite thinking I was forthright and sexually aggressive I was still dilly-dallying about like little Miss Seff. Hey, what can I say? Old habits die hard.

The drive back to his place was funny. He had a big ass, testosterone-fuelled Mustang which *roared* the other cars off the road. Looking at him out the corner of my eye I was so attracted to what I can only describe as his otherness. He was everything I felt I wasn't. It was this otherness, the difference between us, I wanted to explore in more detail. It felt vital, instinctual, juicy – *alive*. After the arid sterility in my relationship this felt like a breath of fresh air. It was all I could do to stop myself from laughing out loud at his brooding seriousness.

Though I wasn't abducted the experience was reminiscent of Persephone being dragged off into Hades' realm to be ravished. And right now I wanted so much to be ravished by the *other*. This was the sort of man who, should I take him home to meet my mum, she'd be appalled by. My mother hates tattoos, *loathes* them. She considers them cheap and tacky. Puritanical, she believes anyone who has them is 'dirty.' And now I had two.

Jean Shinoda Bolen, speaking of the relationship dynamics which a Persephone-identified woman is likely to embark on, says this is typical behaviour of a woman who's engaged in the process of separating herself out from a dominating mother. She says, 'sometimes, Persephone chooses a man of a different social class or even a different race.' As far as my mum's concerned, a man covered in tattoos may as well be from another planet.

I'd like to pause for a moment and say that admitting, publicly, that you've cheated on your partner has to rank up there as one of the dumbest things I've ever done. Along this path I've walked into many situations in which I've known I'm going to be hanged, drawn, and quartered – this is one of them. Truth be told I didn't want to write about my relationship, full-stop, let alone write about cheating on Finn. I'm hardly going to win any fans and I expect zero sympathy (not that I'm asking for it). While writing this book, I suffered nightmares and was terribly conflicted about discussing my relationship. For some unfathomable reason, however, the story demanded I share it (probably so I'd have my arse well and truly kicked, who knows). They say the heart has reasons reason cannot know. For the record, so does the soul. But just so you know, admitting this leaves me feeling anxious and vulnerable. It would have been so much easier if I'd have just left six months earlier (after Women's Invitation). I should never have stayed. Let the stoning begin.

Dropping me off the following morning Tim looked like a deer in the headlights. Admittedly he had borne the brunt of my long pent-up passions, so I was hardly surprised. It'd been a long time since I'd felt so desired by someone. Tim's face left me smiling like a Cheshire cat as I walked back up my street.

But my smile was promptly wiped off my face when I opened the front door into Finn's – the abject sterility in the house hit me full force in the gut. So much so, I doubled over to catch my breath. It was in that moment I realised it wasn't love or pleasure that had held our relationship together, but discipline – *dry* discipline at that. Of maintaining discipline in a relationship, Thomas Moore says:

> **In my practice as a therapist I worked with many men and women who lived their lives out of obligation and remained in painful marriages for reasons of propriety or responsibility. These marriages were sustained by discipline and not by love or pleasure. Many felt that their old and tormenting longings for pleasure with a real partner were selfish and had to be**

overcome. They believed that their lives would be more virtuous, and therefore more meaningful, if they denied themselves the pleasure they craved and remained attached to a partner with whom they felt no joy ... None of them made a connection between the sense of dry discipline that kept them in their marriage and the exciting sexual desire that lured them away from their obligations.

- The Soul of Sex

Moore asks us to imagine what it would be like if we placed 'sex at the top of our priorities in marriage or other intimate relationships.' Though that may sound 'irresponsible or superficial,' as he goes on to say, 'by short shrifting sex we give it a power and autonomy that ultimately comes back to haunt us.'

For me, good quality sex is a form of soul-making. It enlivens and stimulates. It's the bond that holds lovers together. It's the glue that holds a relationship together. Without it the relationship dries up, hardens, and, eventually, cracks - just as ours now had.

The following weekend I picked Finn and his friend up from the airport. I must have had resistance written all over me as, not only was I was late arriving but I was also pretty distant - no surprise considering what I'd done and what I now knew I had to do. Driving back listening to him talk about his holiday I felt sad and conflicted. The only thing I could think about was how I was going to end the relationship and when.

A couple of days later I had a Big Dream in which I am in an East European country. I cross a vast river (called the River Minx) on a light rail transport system. I'm worried I won't be able to cross as the river seems so wide and there doesn't seem to be a bridge. But we do so and easily. When I arrive on the other side it feels like the Underworld. Despite being dark and foreboding it's not scary. I see wild, gypsy-like women, whirling and twirling, dancing beneath viaducts. I say to my female companion that though I'm not afraid, I feel overdressed. We get back on the tram and cross back over the river. The sun is shining, the views are magnificent. I am in awe at the breadth of this vast, sweeping river which is fed by two wide tributaries.

In the next scene I have to jump across a wide abyss. If I miss and fall, I'm dead. I jump it effortlessly. When I look back, there are women stood looking at me. I tell them to jump, that I can help them and that, if they make the leap, they'll be okay. One by one they jump - and I catch them.

In *Man and His Symbols*, Marie-Louise von Franz says, 'Crossing a river is a frequent symbolic image for a fundamental change of attitude.' Furthermore she says that 'The Self usually appears in dreams at crucial times in the dreamer's life – turning points when his basic attitudes and whole way of life are changing. The change itself is often symbolised by the action of crossing water.'

This was the first dream I'd ever had in which I'd crossed all the way over a river – but not just once, *twice* (knock, knock). In my last bridge-related dream, the Golden Gate Bridge in San Francisco, I'd only made it halfway so this was progress.

My comments to my female companion regards feeling overdressed when I arrive in the Underworld was reminiscent of Inanna's descent into the Underworld. As she descends down through each of the seven gates of hell she is stripped naked. The wild, gypsy-like women also reminded me of descriptions I'd read of Ereshkigal as being the other, neglected side of Inanna. In the UK, Romani – particularly East European Romani – are often shunned, considered outsiders and live on the fringes of society. So here I was, not only crossing a threshold, but reconnecting with these shunned, outsider aspects of the feminine (further amplified by the name of the river – 'Minx'), and doing so without judgement and without fear.

Most heartening of all was that I was easily able to go back and forth, across the river – a motif reminiscent of Persephone's descent to the Underworld and eventual return of which Bolen says:

> **Once a Persephone woman descends into her own depths, explores the deep realm of the archetypal world, and does not fear returning to re-examine the experience, she can mediate between ordinary and nonordinary reality ... If she can transmit what she has thus learned, she can become a guide for others.**
>
> **– *Goddesses in Everywoman***

Despite the personal challenges I faced in my relationship, this was an encouraging dream. Keep going, I felt the Self was telling me. This is why I feel it's so important to work with dreams. As I've said before, they are your soul speaking. Question is, are you willing to tune out the world so you can put your ear to the Great Below and 'listen in' to the Dreaming Psyche's whisperings as it calls you, beckons you deeper into your life?

A couple of nights later while out running with my friend, Ellen, I told her I'd made up my mind to leave. On hearing this she invited me to stay at her house while I sorted myself out. She knew I only had a little money, but it was okay. The house was stood empty, she said, so it may as well have a loving occupant.

'You can't go back home yet,' she said. 'Besides, your book really helped me and you've become such a good friend. It's the least I can do.'

Her offer was humbling. But looking back it was also serendipitous – particularly when I think about how we came to be friends in the first place. In the Hero's Journey the hero is supported by allies who offer help, often at significant, pivotal moments. I believe Ellen was one such ally.

Because Finn spent so much time on the road commuting to and from work he'd suggested I have a sign made for the back window of his car advertising my book. Finn's next door neighbour, Mart, had seen the website address and, curious, looked it up to see what it was about. On reading the book's synopsis on my website he'd ordered a copy of the book for his girlfriend, Ellen, who'd read and loved it.

I sometimes forget what a big deal it is when you've read a book which has left an indelible impression on you. Even more so when you discover the author and protagonist lives next door to you. After all, how often does that happen? Ellen later told me it took her a while to pluck up the nerve to say something to me. But I liked her from the first time we ever spoke and invited her to run with me whenever she fancied it. As the year wore on we'd grown close, rambling on, running together through the neighbourhood and local countryside.

When she offered me her house as a temporary refuge, I thanked her before politely refusing and changing the subject. But when she made her offer again this time more forcefully, at the end of our run, something in me knew I had to pay attention (knock, knock). Momentum was building. I thanked her and told her I'd think about it. Little did I know I wouldn't have to think about it for very long – especially as, that night, I had another Big Dream.

This time I am in Manhattan. It is night-time and, all around me, buildings are collapsing, narrowly missing me as they crumble and fall.

In the next scene I am in a long narrow corridor. It is pitch-black and I can see nothing. Suddenly, a dog (beagle) appears, wagging its tail, encouraging me to follow it. I follow it until I come to a door. When I open the door I step out onto a sunny street full of people who, momentarily look at me before continuing their business. Across the street I see a travel agent.

In the final scene fireworks are exploding in the sky.

The last time I was in Manhattan in a dream as I knew the towers were about to collapse I'd made a run for it and escaped the subsequent fallout – but not this time. This time I'm in the thick of it. Though I'm not hurt, there's no escaping the fact the world around me is crumbling.

In the tarot the Tower represents sudden change, disruption, downfalls. This is the card of transformation as old structures break down. Curiously, in the Triple Goddess Tarot, the Tower is known as Kundalini

Rising. I say 'curiously' as, during this time I was struck with, what can only be described as the scratchies. Good Lord, I thought I had body lice. There was no rash but I couldn't stop scratching, day and night, scratch, scratch, bloody scratch. And apparently I wasn't the only one – Hilly, my teacher, was experiencing it too.

'Kundalini,' she told me when I mentioned it to her. 'Your energy's changing, rising. It's like a snake shedding its skin, letting go of what it no longer needs. This is the worst I've ever had it, though. But I'm not surprised – that last workshop was particularly powerful.'

But what really caught my attention, when I looked up the side-effects of rising kundalini energy – known as 'Kundalini Syndrome' – was that one of the symptoms, alongside this intense scratching, was tachycardia attacks. This stopped me dead in my tracks. As a Reiki teacher I don't know why I'd never considered that these attacks might have something to do with changes in my subtle body. But why not? I'd had enough strange experiences with my dalliances in subtle body work to know how weird things could get at an energetic level.

As for the rest of the dream? In many cultures dogs are considered psychopomps (which literally means, 'guide of souls' and is also one of Hermes' names). In Jungian psychology psychopomps mediate between the conscious and the unconscious. In many myths they guide the newly deceased to the afterlife and help provide safe passage. They also introduce the newborn soul to the world. This life-death-rebirth motif was further amplified, in my dream, by the long, dark corridor along which I was led, itself symbolic of the birth canal and, ultimately, rebirth (especially as there was a door at the end of the corridor which opened to the light).

In essence, the dream was telling me my life was crumbling and everything was falling apart – a fact from which, this time, I couldn't escape. Oh, and that I was about to die to my old life but, eventually, I'd experience a rebirth. Fabulous news. Just what I wanted to hear. As for the fireworks? They'd make sense later.

Later that day I had lunch with Tim after which he finished off my tattoo as it needed touching up (and that's not a euphemism). That was the last time I ever saw him. Though I would have liked to have seen him again in my heart of hearts I knew what his arrival in my life had symbolised – *change*. The archetypal third that is the alchemical goddess, Aphrodite had, together with her son, Eros, done what had long been necessary: shaken up a painful, long outdated situation. Now, whether I liked it or not, that situation was about to take another step forward.

I'm not good at lying so Finn must have known something was up with me pacing about the house as I was. When he asked me, later that evening, what was going on, I knew I had to tell him it was over. But this time, it was over for good – never an easy conversation to have.

What made this conversation more difficult – besides the fact that I'd betrayed both him and our relationship – was that, despite everything we'd put one another through, despite the apparent lack of tenderness and affection between us, I realised I'd come to love him. Not in an idealising romantic, rose-coloured glasses way, but in his perfectly flawed way.

Just a month earlier I'd been stood at the living room door, staring down at him while he was lying on the couch watching TV, when it hit me – I loved him. He didn't have to do anything or be anything to impress me; I didn't care what position he may or may not have had at work or how much money he may or may not have earned. I realised that him just being exactly who he was in his flawed humanness, was inherently lovable. That him just being him, was enough.

In that moment I realised that none of us are perfect, that we're all flawed, that we all fuck up, but that doesn't make us any less worthy or deserving of love. We are – each and every one of us – beautifully human. But as I'd discovered at my most recent workshop, it takes great strength to receive, to consciously surrender, and to yield to the penetrative love of another. Even more so if we don't love ourselves or believe we are unlovable. Because if, at essence, I don't love myself, how could I possibly believe another would even accept me, let alone love me, warts and all? So we adopt defensive positions, close off our hearts, and attempt to control others with power-oriented tactics.

Now, here I was, like Psyche stood with her dagger poised over Eros's heart, about to deliver the final death blow. But first I needed a little time to compose myself and gather my thoughts. So I went for a walk – a *long* walk. I told him we'd talk when I got back. While out, I texted both Bing and Ellen: Bing for moral support and Ellen to let her know I might be taking up her offer after all – and sooner rather than later. But when I saw fireworks exploding in the sky I took it as a sign that tonight was the night.

I felt so nervous. Ending a relationship is never easy. The irony was this was the week we were supposed to be in Australia preparing to get married. I'd called off our engagement a year earlier, though, on account of something he'd said to his friend who was contemplating divorce.

He'd told me he'd told his friend that the worst thing is leaving the mother of your children but that it's 'not as big a deal' (or words to that effect) if you haven't had any together. As comments go, it left me feeling cold to the bone.

For me there is no sliding scale of love. Children or not, married or not, if you've loved someone, *really* loved them, ending a relationship is nothing short of heart-breaking at the best of times. Yes, if there are children involved there are far more considerations to weigh up, more hearts to break, more disruption caused – I'm well aware of that. But it was the cold, detached indifference with which he announced his opinion that immediately led me to tell him I didn't want to marry a man who seemed, to me, so hard-hearted.

With this in mind I figured he probably wouldn't care that much about me ending our relationship. We weren't married. Neither did we have any children. Even when we were 'engaged,' he'd never mentioned it to anyone – not to his children, not to his best friend, not to his family. Things only changed when I raised the matter during an argument. So when I told him I wasn't happy, that I hadn't been happy for a long time, that nothing had changed between us since the last time we spoke, and that I wanted to end the relationship, I was surprised to receive a rather cutting reaction and a few surprising revelations.

He told me I made him feel invisible. Familiar with my belief about music sometimes having messages for us, he told me he'd just heard Alison Moyet's song, *Invisible* playing on the radio and realised that that's how I made him feel. This, it seems, was largely on account that I went to Tantra workshops and had Spanish lessons.

I was stunned. The Spanish lessons I did one evening a week (twice a week in the run up to our holiday). He also went out drinking one evening a week with his friend but that didn't seem to count. As for the workshops I did with Shakti Tantra? I'd done three long weekends over the course of the past eight months. That I'd turned to Tantra in an attempt to kindle some warmth and affection for myself, largely on account of the fact he'd distanced himself from me, seemed to be beside the point.

We didn't argue. Instead I listened to what he had to say. I said nothing in return. After all, what could I say? But it's like I've said: when you turn your attention back on yourself, for whatever reason, it never goes unnoticed. After he'd had his say he went to bed. And that was that.

We didn't speak the following day. In fact, it wasn't until two nights later that we resumed our conversation by which point I'd started packing and had arranged with Ellen to go and see her place. I think it was my packing together with my quiet, focused, and undramatic manner that made Finn realise, this time, I wasn't kidding. This time there was no anger, no irate Ares, just me, Thea. And Thea was packing up and shipping out. He asked me if I was leaving. Without any drama I told him, yes, I was. And that was that.

The following day I went with Ellen to see her place. When I saw a stained glass peacock on the front door I took it as yet another sign that this was definitely the right thing to do and the right place to move to. On my return though I was greeted by a very different Finn. Realising I really was leaving and had now made alternative living arrangements, he asked if he could talk with me. This was when it all came out – namely, the truth.

He said he took back his comments that I made him feel invisible and that he resented me learning Spanish and Tantra. He was angry, he said, that's why he'd said those things. I said nothing. He then went on to tell me that he loved me and was proud of me, my achievements and everything I'd done; that, in fact, he told everyone he was proud of me. The only person he'd never told was me. For reasons he couldn't explain he'd always held back.

He told me he'd even held back on replying to a text I'd sent him a couple of months earlier regards the fact it had been three years since we'd bumped into one another (again) and, subsequently, gone on a date. He'd ignored it. I'd forgotten I'd even sent the text. But he hadn't. He'd deliberately withheld replying – a fact he'd been carrying ever since.

It was only later, on reflection, I realised that this withholding of compliments and praise is what my mum's always done (and continues to do). I can't remember the last time my mother praised me for anything I did. As a child you want your parents to see you, to mirror you, to cheer you on. But Mum had, on more than one occasion, deliberately withheld her love or support for my endeavours.

Take, for example, the time I graduated from acting school in my early twenties. On account of an argument we'd had beforehand, she'd refused to attend my graduation. My aunt came together with my boyfriend at the time, but mum refused. At the time her opinion still mattered very much, so for her to withdraw her love and support – especially at such an important moment for me – was about the most hurtful thing she could do. She later told my aunt she'd regretted her actions, that she'd felt awful for doing what she'd done. Later still, she apologised to me in a half-arsed way. But it was too late.

Now, here was Finn telling me he'd done near enough the same thing – deliberately held back, deliberately withdrawn his affection. Like mum so long as all my attention was focused on him I would be loved. Well, if you can call it that. Because, as I was now realising, this wasn't love – this was about power. As Jung said: 'Where love rules, there is no will to power, and where power predominates, love is lacking. The one is the shadow of the other.'

But where Finn had withheld his hand, others were holding out theirs. Besides dear long-standing friends like Bing, new friends, like Ellen, were holding out their hands in support. Then there was Big – a man who had no qualms in being generous with his praise. As far as he was concerned, a job well done was a job well done. And as far as he was concerned, I was doing a good job.

215

But it's what Finn said next which really unnerved me. He pulled out a novel he'd been reading on holiday and read aloud a couple of excerpts which, he said, summed up his attitude about how he'd always loved me and felt he'd missed his chance at marrying me. In other circumstances this would have been terribly romantic, but not now. To be fair, the words he shared were moving and heartfelt. But it was when he said he'd been overcome by a sudden sadness while on holiday, as though something had died, that my heart stopped. Though he didn't ask, I reckon he knew something had happened. I've always felt we were bound up with one another on some karmic level.

By this time he did seem really upset, but after months of being emotionally and physically neglected I was numb to the core. He was right, something had died – our relationship. Though I knew I'd always love him at the profoundest soul level, we were done.

If I thought the revelations were over, though, I was very much mistaken as I was about to hear yet another – this time, from my mum. Later that night I'd dropped by my parents' place to pick something up. Mum asked me how the workshop had gone. Though I didn't go into any detail I told her I'd loved it and that it'd been a gift to move into a deeper, more loving relationship with my body to which she replied – and I quote, word for word – 'I don't like women's bodies. I don't even like my own.'

I was *speechless*. In fact, as she spoke, she put her hand up to her mouth in, what looked like, an attempt to stop the words from spilling forth but it was too late. We looked at one another for a moment before she attempted to divert the conversation elsewhere. But it didn't matter. The truth was out.

Her comments may go some way towards explaining where my own sense of bodily self-loathing came from. Culture had a role to play in it, for sure. But if your mother didn't like her own body, how could she ever fully love and accept that of another's – namely, yours? Speaking of such children whose bodies hadn't been adequately mothered, Marion Woodman says:

> **They have no sense of everlasting arms to uphold them through the crises of life; the early matrix with the mother isn't there. That deprivation propels them to make violent attempts to hold onto life; momentarily they may do so, and then sink back into a lethargy of nonexistence. Their existence is precarious at best because they have no sense of a daily continuum. Such girls seek husbands who will provide that loving day-to-day cherishing, and therefore in marriage they may lock themselves yet again into the mother they sought to escape.**

> **– Addiction to Perfection**

Before I began my enquiries into depth psychology, my subsequent work with dreams and later, body work with Shakti Tantra, this description just about summed me up. As far as I'm concerned what she's describing above is the Handless Maiden or the Kore as nameless maiden (before her initiation). It also describes Psyche who, every time Aphrodite sets her a task, initially responds by attempting to kill herself. But as Woodman goes on to say:

> Of course, children have to recognise negative as well as positive feelings towards their parents, but most of us, at some point in analysis, realise that our parents were in a worse situation than we. Many of them knew they were trapped, but they had no means of finding a way out. The sins of one generation were visited on the next; that is the human situation, and to the extent that parents are unconscious, their children suffer. It is the task of mature individuals to differentiate infantile imagos from the actual parents, to differentiate what was wholesome in their heritage from what was destructive, and to forgive … The task which her own mother may have failed to perform, she must perform. That is the new consciousness, the giant leap, the healing in her own life which she is being called upon to incorporate.

– Addiction to Perfection

As was evidenced by my recent dream, this was the 'giant leap' I'd clearly taken. As far as I'm concerned, there comes a point when you have to stop blaming others for what they may or may not have done and start taking responsibility for yourself. It's not an overnight process. By the time all these revelations came spilling out I'd been grappling with this material for over eight years mostly by myself. Nevertheless, it's a necessary one.

Regards Woodman's comments about the sins of one generation being visited on the next, my aunt tells me that my grandma was notorious at playing her children off against one another. She didn't care as she was closest to her father so it washed straight off her back. But as mum was the youngest she was singled out for favouritism and was often used as a pawn when it came to family power plays.

This realisation – of power dynamics – later led me to re-evaluate something mum had told me as a young child regards the fact she'd left me with foster parents. But why would she tell me that? I was only a couple of weeks old when she'd done so and it had only been for a week. I need never have known. Power, that's why.

As an only child who didn't know my father, my mother was my whole world. Despite also being raised by my aunt and uncle, all the power lay with mum. In my eyes she was my entire world. In my little head if anything happened to her, I'd be left alone – *orphaned.*

Growing up, this fear led me to court my mother's approval and to always try and win her graces. So long as I made myself fit her ideal image of me (real or perceived), made her the centre of my world, everything would be okay. But as soon as I made a move she disapproved of she'd threaten to withdraw her love and would make such statements as, 'We're finished.' Though she'd kept me away from her own mother, as she knew full well what she was capable of, it was too late – the sins of the earlier generation had won out.

Which is why, no matter how much it hurt, no matter what shit was dredged up, I wanted one thing and one thing only – to come clean with myself. I didn't want to go through life wailing and flailing, blaming everything and everyone else for what I perceived I lacked. So when Finn physically withdrew his affections – deliberately, as I was now discovering – I looked at what I believed I lacked and, with a little help from my books and Shakti Tantra, I began giving those things to myself. In doing so I learnt to treat myself how I wanted to be treated. In short, it all starts with *you.*

As for the revelations? They just kept on coming. The following night, when he got home from work, Finn asked if we could go for a walk so we could talk some more. He told me he'd spoken with his manager and wanted to arrange a three-month career break so he could take some time for himself and for us. I told him this was a waste of time. If he wanted to do that for himself that was up to him, but it wouldn't make any difference to my decision or stop me from leaving.

What he failed to realise was all this had only been done in response to my actions. But I'd realised I couldn't be in a relationship with someone who only ever acted when push came to shove. I'd spent the past several years initiating, making move after move into the precarious unknown. It's only after you've taken several leaps of faith that you realise just how difficult it is to stick your head above the parapet of the masses and make a stand for your own life. Until he made such a leap I didn't feel he'd understand how truly challenging it is, how vulnerable it leaves you feeling. I was tired of justifying my decisions, of being made to feel I'd done something wrong in wanting to follow my dreams. I was also tired of being alone in a relationship. I'd opened up and shared my heart six months earlier and, still, nothing had changed.

It was then I considered telling him about my affair with Tim. As I mulled over how to broach the subject, he made yet another revelation. Apparently he'd been taking some tablets since the start of the year of which one of the known side-effects was a loss of libido. Despite being explicitly warned about this, he went ahead and took them anyway. That, of course, was his personal business – but, in this case, it also affected me.

So here I was feeling guilty and shitty about the fact I'd just slept with someone else, when he had knowingly undermined the sexual integrity of our relationship for the best part of a year (at least, that's how I saw it). Not only had he consciously held back on saying anything vaguely complimentary to me, but he hadn't considered telling me he'd made a decision which would have a detrimental impact on the level of eros between us. It doesn't justify what I did nor does it make it okay, but it made me wonder: at what point does a betrayal begin?

But you know, by this point, I was so tired of it all I decided not to tell him about Tim. I'd heard enough revelations these past 48 hours to last me a lifetime. In light of all the revelations now coming to the surface it would have been the ideal time to come clean – but I didn't. I guess in that moment I, too, failed the integrity of the relationship by keeping something back. Perhaps, on some level, I didn't want this to turn into a mutual mud-slinging, a tit for tat. The situation was already heart-breaking. Neither of us could eat from the upset of it all. I'd be leaving the following weekend. Until I moved out I wanted to keep things amicable and peaceful. (By the way, he knows now – I wouldn't tell the world, in a book, without telling him first.)

Thankfully, there was no drama, no arguments. We even continued sleeping together in the same bed. Finn was pleasant, made conversation, started asking me how I was, what I'd been doing. In fact, he reminded me of the Finn I met when we started dating again three years earlier. He did seem genuinely regretful. But, as I've said before, he wasn't a bad or malevolent man by any stretch of the imagination – we just didn't fit anymore.

In view of this behavioural change it would have been easy to feel sorry for him, give the relationship another go. But I didn't. In fact, it was a detail from the story of *Psyche and Eros* which reminded me to stay focused, keep moving forward, and not look back – a detail I sum up this way: *Pity is not lawful.*

Erich Neumann speaking of the fourth and final task Psyche faces in which she must descend into the Underworld and face its queen, Persephone, says:

As the tower teaches Psyche, 'pity is not lawful.' If, as we shall proceed to show, all Psyche's acts present a rite of initiation, this prohibition implies the insistence on 'ego stability' characteristic of every initiation. Among men this stability is

manifested as endurance of pain, hunger, thirst, and so forth; but in the feminine sphere it characteristically takes the form of resistance to pity. The firmness of the strong-willed ego, concentrated on its goal, is expressed in countless other myths and fairy tales, with their injunctions not to turn around, not to answer and the like. While ego stability is a very masculine virtue, it is more; for it is the presupposition of consciousness and of all conscious activity.

The feminine is threatened in its ego stability by the danger of distraction through 'relatedness,' through Eros. This is the difficult task that confronts every feminine psyche on its way to individuation: it must suspend the claim of what is close at hand for the sake of a distant abstract goal.

– Amor and Psyche

Of the countless women I've known who have stood on the threshold of metamorphosis the one thing which has stopped almost all of them from moving forward is *pity*. Her partner repents, tells her he'll change, to give him another chance and she, rather than striking out alone, feels sorry for him, and lets him stay (or she stays). At this point tears on his behalf usually seal the deal especially as many women are suckers when it comes to seeing a man cry.

What they don't realise is they serve neither their partner nor themselves by feeling sorry for them. For many women the underlying fear is this may be as good as it gets. It's only a courageous woman who's committed to coming to consciousness who is willing to sever the, often ouroboric, mother-son ties that keep her bound to her son-lover, sacrifice her relationship, descend into her own personal Underworld, and submit to the suffering she will likely experience there. For many women this is the greatest, most challenging task they will face on their personal Hero's Journey.

With regards our relationship so long as I remained 'in the dark,' as Neumann says of Psyche, I 'was the mere companion of his nights, secluded from the world, living only for him.' Though he didn't know what I did I believe Finn resented the work I did with Shakti Tantra because it threatened the unconscious nature of our relationship.

It was, after all, largely on account of the illuminating realisations at the workshops that I'd sounded the death knell on our relationship. It may not have been two envious sisters who encouraged me to sever ties and end my relationship but it was the camaraderie and the conversations shared with my Shakti sisters which forced me to look at my relationship in a new, more conscious light. Finn may not have been a monster but I deserved to be loved – not as a mother-mate but as an equal partner.

This is why the decisive moment for many women is when they are finally willing to end their relationship and move forward without pity, of which Neumann goes on to say:

> **By freeing herself from him with dagger and lamp, which she bears in place of the torch of Hecate and the other matriarchal goddesses, and so surpassing him and her servitude to him, she deprives Eros of his divine power over her. Psyche and Eros now confront one another as equals. But confrontation implies separateness.**
>
> *– Amor and Psyche*

Being left alone with themselves is what puts the frighteners up most folk. Throw in the tick-tock of the biological clock and many women will often settle for less than they deserve. If only they were willing to sever ties, descend into their personal Underworld, and focus on a 'distant abstract goal' they may eventually end up with what their heart truly desires. The only problem with that route is who knows how long you'll be down there (alone in the Underworld)?

This is why the greatest challenge Psyche faces is her fourth and final task in which Aphrodite demands she go down in the Underworld and, as Neumann says, 'carry something hidden beneath the earth up into the world.' The Underworld is a place of death, of suffering, of loneliness, and of countless tests which will inevitably tempt her off her path. ('Please forgive me, I've changed!' 'I realise now what I had in you!' 'I'll do anything to win you back!')

For me, the story of *Psyche and Eros* provides one of the best mythological and psychological roadmaps for any woman who is engaged in her own Hero's Journey – especially as the ending sees her reunited with Eros but at a newer, higher level of consciousness. Here in the real world this doesn't mean you'll necessarily be reunited with the same partner, but it does suggest the level of eros (love and relatedness) with another will be elevated: that it will be at a more conscious, more mature level which honours the psychological work you've, meantime, consciously submitted and surrendered to.

I knew, though, that leaving was absolutely the right thing to do by something Finn said to me on my final night. I was helping him set up his new laptop when he commented on a ring I was wearing. It was a rose gold ring I've worn for years. He'd bought me a gold-plated stacking ring a couple of years earlier but the gold had since worn off, so I'd gone back to wearing my old favourite.

'I see you have that ring on again. It's pretty,' he said, 'Suits you. How long you been wearing it?'

'Months,' I replied. 'I've been wearing it for months.'

With that one comment he summed up the whole problem of our relationship – though he saw everyone else, he didn't see me.

He never did.

FORM AND SUBSTANCE

Having said all that I did waver and wondered if I'd made the right decision – especially now I was alone in Peacock Palace (a nickname my friend, Peej, gave the house on account of the peacock on the front door). Had I been too hasty? Should I have given him another chance?

That question was answered by a dream I had a couple of nights after moving from which I woke up feeling *furious*. I didn't realise how angry I was until that dream brought my innermost feelings to my attention – angry and *betrayed*. As civil as I may have acted during our last week I was obviously reeling inside.

I further knew my decision was the right one on account of an email Finn sent me the following day – an email which confirmed the fact I'd done nothing 'wrong,' after all. He said he'd read the letter I'd left many times and thanked me for what I'd written. He said he'd even been able to read it clearly. (He always said he couldn't read my handwriting – funny he could now.)

He went on to say how I'd opened his eyes and made him realise that all I'd ever said to him was right and that, on reflection, it wasn't so much resentment but *envy* he felt at the courage I had to do what I was doing. He did, however, resent the supermarket as he realised he'd put all his heart and soul into his job at the expense of me. For that, he said, he felt 'so sad.'

He said I'd made him want to be a better person and that maybe my leaving was the best cause of action as this is what he may have needed for him to see himself. Though all this didn't stop his heart from hurting as much as it did or the feeling of loss.

He told me he'd looked at my suggestion regards taking a month off for a holiday and was in talks with work to make this happen. His plan was to take a three-month long career break from the end of January and to spend a month of that time away. He shared a Rumi quote I'd written in my letter – 'what the heart loves, is the cure' – to which he said, 'let me find that out and see.'

Finally, he told me he loved me and he hoped with all his heart that when he came back our paths would cross again and that, this time, he would be ready and I'd still feel the same.

Envy – what a noxious, spiteful, soul-eating emotion. Unlike jealousy, which tends more towards *control* out of fear, perhaps of losing someone or something, envy covets and seeks to *destroy* and denigrate in its attempt to outdo or undo a rival's perceived advantages.

That he felt envy towards me also explains the competitiveness and his ongoing will to beat me at everything, to always be better than me, and to try and do me down ('Why would anyone pay you that much?'). It also explains why, when I confronted him about breaking one of the keys on my laptop (a writer's most prized possession), he just laughed. I didn't let him see me cry.

When I felt envious of my friend, Lisbeth, when she'd entered a 10K (and Sam's ex-girlfriend for having run a marathon), I turned that energy back on myself and competed *against myself* by entering the New York City Marathon and, later, Rome and Athens. Three marathons later my envy had been transmuted into self-confidence.

That renewed sense of self-confidence was what I exuded when I bumped into Finn again. Didn't matter I had no money and nothing to my name. As I was now learning not only is self-confidence priceless, it's also much coveted – especially by those who suffer with low self-worth and low self-esteem. Speaking of this, Ann and Barry Ulanov say:

> The target of envy's attack is not one's doing, but one's being. Cinderella, for example, owns nothing but her work and the attitude with which she approaches it. But her sisters envy her even that. Owning much but doing nothing, they envy her way of being and going about things. They aim to take it out of her, to disembowel her spiritually, so to speak. Seated in her ashes, going cheerfully about her duties, dressed in rags, the suffering servant has an unmistakable allure about her that the envious sisters clearly lack.
>
> – *Cinderella and her Sisters*

My aunt says that, as a young woman, the most common line fired at her was, 'Who does she think she is?' or 'Who do you think you are?' She was confident, that's what. Her pride and inner sense of self-confidence were instilled in her by her father and continued to carry her through life long after he passed away.

If you're confident and believe in yourself, those who aren't self-confident or don't innately believe in themselves or their abilities will either withhold praise where praise is genuinely due, criticise you, or sabotage your efforts in an attempt to bring you down to their level so they might feel better about themselves. This, I'd noticed, was happening to me more and more – especially since Athens.

Those who do believe in themselves and have scaled the heights, tend to be encouraging and supportive. Not threatened by your talents or your success they want you to get bigger, to be all you can be. Big was one such person. So was another new friend, Nina – a woman I'd met at the Michael Meade workshop I'd done in Santa Cruz a year earlier – with whom I'd recently reconnected.

I'd also noticed an increasing number of positive characters were flooding my dreams: rich, famous, successful, handsome, entrepreneurial men with a few Olympic athletes for good measure. For the first couple of months after I moved out, week after week I'd be chatted up by a wide array of world leaders and the super-rich. I wondered what was going on. What did they all want with me? Then it hit me: *I'm* the common denominator – they all like *me*.

These men, I'd noticed, in a series of ongoing dreams, were replacing weak, impotent masculine figures (often elderly) who were either dying or being dumped by strong women. It was these decrepit, barren men, being replaced by more virile ones, who alerted me to a dream I'd had right around the time I'd met Finn.

In the dream I am wrapping a bandage around a man's wounded thigh which has been lanced and is bleeding. I feel a great deal of love for this man. I reassure him and tell him he's going to be okay.

I'd recognised the motif as the Fisher King from Arthurian legend – the guardian of the Holy Grail (a term often used by alchemists to describe the soul). In the tale, the King, a 'suffering man of sorrows' – as Wolfram von Eschenbach describes him in his book, *Parzival* – has been wounded in the thigh or testicles and is unable to move on his own. So long as he remains injured and, as such, impotent (wounded in his generative function – in other words, his creativity), his kingdom, also, is rendered dry and infertile – a barren Waste Land.

The Fisher King was, without a doubt, Finn's personal myth. Not only did he physically embody this myth to an uncanny degree but during his brief artistic flourish he painted old kings again and again. I bought him a medieval, leather goblet one Christmas, so obsessed was he with them. And while we were on holiday I gave him a book to read by Robert Johnson called *The Fisher King and the Handless Maiden* (which he did).

It was only much later – when reading a paper Nina had submitted for her post grad course in which she alerted me to the King as the 'suffering man of sorrows' – that I realised why I'd also left Finn a song to listen to by City and Colour called *Sorrowing Man*. I couldn't understand why I'd felt so compelled to leave it along with my goodbye letter but I felt he should listen to the song and pay close attention to the lyrics.

Thinking back, I wondered if my dream of three years earlier had portended events about to unfold in my relationship with Finn – namely, that our relationship would somehow help heal my own wounded inner masculine. This 'increased potency,' so far as my inner masculine was concerned, was further confirmed by a dream I had after I moved out in which a famous male porn star pursued me (and we all know how virile *they* can be) and in another dream in which a young Egyptian servant cums in his pants after giving me a breast massage (uncontrollably and unendingly too, might I add – an image which left me chuckling away to myself for the rest of the day).

But I hadn't 'healed' him. If anything I'd walked out on him, sacrificed him. Aha! There it was – *sacrifice*. It took me a year to spot this and to fully own and accept responsibility for the part I played in the breakdown of our relationship. Because, besides my fling, I had a role to play – namely, a *mothering* role.

Unbeknown to me, when I wasn't looking, I'd started mothering him. As I neither have nor want children, I assumed I was immune from this Mother archetype. Oh dear. How naïve was I? Because when I wasn't looking it seems Mother had crept in the back door and started running the joint as M. Esther Harding reminds us here:

> A woman who has not yet 'sacrificed the son,' that is sacrificed the instinctual maternal within herself, may have no actual children, but will nonetheless carry the maternal attitude into her relationships. She is under an inner compulsion to mother all for whom she cares. She cannot bear to see anyone unhappy or in difficulties. Motherliness dominates in her. She never realises that her inability to accept hardness for her friends reflects her own inability to face the hard things of life for herself; still less does she appreciate the fact that her oversolicitous attitude towards them cultivates their worst weakness, throws them back into childishness and self-pity, by which a man's very manhood is undermined. By this attitude she robs her son of his individuality. He is made soft, feminine. He is rendered impotent, all his virility is drained out of him. This is the false castration through the mother by which no redemption is achieved.
>
> When, however, a woman has the courage to say 'no' as well as to say 'yes,' when the negative or black side of Eros has a place beside the light side, then the son as well as the mother may be redeemed by the sacrifice. For when he meets with her refusal to pamper and consider him and save him from hardship, he gains thereby the power to meet the real

difficulties of the situation for himself, provided he accepts the reality of the situation and renounces his demand that she mother him and give him what he needs.

– Women's Mysteries

I think this Mother archetype first appeared when I took over the cooking. Before I moved in, Finn did all the cooking. Not wanting to slip back into playing a daughter role to my daddy-lover, however, I stopped pretending I couldn't cook. Though not something I particularly enjoy, if I put my mind to it and follow recipes I'm not bad at rustling up meals.

But what's that saying? The way to a man's heart is through his stomach? It's enormously satisfying seeing someone enjoy your efforts. Though if I'm being ruthlessly honest with myself, looking back, I can see there's an incredible amount of power bound up in the maternal instinct. It wasn't power I was consciously aware of at the time; again, it's only on reflection I can see it. Still, it was there.

Where this tipped – and, again, I didn't spot this at the time – was when I started to feel I was 'on the back foot.' When my first book failed to be a roaring success and I started feeling bad and guilty about not earning money, I upped the ante on the maternal front. Though I may have told myself I enjoyed cooking, tending the house, and taking care of Finn, it wasn't that – it was about regaining some semblance of power in the relationship.

After all, who doesn't enjoy being cared for and fussed over? Who's going to upset that cosy apple cart? *Here, eat up – no-one can take care of you like I can...* Argh! I'd become just like my friend's wife who wanted to take care of her 'two boys.' I was even picking him up from his weekly nights out. *It doesn't matter what time it is, text me and I'll come and get you. I want to make sure you get home safe.* Erm, why? He's a grown man who's managed perfectly fine getting his drunken, swaying arse home for the past umpteen years. Swaddling him, that's what I was doing. Fussing and farting over him like he was a little boy.

If he'd have asked me to pick him up I should have said, 'Maybe – it depends on what I'm doing. I'll let you know.' Soon, however, he came to expect it. After all, why wouldn't he? This problem was further exacerbated by the fact I never said no. But, as I've said, because I felt powerless, I responded by acting in an oversolicitous manner towards him.

Little did I realise that this did neither of us any favours. Why? Because I was, in essence, undermining his mature manhood – my actions were *emasculating* him. Step (or rather, limp) forward the wounded Fisher King: wounded by a woman who, by her own unconscious actions, were rendering him impotent and unable to help himself.

But it was for him to dig into his own creative potential and figure it out for himself. I couldn't do it for him. As the no-nonsense, unsentimental Crone tells the Handless Maiden as she wails and flails: 'Get it yourself.' Life's tough – deal with it.

On further reflection I noticed that, so long as I supported Finn's artistic endeavours, told him how wonderful his work was, he flourished. Soon as I quietly withdrew my support, however, his creativity shrivelled up. But it's hard enough carrying your own creativity let alone someone else's.

The other glaring problem with this dynamic is that, from a psychological perspective, it's incestuous. After all, no son wants sex with his mother (well, unless you're Oedipus – but that's for another time and another book). Before you know it the idealised, chaste mother-mate is left at home while the son-partner goes off to have an affair with his whore-mistress. No-one doubts he loves his wife; he probably does – but in an idealising, place-her-up-on-a-pedestal, mother-like way. For as Harding goes on to say:

> **This childish demand on his part and the equally undeveloped maternal wish on hers, may serve on a low level of psychological development to produce an alliance between a man and a woman which passes for relationship. But when a necessity arises for something more mature in the situation between them this demand has to be replaced by a greater submission to the laws of Eros.**
>
> **– Women's Mysteries**

The glue of Eros had reared its head in our relationship courtesy of my long-standing commitment to wanting better, more conscious sex – preferably with a man I considered my equal and not a son-partner. So, like Psyche, like Kali, and like Hecate-Artemis, I took my dagger, severed the psychic umbilical cord between us, and sacrificed the relationship casting us both out of the psychic incestuousness we'd been bound up in. (Remember Elle MacPherson in my dream seating the old man in the kitchen? It's a similar motif – the Mother surrendering an outworn aspect of consciousness to the fiery alchemical vessel/kitchen so it can be transmuted.)

So though my desire for hot, passionate sex may have seemed shallow and superficial, my sex drive actually had a lot going for it as it provided the volitional oomph, the necessary lift-off to free me, get me moving again. With the problem dissolved life could flow again – *dissolutio*). Because one thing was for sure – I did *not* want to mother a little boy. Neither did I want to play the helpless little girl to some daddy-lover.

This outer drama was also playing out at an inner, psychic level as evidenced by the interplay between the masculine and feminine energies in the dreamtime. When I first began studying depth psychology I connected with different aspects of the masculine. First up were a series of adventure dreams with Daniel Craig as James Bond (a few steamy ones, too). Then that side of things took a break while I worked on and reconnected with my inner feminine during which I had a series of lesbian dreams. Then it was back to the masculine but at a different level (the orator – as symbolised by Barack Obama). Then Michelle appeared with him. (None of this, by the way, was under my conscious control – I just watched what was playing out in my psyche.)

The Dark Mother appeared next, swiftly followed by a long series of dreams with Prince William and Kate Middleton who prepared for their wedding and later got married (hieros gamos, the *coniunctio* – the sacred marriage). The last dream I'd had with them was while I was on holiday in Spain. In that dream, he (Prince William) stood back and watched, proudly, as his Duchess stepped out and assumed her public role with ease and grace. In short, she was ready.

Now, too, it seemed the Old King of my psyche was dead – as symbolised by the impotent, decrepit men now being replaced in my dreams – and a new, more virile masculine figure was stirring (The King is dead. Long live the King!).

In the week before I left Finn's I'd dreamt of a divine child – a hermaphroditic walking, talking baby who mysteriously emerged from underneath a table. This baby was incredibly loving towards me. It was a charming baby, drawing everyone together with hugs and loving embraces. I felt blessed that it would attach itself to me (I carried it on my hip). Hermaphroditus was the child of Aphrodite and Hermes and embodies a balance of masculine and feminine energies – yet another symbol of the *coniunctio*.

Just as positive was the fact I'd been orphaned in a dream and left alone to study law in central Manchester (the city in which I was born and which I often associate with the Self – the totality of the psyche as opposed to Manhattan which, for me, tends more to symbolise the ego/persona). In essence, I felt I'd withdrawn my infantile projections and was now following the inner law of the Self – in other words, I was being Self-guided.

In another dream, my uncle (the man who raised me and who essentially is my father) got into bed with me. As he attempted to cuddle me I got straight out. No siree – no more daddy-lovers, thank you very much! (I'm well aware, though, that that isn't the only way to look at that dream.)

Despite all this subterranean night-time action not a whole lot was going on in my waking life. I'd retreated into the private folds of Peacock

Palace and rarely went out. In many ways it was my chrysalis. I felt a darkening, a veiling, a drawing in.

I knew something was up by my inexplicably, strange mood. On the one hand here I was single and living alone armed with my bag of tasty Aphroditic tricks with which I could now do whatever I liked, whenever I liked. Except I didn't want to do anything with them. Or did I? I wasn't sure.

On the one hand I *thought* I did (or should) especially as, all around me, everyone seemed to be having sex. Bing had a new boyfriend who she disappeared into for several weeks while they 'bonded' (and that's an understatement – she's a randy little bugger). Our last workshop had also blown the lid off several other women's sex lives and they were now out there, going for it. Even my next door neighbours regularly engaged in what I called Fuckfest Wednesdays during which the female of the species went on and on and *on*, shouting out and wailing her seemingly endless orgasms up the walls – orgasms which managed to reach through the living room, across the house, and up the stairs before, finally, reaching an ear-shattering crescendo in my bedroom where Tess the Tantric Tortoise, here, was trying to get some sleep.

Having said that I would like to share something I regularly indulged in once I was left alone with myself. When Ellen first showed me around the house, as soon as I clapped eyes on the giant mirror which faced the bed I knew it was a sign for me to face one of my final sexual edges: watching myself self-pleasure. I have to admit, it took me a while to rustle up the courage to look myself straight in the eye and face myself square-on like that but once I did *damn* was it hot. Suffice to say I recommend you try it sometime.

As for taking a lover? No. Nothing. I could have. There had been opportunities. But as much as I thought I should be taking advantage of singledom – especially now I was a budding Tantrika – I didn't.

It was only after three months that I finally shacked up with some of my Shakti Tantra sisters and went to the opening of an erotic art exhibition in Liverpool. Getting ready and dressed up for this night was another moment I particularly enjoyed.

Before embarking on the women's workshops I'd always had issues with my bum. By this I mean I was reticent about overtly displaying it and putting it 'out there' in a pair of skinny jeans, say. Truth be told I'd never worn a pair of skinny jeans in my life. I always thought they were for girls and women with leaner, lither legs. Then I remembered a woman I'd seen who'd paraded her fine, voluptuous backside up and down the stage of a concert I'd recently attended. She wouldn't know it, but just by virtue of putting those jeans on and proudly and unashamedly flaunting her tush, she'd inspired me to do the same.

In the past Finn had been critical of some of my clothes choices, especially jeans. But now I was single I could wear what I damn well liked. So I bought myself my very first pair, slammed on a new pair of high heels and with a slink in my step and a wiggle of my skinny jeaned, shrink-wrapped ass, I hit the town.

In heels I stand at six foot. To be willing to stand up and jut out so prominently, further echoed my burgeoning confidence. But I liked it. I could hold it now. I couldn't handle the attention it invariably attracted before, but I didn't mind it now. So what if people look, I thought?

Anyway, I'd arranged to stay with Sarah, the honey-voiced one that night. So, at the end of the night, when I got talking to a guy I thought was a bit of all right and who I found out was also staying at Sarah's, I made up my mind that perhaps it was time I move on too – especially since Finn had wasted no time in doing so.

Something told me he was seeing someone. I don't know, call it intuition but I sensed something had shifted. My first inkling was when I called round to see one of my old neighbours to say goodbye as they'd been away on holiday the week I'd moved out. I explained what had happened and that I'd moved away when Colin said to me, 'Oh yes, he had flowers delivered recently.' Then he stopped. I looked at him. He looked at me.

'Finn? Flowers?' I frowned in puzzlement. 'Finn doesn't buy flowers. He's never bought them. Maybe he's taking a career break after all and his personnel department have sent them.'

It was only later, New Year's Eve to be exact, when Ellen dropped by to show a viewer around (her house was on the market) that I found out he was, in fact, seeing someone. I had to press her for it but in the end she told me.

'Yes, he is,' she said. 'It happened pretty quickly. Even Mart was surprised at how quick he moved on. He's been walking about the neighbourhood with her, holding her hand...'

Of all the things that could possibly piss me off, this was it – the hand holding issue. As for the flowers? They were obviously for her. She asked if I was alright. I lied, told her I was. But inside I was *so* angry (says the woman who slept with someone behind his back and, subsequently, ended the relationship – someone mention hypocrite?). Judging from the speed with which he'd met her I could only assume he'd met her at work. I wondered if my dream from months earlier about him flirting with someone from work had, in fact, been prescient after all.

Back at Sarah's place Oscar and I had ramped things up several notches on the flirt-o-meter scale to the point I knew he definitely liked me. After Sarah showed me to my bedroom and disappeared to show her other guests to their rooms, I slipped straight back out and knocked on Oscar's door.

As usual I beat about the bush until he made a move on me to which I immediately acquiesced. But it was a decision I instantly regretted. Not because there was anything wrong with him or because he did anything wrong but because I didn't want *this* anymore, by which I meant casual affairs, one-night stands. This was why I'd been holding back these past three months.

The last time I was single was when I was training for the marathons. After the Rome Marathon I'd lost a lot of weight which resulted in a newfound confidence in my body and sexuality. Though I'd made a promise to myself to stay single it wasn't long before I succumbed to the odd sexual snare or two - snares I participated in not so much because I wanted to, but *because I could.*

My attitude was: *I've lost all this weight, why shouldn't I go out and enjoy my body? I'm entitled to it.* But on reflection I realised there was something eerily reminiscent of this attitude to when I'd told my work colleague that I'd bought a Louis Vuitton purse *because I could.* It smacked of defiance, entitlement - like I'd somehow earned the right. Now, though, it felt puerile.

I was at a place where it would have been so easy to take advantage of the situation I now found myself in. I knew so much more about my body and my pleasure. I'd just unleashed a long-repressed, long-shamed aspect of my sexuality and womanhood. I was single. I lived alone. The conditions were ripe for me to go for it. But as I was now realising that wasn't why I'd signed up for the workshops with Shakti Tantra. After all, I didn't need them to give me permission to be lascivious. So what was it I was looking for then? Was it just better sex? Or was it something *more?*

Though Oscar wanted to see me again I wasn't interested. I was done with the casual liaison portion of the programme. There was no longer any beauty or meaning or depth in such encounters for me. This was when I thought back to the story *The Prostitute and Pearls of Wisdom* and, in particular, this idea of holding out or, as the story puts it, 'wait for the pearls.'

In the story you may recall the disciple advising the sister to turn away all those who call at her hut unless they bring her a 'bag of pearls of the highest water.' Because it's a story and, as such, happening in the eternal now of the dreamtime, the action is condensed and takes place in one night. So when the story says, 'the night was progressing and the stars were rotating, and the darkness was gathering deeper and deeper into the depths of this long, dark night,' back in the realm of our waking reality, we can assume the action takes place over the course of several weeks or even months, with a 'long, dark night,' symbolising a dark night of the soul – a process not exactly renowned for its swiftness.

The sister's deepest fear is she'll die in 'a simple poverty of utter isolation.' I thought back to my own attitude and how I'd always sold myself cheap especially in personal, intimate relationships. But I was single now and I knew that road and where it led all too well. I wondered, then, what would happen if I, too, 'waited for the pearls?' Would holding out really attract the attention of the divine? Would such a thing even be possible in the mundane reality of daily life? If so, what would that look like?

In stories and dreams pearls are often symbolic of the feminine essence (but not always, so don't get hung up on that – it depends entirely on context). In *The Book of Symbols* we also learn that, 'In the Gnostic Hymn of the Pearl, the pearl is the gnosis of "self-acquaintance" that reunites the soul forgetful of itself with its divine origin.'

So after she has suffered through a long, dark night, when Brahma eventually turns up, rather than pay her with money, he honours her true value and feminine essence by giving her pearls, after which she (soul) is united with Brahma (divine) in a sacred marriage.

If I was going to test this out, see if it was true, it would mean I'd have to hold out, *really* hold out, turn my sexual instinct back on itself and abstain from sexual liaisons. This may mean suffering through another long, dark night of my own (as if I hadn't enough of those already), but with my next workshop – Women of Substance – now a month away, I figured now might be as good a time as any to curb my sexual appetite.

The more I thought about it the more it seemed the right thing to do, this saying *no* to oneself. There was something about the self-discipline and sacrifice it entailed which reminded me of the sacrifices I'd made ahead of Athens. Back then I'd decided to sacrifice all comforts (fuel belt, GPS watch, company) and face my fears head-on – those fears being loneliness.

By consciously approaching that third and final marathon as a ritual I'd transformed what may have otherwise been a profane, run-of-the-mill event into a sacred, transcendent experience. But I doubt that would ever have happened had I not reflected on the lessons I'd learnt in New York and Rome and carried them into Athens. First, though, I'd had to come clean with myself, work with my hang-ups, my fears – in other words, my *prima materia.*

My psyche's raw material, which was ripe for being transmuted, was my fear of being left alone with myself (orphaned, you might say) with no-one to support me or be there to celebrate my big achievement. Prior to that, I'd always wanted someone with me (Sam in New York), someone to cheer me on (Bing and Lisbeth in Rome). But in Athens I decided not only would I go it alone, but that I'd strip away all comforts. That's what I meant by coming clean with the moment. No more of this infantile wailing and flailing. No more 'Look at me mummy! Look at what I've done!' (What's implied there is if you don't look at me, how will I even know I exist?). I needed to stop looking for others to parent me and start parenting myself.

But it was only once I'd let go of all false attachments, only once everything had been stripped away and I crossed the finish line in Athens that I realised, for the first time in my life, that I wasn't alone; rather, I was rooted in myself. Put another way, I was rooted in the Self.

Not only did I now understand this psychologically but it was an acute visceral experience I'd felt surging up from the soles of my feet, flushing my genitals before finally flooding the rest of my body filling me with an unshakeable sense of Self such as I'd never felt before. Had I not travelled alone, had I not stripped away all outer supports and faced my personal fears head-on I doubt I'd have ever had such an incredible, life-changing experience.

It's only when you reconnect with your authentic inner taproot that you stop clinging, stop hanging on to other people and to the things of the world. That was where my deep-rooted, unshakeable sense of inner conviction and self-belief stemmed from. In that moment I knew, soul to bone, that I AM. Never again would it matter what possessions I did or didn't have, how much money I did or didn't have, whether or not I was with someone. I was no longer defined by my possessions or my relationships or my bank balance; stripped of everything, stripped of all false attachments, I felt myself rooted in the Self, the true I AM - and the only one that really matters. All else is ashes and dust.

Of course, no sooner had I had that realisation than it was tested. Every hero, after all, once they've tasted the ambrosia of eternal life or stolen fire from the gods faces the challenge of bringing that truth back to share with the rest of the world. I was no different. Not that I saw it like that. I didn't think I was Prometheus - I was a woman from Manchester who'd just run a bloody marathon. Let's not get too excited about it.

But judging from Finn's aggressive pursuit of me I'd obviously discovered something that others wanted for themselves - something *priceless*. This was where my next challenge lay: now I'd connected with this inner taproot would I sacrifice it for love, for comfort, for the sake of a relationship?

When it came to such a test the Self couldn't have picked a better adversary in Finn. He was, after all, someone I'd known a long time; someone I trusted and had always felt fondly of. But though he'd taken me to the brink of my own self-belief when push came to shove I turned away from him and turned back towards the Self. Why? Because I knew that, should I betray the Self, I'd also be betraying myself and, consequently, everyone else around me – something I could never do. For me, self-integrity (Self-integrity) matters. 'To thine own self be true,' Shakespeare wrote. Rarely has a better piece of advice been imparted.

After this workshop (Women of Substance) it would be six months until our fifth and final workshop, Ecstasy. Once again, I realised I had a unique opportunity to come clean with myself and make the most of this time by making another conscious sacrifice.

This time, however, the fear I faced was holding out and 'waiting for the pearls.' Prior to this my unspoken belief was, if I don't *do* anything to make a relationship happen, if I'm not out there hustling, manipulating, flirting, attempting to control others, attempting to control situations I'll be forgotten about, left alone. Looking at it it's yet another take, another aspect of the fear I faced heading into Athens – except, psychologically speaking, this was on a bigger scale.

I say bigger because, like everyone else, I enjoy companionship. But I don't want companionship because, deep down, I'm afraid of being left alone with myself – that would be selling both me and the other person cheap. It would be a profane transaction based in fear, not love. This was the challenge the sister faced in the story while she waited through her long, dark night. Could she stand to be alone with herself no matter how long she had to wait? Even if that meant 'dying alone in a simple poverty of utter isolation?' The thing about real life is you could be left alone with yourself for a long time. Who knows? It could be months, years maybe.

This is a challenge which brings up all sorts of fears, the main one being, do you like the company you keep when left alone with yourself? *Especially* when you're left alone with yourself?

In Athens I'd been alone for a week. But consciously forgoing all relationships and being single for months or years while I waited for the pearls especially now I was armed with my recently revitalised sexuality and my Aphroditic toolkit with its bells and whistles which I wanted so dearly to share with a beloved? Ay, ay, ay, talk about ramping it up to the nth degree.

Then there'd be the tempters. Those who, like the sister in the story, I'd likely be presented with who didn't have the pearls. But like Psyche who must first submit to a series of tasks before she can be reunited with Eros at a new, elevated state and the prostitute who must also endure and hold out for something with more meaning and value I knew that, like Artemis with her bow and arrow, I also had to focus on a far-distant goal and not compromise myself by giving into temptations.

I knew I was on the right track by the almost instant kickback I got from my sex drive. Good grief it shot through the roof. It wanted satisfying, dammit! If it could speak it would have said, 'Get outta my way – don't you stop me!' On arrival at my workshop I shared this in the opening circle to see what my teacher had to say about it.

By the way, here's the online bumph from Shakti Tantra's website for Women of Substance:

> **This three-day workshop is a turning point on the Shakti Tantra women's journey where we meet the demons that limit our pleasure. We start to transform our unconscious games so that we can enjoy the eroticism of our power, allowing us to merge into a deeper and more expansive experience of pleasure – the marriage of body with spirit.**

Reading that now is interesting to me because, if I'm being honest, I didn't read it at the time. All I knew was there was a workshop on the horizon and that was pretty much that. After my Dionysian fallout at the previous workshop this one didn't seem to register as much. I think, primarily, because I felt myself slipping into a quietened, subdued state I can only describe as *wintering*.

In the opening circle I shared that I felt 'my sex was on fire.' That's how it felt – *on fire*. Never one to beat about the bush, Hilly asked, 'Do you want to fuck?'

'No. It's not that,' I replied. I'd tried that out with Oscar a month before and knew that wasn't it.

'Have you asked your body what it wants?' asked Sarah, the honey-voiced one.

'No,' I replied.

'Well ask it,' she went on. 'In particular, ask your yoni what she wants. After all the body has its own wisdom: a wisdom we all need to listen to more often.'

What was confusing to me was while my body did want to fuck, my head didn't. I was embroiled in an inner civil war: Abstract Ideals versus Bodily Instincts. This was when I discovered I was absolutely working with the right substance – the right *prima materia*. I'd turned myself into a one-woman alchemical laboratory as I turned myself back on myself so I could transmute my base instinctual desires into, hopefully, one of devotion.

In fact I'd go so far as to say that this was where my true Tantra journey began. Because this was no longer about finding my pleasure in my own body or with another: this was about moving towards a deepened relationship with the Other – the marriage of body and spirit; a hieros gamos, the greater *coniunctio*. This was the something more I'd always wanted.

I'm not sure if Shakti Tantra follow Women Behaving Badly with Women of Substance deliberately. I mean, it's obvious they know what they're doing - when you're in the workshop that's self-evident. What I mean is after the Dionysian explosion at Women Behaving Badly it would have been so easy to get stuck at the level of the sacral chakra (*swadhisthana*) - the chakra associated with sexuality and pleasure - and run out into the world in a frenzy tearing through all the flesh you could sink your claws into. But as Marion Woodman says, 'On the journey, individuals recognise their animal passion and, like children, tend to live it out. However, raw instinct tends to become more raw. Society would be anarchy without personal discipline.'

You may have noticed, in our wee folktale, that it's the disciple who advises the sister to hold back, restrain herself. In doing so what was once a profane situation is, with time, transmuted and transformed into a sacred one. In a way he's a personification of her sense of discipline (disciple, discipline - the clue is in the words).

From an alchemical perspective what you're looking to do is transmute those three self-serving, instinctually-oriented lower chakras and redirect them so they're in service not to one's ego (I, me, mine), but to the heart (we) - the seat of the Self. They couldn't have picked a better workshop name than Women of Substance, because this was the level where I took the substance that was my base, sexual desire and consciously began transforming it.

In alchemy the saying is: *Sublimate the body and coagulate the spirit*. In other words raise (sublimate) the body and, with it, the base instincts (bottom three chakras) and draw down spirit (top three chakras) so they meet and merge in the middle chakra - the heart. When a true permanent transformation takes place your heart becomes, what the alchemists call, the Philosopher's Stone - this is the place where the true inner marriage of Shakti and Shiva (Tantra) or King Sol and Queen Luna (medieval alchemy) takes place. Catherine MacCoun puts it this way:

The heart is now the meeting place between intention and will, between heaven and earth. Empowered by all the other centres, its energy streams outward into the world. It is brilliant with the intelligence of heaven-inspired intention and sonorous with the power of the earthy will. Like a diamond, it is indestructible, cutting, and radiant. It loves bravely, shrewdly, mightily, and magically. It has become the philosopher's stone.

– On Becoming an Alchemist

237

None of this can be done, though, until you've sufficiently 'got your rocks off,' got it all out of your system. Take Gautama Buddha. He was born into a royal Hindu family. It is said that his father, King Suddhodana, wanted his son, Gautama, to be a king. Not only was he presented with everything he could ever want or need, but it's also said that his father demanded he be shielded from religious teachings and human suffering.

This didn't work and once Gautama saw that we get old, that we suffer, and that we eventually die, he turned his back on his position of tremendous wealth and privilege and assumed the life of an ascetic. This time he took things to the other extreme depriving himself of all worldly goods, including food.

After much suffering he realised that extreme asceticism didn't work either. This was when he discovered what Buddhists call the Middle Way – a path of moderation away from the extremes of self-indulgence and self-mortification (asceticism). By all means enjoy the things of the world – but don't get too attached to them and certainly don't allow them to define your sense of identity.

The suffering most people experience is due to their obstinate clinging to the material world. Take it all away and many are left feeling bereft and worthless. But as I'd learnt in Athens, sometimes you have to get rid of everything before you're able to reconnect with the innermost taproot that is the Self ('I am the true vine,' Jesus said). Once you've reconnected with that taproot, never again will you cling to this material world or allow it to define who you are. Whether you possess belongings or not, like I discovered in Athens, you will know I AM.

Where many spiritual folk go wrong, however, is in trying to bypass the body in their attempt to 'chase the spiritual ace.' What they fail to realise is even Buddha had a rare old time, lording it up before he eventually turned his back on it all. In my case I had to get my sexual rocks off before I could even contemplate turning toward the within. It was an issue I had to bang away at (pun intended), until it lost its lascivious lustre.

Big is another wonderful example of this. He's worked his way to the top of the ladder and had it all: the Aston Martin, several multi-million pound properties, the fancy lifestyle. So when someone like that says they've had enough, that it's not all it's cracked up to be and starts talking about doing something with more meaning, I know he's ripe for transformation. Now his ego's satisfied he can start to sate the Self.

Don't get me wrong he still likes nice things, just as I do, but he no longer defines himself by them. I watched with amusement as he took great delight in downsizing and streamlining his life much as I had years earlier when I'd sold my house and got rid of most of my belongings. When he texted me a photo of a storage unit filled mostly with his books and a few other personal belongings it was like staring at a snapshot from my own life.

But you have to have had whatever it is your heart desires and experienced and exhausted it to the utmost degree before you can even *think* about trying to transcend it. So, to be clear, there's nothing wrong in wanting to stake your claim, make a ton of money, attain a position of power, achieve the fame, or have all the sex in the world. Because it's only when you've stuffed your face and had your fill that you may eventually discover that it's not all it's cracked up to be. That's where the *something more* comes in.

My first turning point, remember, was realising I'd bought a Louis Vuitton purse for no other reason than *because I could.* Next up was realising I'd been having sex *because I could.* In and of themselves there was nothing inherently wrong with what I'd done. It was only once my attitude towards them changed that I was finally able to step beyond them and start looking for the something more. But you can't skip that first ego-oriented step. That's why you have to be careful when it comes to purifying and transmuting base, instinctual desires as Edward Edinger reminds us here:

> **The necessary frustration of desirousness or concupiscence is the chief feature of the calcinatio stage. First the substance must be located, that is, the unconscious, unacknowledged desire, demand, expectation must be recognised and affirmed. The instinctual urge that says 'I want' and 'I am entitled to this' must be fully accepted by the ego. There can be no proper calcinatio, as distinguished from masochistic self-flagellation, until the proper material is at hand.**

> **– *Anatomy of the Psyche***

In other words there can be no burning away of false illusions (*calcinatio*) until you've got something to burn in the first place. Because I was done with the casual sex portion of the programme I was ready to take it to the next level.

At the time I had this realisation I'd been on my own Great Round of Transformation for just shy of nine years. Others on the women's programme may need to spend much more time – years, perhaps – thoroughly exploring their personal pleasure and fulfilling all their wildest, sexual fantasies before they can even think about transcending them. Not that the pleasure stops – it absolutely doesn't. It's just that the tenor of the pleasure changes. It becomes more subtle, heart-based – less 'me' and more 'we.'

The Women of Substance workshop further compounded the fact that I was ready to up the ante, especially as much of what we did reminded me of the work I'd done at my method acting course years earlier: exploring demons, working with the shadow, and whatnot. Throw in years of depth work and an ongoing commitment to self-reflection courtesy of journaling and dreams, together with my 'sex on fire' that was now demanding I satisfy its 'I wants' and I was ripe for transmutation and transformation.

Here's the blog I wrote about my workshop experience:

WOMEN OF SUBSTANCE:
WORKSHOP REVIEW

'And your body is the harp of your soul, and it is yours to bring forth sweet music from it or confused sounds.'
– Kahlil Gibran

Women of Substance is the fourth of five levels of the women-only workshops Tantra organisation, Shakti Tantra offers. For me, this level took a different turn – inwards.

Up until now each level has felt somewhat outward oriented. That's not to say there haven't been moments for reflection, introspection, and contemplation (there has); rather, this was the level where we began to explore – within a beautiful, safely contained setting – the deep-rooted mental, emotional, and psychological demons that deny our pleasure and constrict our relationships with ourselves and others.

As far as I'm concerned just getting this far shows you're a Woman of Substance. Everything we encountered and experienced during the three-day workshop took us deeper into the unexplored and energetically blocked recesses of our bodies and psyches.

You may wonder what we got up to. As always my lips are sealed. This isn't something you could understand from a cool, uninitiated distance. You have to breathe it, feel it, cry it, laugh it. You have to drop the shit, shake it off (which you do at each of the preceding levels). By the time you reach this level, you do wonder what else they could possibly throw at you, what stones are left unturned.

As per usual, they have plenty.

Though don't let me give the impression it was all hard work. There was one structure that made me so happy, so grateful to be alive, I cried smiles. Never has my body felt as nourished as it did after experiencing this particular exercise. Never. I sparkled and shimmered, undulated and laughed. Damn it felt good. I've long intuited the body harboured many delicious secrets; that it was capable of producing melodies and harmonies so sweet, so skin-tingingly exquisite... but only if you're open and relaxed enough to consciously receive. And therein lies the challenge – to believe yourself worthy and deserving of receiving the loving, undivided attention of another (which is what the work at each of the previous levels is all about – preparation, preparation, preparation).

The other thing about being open to receive is it spreads its tentacles and doesn't remain contained in just one area of your life. I've always said transformation cannot be conveniently compartmentalised – change changes everything. So since level three where the nut was finally cracked and I understood, experientially, that it takes great strength and courage to be vulnerable and open enough to consciously receive, my mantra today, albeit quiet, is 'I do deserve.'

This workshop also further reinforced that the body isn't something 'bad,' something to be punished, flagellated. It's a magnificent, beautiful, sacred manifestation of the divine. It's worthy of being respected, celebrated, enjoyed.

Throughout this process I've gradually come to love my body. Little by little, step by step, I've fallen in love with her. And I don't mean that in a trite, clichéd way – I mean that from depths I never felt before I did this work. Where I once beasted her with arduous exercise regimes, hid her in shame, filled her with junk, I now revel in her beauty, marvel with a heart wide open at her sensuous nuances.

Bring on the fifth and final week-long level – Ecstasy.

THE YEAR WITHOUT
A SUMMER

As winter turned to spring I knew it was time to surrender, go with the flow, and move back to my parents' home. Not that I minded. Well, I did and I didn't. On the one hand I felt like a failure (in the eyes of the culture, at least). Here I was, a thirty-five-year-old woman living back at her folks – *again*.

On the other hand it dawned on me that in the Great Round of Transformation everyone, when they've come full circle, must return to where they first started. How else will they be able to see if they've really changed? Wasn't that the whole point of the hero setting out on their journey in the first place?

It was now nine years since I'd first left home after realising I needed to get away from mum and figure out who I was when no-one was looking; nine years since I'd dissolved into a wailing heap of hopelessness at my doctors and walked away from my job with the toady, two-faced boss. Now we'd see whether or not I'd really changed.

When it comes to personal transformation more often than not it's the small things you really appreciate. So the fact I finally had my own bedroom at the opposite end of the house from mum symbolically summed up the psychic umbilical that had been severed in our relationship. As a child, I'd never had my own bedroom. I had to share with mum. As my aunt had worked from home as a machinist making bags, her workroom occupied the third bedroom – a bedroom I'd long wished had been mine. But she'd long since retired which meant that, finally, it *was* mine. Many ghosts were laid to rest the first night I slept alone in my own bedroom. Many.

But the changes went way beyond that. You know you've really transformed when the people around you – especially those to whom you're closest and who know you best – act differently towards you. Not because of anything you say, either. Not only do they act differently towards you but *they* start acting differently. After all, your change changes *everything*. Gandhi was spot on when he said, 'Be the change you wish to see in the world.'

I noticed, for example, how my family started taking better care of themselves after I moved back in. The difference was so swift and marked, it was downright amusing. Drawing inspiration from the organic skin products and low-toxin cleaning products I brought back with me they soon adopted many of the same practices as me. Before long they were bathing in Dead Sea and Epsom salts and slathering themselves in coconut oil. I hadn't said a peep about what they should or shouldn't do with their bodies (none of my business) – they just watched and drew their inspiration from me.

Soon my aunt joined me on my daily walks as I introduced her to a nearby urban trail she'd never seen before. After feeling left out, mum joined my aunt instead and I powerwalked alone in the evenings. Before long, my uncle got in on the act and joined my aunt at the weekends when he was off work. Of all the changes I noticed, this reconnection – between my aunt and uncle – was the most heart-warming, as it was first time they'd gone out walking together since I was a child.

Anyway, next thing you know I've acquired a new nickname – Professor Peabody. My aunt decided it was a fitting name as she regularly remarked on how much I'd grown and learnt since I'd been away. 'Where's Peabody?' my aunt or mum would ask if there was something they wanted answering. 'She'll know.' Again, this was a turnaround. Not only had the 'little one' grown up, but her opinion was now being sought on a wide and diverse range of matters.

'It's because you don't preach,' my aunt said to me one day when I asked her about the Peabody moniker. 'You don't make me feel stupid for asking. And you explain it in simple terms. You're down to earth,' she said. 'And considering I'm twice your age, I can't believe how much I've learnt from you about people and psychology. It's all so fascinating.' Like I've said before, it's good to be seen – seen and cared for.

Because that was the other thing my family did – took care of me. If there's one good thing about living back at your parents (mine, anyway) it's that they have systems and schedules for everything. My aunt, being the Crone that she is, runs a tight, well-organised ship you can set your watch by.

So when my tooth flared up and I had to return early from a trip to London to visit the emergency dental hospital, my aunt chaperoned me for emotional support. ('You looked bloody awful,' she said, 'I felt so sorry for you, you poor thing.') This wee tooth, though, came to play a significant, symbolic part in my gradual *putrefactio* and eventual *mortificatio*.

I'd been suffering with toothache for years but hadn't done anything about it. Each time it flared up I stuffed the pain back down with painkillers. But over the past year the pain had gotten worse and worse until, during a trip to London, the crown of the tooth sheared clean off leaving my now very angry and inflamed nerve exposed.

I have *never* known pain like it. I felt like Edvard Munch's painting, *The Scream*. For someone who has never had a filling in their life and no bad dental experiences this felt like I'd saved them all up for one epic tooth breakdown. It was this experience which stopped me dead in my tracks and put me on my back and in my bed – which, I soon realised, was *exactly* where I was meant to be in preparation for my dark night of the spirit: back at home under my parents' care. Because this was when it all turned to shit. And I mean *literally* turned to shit.

This is what happens when you start poking about in the depths of the psyche. After all, there can be no inner transformation, no coming to consciousness without some sort of healing crisis – the healing crisis in question being a *spiritual crisis*.

Our modern day culture knows little if anything about such experiences. Actually, we do – we just call it depression. Except this wasn't a depression – this was *putrefactio* as the medieval alchemists called it (a stage also known as fermentation).

If you don't work with your dreams and your psyche is suddenly subjected to an overhaul (aka 'extreme makeover') you'll most likely think there's something wrong with you and head to the doctor who, in most cases, will prescribe you anti-depressants. There's only one problem with this: you're not depressed – your psyche's *fermenting*. Welcome to the life-death-rebirth mysteries.

I knew I wasn't depressed because my mood was reminiscent of how I'd felt during the dark night I'd experienced several years earlier when I turned away from the gross, material world and gravitated towards subjects of a more spiritual, esoteric nature.

Such behaviour (seeking solace in spiritual subjects) is typical of a soul's dark night in that you seek solace in the ethereal Other. It feels like the lamentation of the soul precisely because it *is* the soul which is suffering. The soul, now realising something's missing, looks for something more, looks for its spiritual beloved (Self) with which it longs to be reunited.

It's at this stage many people correctly intuit that what they seek isn't in this world (i.e. not tangible). So, they loiter in the self-help section of the book store (while hoping like hell no-one sees them there), dabble in spirituality, light incense, or wonder if they should pursue a 'cool' religious path like Buddhism.

The old mythological idea, however, is it's only once you've suffered through a dark night of the soul that you become eligible (for want of a better word) for what St. John of the Cross called a 'dark night of the spirit.'

If you think a dark night of the soul is bad it's nothing compared to a dark night of the spirit. In the former the emphasis tends to be more on getting a higher perspective (*sublimatio*) by seeking solace in more spiritually-oriented subjects. But in a dark night of the spirit, inspiration dries up as the soul is suddenly dumped, dropped from a great height, and abandoned. After all, what goes up, must come down.

Whereas during the soul's dark night you tend to berate yourself for your meaningless life which usually causes you to turn away from the things of this world, a dark night of the spirit – its darker, spirit-zapping sibling – has you questioning *everything*.

Say, for example, you've been studying Taoism. All of a sudden you may feel like it's a load of crap. You lose faith in the teachings and wonder what you ever saw in it in the first place. In much the same way the material world lost its lustre during the soul's dark night, the spiritual world now loses its brightness leaving you feeling like the guiding light that has so far sustained you has been blown out and, with it, all hope and optimism.

But now you're stuck because on the one hand the things of the world no longer interest you the way they once did and even if they did, you haven't got the wherewithal to deal with any of it; on the other hand, the things of the spirit have lost their sheen too, leaving you feeling hopeless and wondering why you ever bothered pursuing a psychological and/or spiritual path in the first place. Betwixt and between, you're left wandering alone in a spiritual Twilight Zone. This is the stuff existential crises are made of.

What makes this stage hard to accept is that there's nothing you can *do* about it; rather you're forced to 'let go and let God' and surrender as the Other sets about simultaneously dismantling and restructuring your psyche in preparation for greater, yet unknown tasks. After all 'you' in the ego sense didn't consciously create the body you inhabit just as 'you' don't consciously pump the blood around your body or grow a baby – the Other does that; the not you (there can only be a 'you' if there's a 'not you,' right?). C. S. Lewis puts it far more eloquently than I ever could:

> Imagine yourself as a living house. God comes in to rebuild that house. At first, perhaps, you can understand what He is doing. He is getting the drains right and stopping the leaks in the roof and so on: you knew that those jobs needed doing and so you are not surprised. But presently He starts knocking the house about in a way that hurts abominably and does not seem to make sense. What on earth is He up to? The explanation is that He is building quite a different house from the one you thought

of – throwing out a new wing here, putting on an extra floor there, running up towers, making courtyards. You thought you were going to be made into a decent little cottage: but He is building a palace. He intends to come and live in it Himself.

– *Mere Christianity*

So during this second dark night you turn down the volume on your life and 'get out of the way of yourself' so as to allow the Other to do the necessary interior renovations in preparation for your eventual rebirth – easier said than done. After all, here in waking reality people have jobs to go to, mouths to feed, and bills to pay. But that doesn't lessen the feelings of loss or abandonment you may experience during this time.

Because this was how I felt – *abandoned*. Abandoned and betrayed (*I've done all this work, given up everything and for what!*). In my journal, I called this period the Garden of Gethsemane as it was all I could do to stop myself from crying out, 'My God, My God, why have you forsaken me?' Not that it happened overnight. I'd felt this veiling, this *darkening* (*nigredo*, the blackening) drawing in since I moved into Ellen's. I didn't want to go out as for the most part I wasn't in the mood. Everything felt like too much of an effort. I just wanted to be left alone with myself.

This is why, in many indigenous cultures, the dark night of the spirit is usually left to the shaman – the healer, the outsider, the one who lives alone on the outskirts of the village who mostly keeps to themselves. Let them suffer the psychosis and tell the rest of us about it when they return to the land of the living – that's their 'job' after all.

The advantage traditional tribal cultures have over us more 'modern' technologically-oriented folk is that when someone in the tribe seemingly starts to lose the plot the shaman, all-too-familiar with the tell-tale signs of initiation, plucks them out of the tribe and packs them off to help them deal with it. He or she knows the territory because they've been there, seen it, got the T-shirt – often several times over.

In many cases the initiate is isolated and left alone to endure their spiritual crisis. Joseph Campbell, on his audio lecture, *The Inward Journey* talks about a shaman leaving an initiate alone in a tiny igloo for thirty days reappearing only every ten days to give some food to this fellow. The shaman correctly grasped there was nothing he could do except support the initiate as he endured the supernatural visitations which were now pounding at his psyche's door, day and night. His igloo served as his spiritual chrysalis, a tomb-womb in which he died and was later reborn.

Such an experience, when someone is suddenly 'called' and starts to feel as though they're losing their mental marbles is called an *auto-shamanic initiation.* The thing with these experiences is you can't choose them. Neither can you will them to happen (as if you'd even want to).

If you've gone the distance on your own Great Round of Transformation, stuck at it for years, this is the eleventh hour part of the journey when everything dies. And I mean *everything.* As earlier mentioned in *The Writer's Journey*, Christopher Vogler says if the Ordeal (in my case, the sacrifices I made going into the Athens Marathon) is the mid-term exam, then the Resurrection is the final, end of year exam. ('Thought you felt lonely and abandoned during the New York City Marathon?' said my Dreaming Psyche. 'Well wait 'til you get a load of this.')

Because – and here's the thing about personal transformation – if you're committed to going the distance, even if you're not sure where the hell it is you're going, there'll come a final test to see just how serious you are, see if you really did learn from lessons and mistakes made along the way; see how serious you are about this metamorphosis malarkey; see if – and this is what it ultimately boils down to – your old self has *died.*

Whatever it is you're destined to do you have to be strong enough to do it – mentally, emotionally, and physically. You have to prove yourself equal to and worthy of it; that you're willing to do the hard yards; that you're able to face into it with the strength, grit, and determination required; that you want it no matter how high the odds; that you're not going to bail out at the first sign of trouble. Trust me, at this stage life's going to throw just about everything it has at you. I've a half mind to rename this stage Canyon of the Wrecking Balls as it sets about pulverising your psyche to a pulp.

Based on my own experience and that of those around me who have also been mentally, physically, emotionally, and psychologically stripped to within an inch of their sanity, this is the place sacrifices have to be made whether we like it or not; where businesses fail and jobs are pulled out from under us; where the knives come out and gossips, detractors, and naysayers seize upon us with a Menaedic frenzy; where relationships are stained with tears of disillusion and disappointment; where money dries up along with our motivation; where our health falters and illness descends; where pets die, homes are downsized, and court cases are brought against us. And on, and on, and on it goes.

In fact there's a hexagram (23) in the I Ching – the ancient Chinese divination system – called, among other names, *Stripping* or *Splitting Apart* that corresponds with this stage about which Stephen Karcher says:

When you beautify things, the obligations of the old come to an end. Strip the corpse. Accept this and use the energy of Stripping. This means someone who strips away the old.

The root of Stripping is knife. It represents stripping off skin and flesh, slicing into the body and revealing the bones, uncovering the meats offered in sacrifice. There is deprivation and loss of direction and focus, imaged as a period of time spent in the grave. The outmoded and decadent spirit is displaced in preparation for the return of the new.

– *Total I Ching*

In Tarot it's the grim reaper himself, *Death*, wielding his crap-cutting, cord-severing scythe. Of death, Edward Edinger says:

[Mortificatio] literally means 'killing' and hence will refer to the experience of death. As used in religious asceticism it means 'subjection of the passions and appetites by penance, abstinence, or painful severities inflicted on the body'... Mortificatio is the most negative operation in alchemy. It has to do with darkness, defeat, torture, mutilation, death, and rotting. However, these dark images often lead over to highly positive ones – growth, resurrection, rebirth.

– *Anatomy of the Psyche*

Altogether now: happy, happy, joy, joy!

During this period dreams (nightmares) may consist of unflinching brutality, dismemberment, great floods, fires, descents to the underworld, and corpses stripped back to the bones. In your outer waking reality what you no longer need will be taken away. This includes material belongings. Relationships, too. We need only look at autumn to see nature stripping back in preparation for the greatest dark night of all – *winter*. Of shamanic initiations Mircea Eliade says:

We may give all these psychopathological crises of the elected the generic name of initiatory sicknesses because their syndrome very closely follows the classic ritual of initiation. The sufferings of the elected man are exactly like the tortures of initiation; just as, in puberty rites or rites of entrance into a secret society, the novice is 'killed' by semidivine or demonic Beings, so the future shaman sees in dreams his own body dismembered by demons; he watches them, for example, cutting off his head and tearing out his tongue.

– *Rites and Symbols of Initiation*

So it was, in the back bedroom of my parents' humble home in inner city Manchester, that I quietly went out of my bloody mind. Well, not *quite*. Thanks to the years of study I'd put in, when the demons finally came a-knocking I was somewhat 'prepared.' Not that I ever expected something like this would happen to me – after all, why should it?

I once heard told that Jung, suspecting one of his analysands was, herself, heading towards such an auto initiation, loaded her up with all the books on mythological motifs and religious symbolism he could find and recommended she brush up on it, quick smart, so that when she was flooded by the contents of the unconscious she'd have an idea of what was happening to her and wouldn't be drowned by this king tide. Suffice to say it worked and she later went on to become a psychotherapist herself acquainted as she was, now, with the Underworld.

Before she descended to the netherworld Inanna made arrangements with her loyal servant, Ninshubur, to come and get her if she hadn't returned after three days. We might look at this motif as being symbolic of the prior arrangements ego consciousness (symbolised by the bright sister, Inanna) makes by means of preparing itself before it succumbs to the unconscious (netherworld). If she hadn't made such arrangements it's unlikely she'd have ever returned to the topside world of consciousness (something which can and often does happen when people have breakdowns from which they never recover).

I knew something was really up with me when I felt my energy drop and apathy set in. I stopped reading my psychology books and read novels that required little to no mental effort. I rented a ton of movies and caught up on several old TV series I'd fallen behind on. I slept longer. I couldn't even be bothered to go on Facebook to see what everyone was up to. I just didn't *care*.

But it was when I had the following dream that I knew 'work' was about to start on my psyche. In the dream I am working for a government organisation as a policy maker. I ask if I can cut my hours so I can concentrate on my studies outside of work (depth psychology). My request is accepted. In the next scene I have difficulty writing the word MAINTENANCE on a form. I keep writing it and writing it. In accordance with my request my salary is also cut. Although expected it is still a shock.

In my notes about this dream I wrote, 'ego (policy maker) is temporarily stepping down while the psyche undergoes maintenance.' It was this dream which marked the beginning of a three-month long period of what turned out to be the richest, most intense, most profound series of dreams I've experienced since I started working with the psyche.

That this dream accompanied my tooth being yanked out in a procedure that I had to watch while two dentists sweated over me for an hour had initiation written all over it. The extraction of teeth is a classic symbol of initiatory rites (dismemberment) as *The Book of Symbols* reminds us when it says, 'sometimes, in initiatory rites, teeth were knocked out, suggesting that something of the old way of being had to be sacrificed in order to engage a new reality.'

Silly as this may sound I really didn't want to let go of that tooth. I'd been warned, back in 2002 when I had all four of my wisdom teeth removed, that this day would come. I'd had my wisdom teeth removed because they wouldn't stop growing and had begun to impact on my other teeth. After they'd been removed my dentist noticed one tooth had been traumatised and weakened by my, now extracted, monstrous molars. It was only a matter of time, he said, before it would eventually crumble and have to be extracted, too.

Ten years later, almost to the month, it did just that. But what really bothered me was I'd be left with a great big gap at the back of my mouth. Immediately after the extraction I discussed, with my dentist, the possibility of getting an implant.

'No-one can see it,' he said, looking at me as though I'd had a few too many anaesthetic injections. 'And it's not exactly cheap, either.'

My concern, however, was how it would affect my speech. It's amazing how subtle a difference the alignment of your teeth can make to the way you speak. Remove one and you can really feel the difference as your tongue lashes about in the gap once occupied by two molars. Then there was vanity. I like my teeth so this loss cramped my smile style whether anyone could see it or not.

As the weeks went on and I increasingly recognised what was going on in my psyche and that I was, in fact, undergoing something akin to an initiation, I decided to leave the gap as a mark of this period of my life. It has affected my speech, yes. It's ever-so-subtle but I can tell. I struggle saying certain words now, but that's okay. I also kept the tooth. I plan on having it made into a necklace, one day, as a further reminder of the time I was dismembered in the dentist's chair (because I'm somewhat twisted like that).

It was another dream which announced the fact my three-month long 'psychic overhaul' was now complete (halleluiah!). In the dream I am at a petrol station and my car has been fully refuelled. In the next scene I am finishing off a house renovation in Manhattan. There was a lot more to this dream but that's the essence of it.

You may recall the buildings crumbling all around me in Manhattan just before I broke up with Finn. Here we have the completion of the building work which has since taken place – most of which, judging from the many dreams involving builders and building sites, happened during this three-month period. It seemed my psyche was telling me I now have a new sense of identity (The King is dead. Long live the King!).

250

To give a flavour of what the psyche looks like while it's undergoing a simultaneous deconstruction (death) and reconstruction (rebirth), here are several dream snippets that took place during this period together with some brief notes of what these images/motifs meant to me:

- *I am in a hospital in Manhattan.*

This followed the maintenance dream and suggests my ego/persona is undergoing a psychic surgery of sorts.

- *I dream of profound blackness. I awake feeling deeply content and profoundly rested.*

Nigredo, mortificatio, and tomb-womb symbolism.

- *I am in a church graveyard at night. There is a male ghost I can clearly see and communicate with.*

Lifting of the veil between the worlds. Heightened ability to communicate with the Other.

- *A black woman wearing a green dress and silver jewellery is brutally mutilated in a knife attack to her face.*

Dismemberment of the persona as represented by the mutilation of the face. Green symbolises new growth, rebirth. Silver jewellery may symbolise the feminine.

- *White walls are being painted red.*
- *My family take in a guest for the Olympics. He mentions something to me about a ruby.*

Rubedo symbolism. The white of the *albedo* is being tinctured by the red of the *rubedo*. This symbolises the *blushing* also known as the 'blood-marriage' – the Word is finally being made flesh. This motif, of white rooms being painted red, appeared in several dreams.

- *A friend who is a tour guide is briefing me on my Tantra intentions for the next year when, suddenly, I am blinded by a light so bright and so intense I can't see.*

This dream left an incredible impression on me. I wondered how my eyes, even though I was sleeping, could experience the same physical sensation as if they'd been open and I'd been staring at the sun for too long.

251

- *I am stood talking to Michelle Obama in the kitchen about a speech I've just watched her give. While talking, I am embarrassed to find a mouse infestation under the sink. The mice are scratching at the grout between the tiles, tunnelling down. The hole they've made is huge. I fill the hole with water and try and drown them. There is one white mouse which looked a bit punkish, sporting a Mohican and lots of baby mice jumping about behind the washing machine which were breeding fast.*

I had a lot of mouse animal symbolism during this time. Of mice, from *The Book of Symbols* we learn that, 'they personify the labyrinthine restlessness beneath the surface of things ... mice are suggestive of the small, invisible, intricate workings of the unconscious to overcome obstacles, even without our conscious participation.' Remember Vasilisa's doll, Psyche's ants, and Cinderella's birds? Here the mice symbolise the same thing for me.

- *A friend who is a make-up artist is helping me prepare for a celebratory party. Elsewhere in the dream, Cinderella is mentioned.*
- *I see a sheer tunic dress in a shop window. The shop owner recommends against me buying it as she says I have a large bust and it wouldn't flatter me (I'd look like a sack). She recommends a more streamlined dress. At the end of the dream a member of my staff received a call from Givenchy offering me a tailor-made gown.*
- *I am working as waiting staff. I want to leave early but stay on until the very end of the shift at which point I am offered a 'Cinderella' luxury tropical holiday package which would leave immediately.*

Watch out for a change of clothes in dreams and stories: they often represent a change of state. Think of the movie *Pretty Woman* when Julia Roberts's character goes shopping. 'You shall go to the ball!'

- *There are many builders who are building an observatory in the middle of an airfield. They complete it incredibly fast and celebrate on finishing.*

Reconstruction, reconstruction, reconstruction. There were countless interior design, renovation, and construction dreams during this period.

- *I am running laps around a square-shaped garden in the centre of Manchester.*

(The square is a mandala which, in Jungian psychology, often symbolises the Self – a motif further amplified by the fact the dream was set in my birth city.)

- *I am preparing to get married in a stately home. Mention of TV series, Coronation Street. My groom is a dark-skinned, unknown man. I express concern at the venue not being religious/spiritual enough. I complain my dress is too elaborate for such a venue. I realise I'm afraid and am making excuses. The marriage is going ahead whether I'm ready or not. It is already booked and paid for. The groom tells me I can't back out now as we have 5,000 guests coming to the reception.*

This was a Big Dream. What particularly caught my eye, though, was the number '5,000'; especially as a couple of nights earlier the number '50' had been highlighted. This hundred-fold increase alerted me to an alchemical stage called *multiplicatio*. Jesus's miracle in which he fed the 5,000 symbolises *multiplicatio* about which Edinger says:

To some extent, the consciousness of an individual who is related to the Self seems to be contagious and tends to multiply itself to others. The I Ching speaks of such a phenomenon:

Contemplation of the divine meaning underlying the workings of the universe gives to the man who is called upon to influence others the means of producing like effects. This requires that power in inner concentration which religious contemplation develops in great men strong in faith. It enables them to apprehend the mysterious and divine laws of life, and by means of profoundest inner concentration they give expression to these laws in their own persons. Thus a hidden spiritual power emanates from them, influencing and dominating others without their being aware of how it happens.

– Anatomy of the Psyche

This further reminds me of what D. T. Suzuki says about the old man who has achieved Satori (enlightenment) and for whom the cherry trees blossom wherever he goes:

Entering the City with Bliss-Bestowing Hands, the last of the 'Ten Ox-herding Pictures' of Zen Buddhism, represents the culmination of individuation: 'And now having moved through the stage of emptiness, and also having seen God in the world of nature, the individual can see God in the world of men.' Enlightened mingling in the market place with 'wine-bibbers and butchers' (publicans and sinners), he recognises the 'inner light' of 'Buddha-nature' in everyone. He doesn't need to hold himself aloof nor to be weighted down by a sense of duty or responsibility, nor to follow a set of patterns of other holy men, nor to imitate the past. He is so in harmony with life that he is content to be inconspicuous, to be an instrument, not a leader. He simply does what seems to him natural. But though in the market place he seems to be an ordinary man, something happens to the people among who he mingles. They too become part of the harmony of the universe.

– Manual of Zen Buddhism

The blossoming of the cherry trees is another motif of *multiplicatio* in that he's able to 'influence and dominate others without their being aware of how it happens.' In other words it's not what he says; rather, his sheer *beingness* allows others to reconnect with their own innate source. The Self shines forth through him (radiates from him, you might say) without him even having to say or do anything. You might say that in his presence individuals are made to feel like a 'flower that has got its bloom back' (as one friend described it).

But to achieve a true sacred marriage – the inner marriage of soul and spirit, Shakti and Shiva, the Great Coniunctio, the Philosopher's Stone – your ego has to die to its old, infantile self-serving wants and desires and surrender completely and unquestioningly to the Self.

This is why this final Resurrection ordeal is experienced as death because, from the ego's perspective, it *is* a death – it (ego) must sacrifice itself in order to give its life over to the Other (Self) which is why you'll be taken to the absolute brink and have everything stripped away. (And to think this all started with me wanting better sex. Honestly.)

Question is, are you going to try and hold on to your material belongings, your job, your car, your house, your position at work? Are you going to wail and flail and cry out in self-pity, 'It's not fair' and 'Why me?' Or are you willing to sacrifice it for the Self?

Most people want what I call 'transformation lite' – they want all the perks without having to make any of the sacrifices. Well I have news for you – it ain't happening. ('Just how much have you got to give up?' Bing asked me one day. 'Everything,' I thought.) It's not for no good reason they call it the Hero's Journey, after all.

Anyway, as mentioned, these dreams are a mere taster of what went on during this time. What made this period even more challenging was how, apart from my sore mouth, everything in my life seemed to die, pack up, or break down. Neither was I making a bean – nothing, zip, nada (something my maintenance dream had warned me about). I'd had a couple of clients but since I'd moved back to my parents' place everything had gone quiet on that front, too. My life felt like tumbleweed.

But one of my darkest moments coincided with a dream in which a group of people had been hanged from trees by a godfather-like figure in an act of retribution. One of the men reminded me of the actor, John Goodman.

I don't think I have to spell out which 'good man' was hanged from a tree (another symbol for the cross). But the hanging symbolism didn't end there. Later that night I watched a movie which, unbeknown to me, featured multiple hangings. Talk about ram the message home. Suffice to say I went to bed feeling pretty low that night. It was all I could do not to start singing, 'You just keep me hanging on.' Because that's how I felt: like I was hanging around – *waiting*. But waiting for what?

What I failed to remember was it wasn't just Christ who was crucified on a cross or Odin who sacrificed himself by hanging on Yggdrasil, the world tree, but Inanna too who, after being killed by her sister, Ereshkigal, was left to hang on a stake and rot (*mortificatio, putrefactio*) for three days (there's that number again – the number of mounting momentum).

Meanwhile, no sooner has Ereshkigal killed her sister than she starts wailing about the place as though mourning herself (which, technically, she is – Inanna being her sister, her bright aspect). In this story we have the ego (Inanna) voluntarily descending, submitting to the depths, and sacrificing itself to the unconscious (Ereshkigal) so that it might die and be reborn.

In a roundabout way this is what I'd done, too. I knew something in me had to die, that I had to sacrifice my old self-serving, lust-driven ways (situated down in my lower three chakras), so that they might be transmuted.

Not that I'd consciously thought any of this through or planned it in any detail. But just as I'd sacrificed all comforts heading into the Athens Marathon when I decided to face my innermost fears head on, I thought I'd do something similar heading into Ecstasy. It's only now, on reflection, that I can see what I was doing. At the time I just thought I'd turn myself back on myself, spend several months celibate, and see what, if anything, happened.

This several month period was definitely the right time to conduct this 'experiment' as all around me everyone (all my friends, everyone on the TV, everyone in the entire bloody world) still seemed to be loved up, having lots of (mind-blowing) sex, canoodling with loved ones, and generally enjoying their bag of Aphroditic tricks. Meanwhile, Tess the Tantric Tortoise, here, was single and living in my parents' back bedroom strumming *I Can't Get No Satisfaction* on my labial lyre like a lovelorn troubadour. The fact I perceived everyone else to be having a good time pissed me off. And I mean *really* pissed me off. It wasn't fair. Nothing was fair. (*What was it I said years ago? 'Make me an instrument of thy peace?' And for what, I ask you? For what? Well SCREW YOU.*)

I knew I'd obviously hit on something by how angry I felt – angry about *everything*. I banged about my box-shaped bedroom like a woman possessed. When I didn't feel as though my psyche was being assaulted I was feeling sorry for myself. What a mixed bag of shitty, conflicting emotions I was. The feeling sorry for myself stemmed from the fact that my heart was still in bits over my breakup with Finn and, try as I might, I couldn't put the damned thing back together again. As the year wore on it seemed to get worse and *worse*.

It was this hypocritical behaviour which puzzled even me. I'd had a fling, I'd ended the relationship, I'd since decided to sacrifice all sexual liaisons for a poxy seven and a half months (from my liaison with Oscar through to Ecstasy) and now here I was feeling sorry for myself. Sorry, skint, and spotty.

The acne outbreak I experienced during this time was, hands down, the worst of my life. Not even as a teenager had I experienced anything like this. I caught my aunt peeking at me one day from out the corner of my eye while we were out walking together.

'What are you looking at?' I hissed.

'Nothing,' she said. 'Well, actually, your jaw. Are they sore? They look it.'

Because these weren't spots – these were boils: boils oozing puss all over my jawline and neck. This was a healing crisis par excellence. All the shit was coming to the surface. I looked *awful*. So even if I'd wanted to engage in any sexual shenanigans, I'd have had no chance as no man would have come near me with a barge-pole (except, perhaps, to lance one of my boils). It's like Catherine MacCoun says:

> **Alchemy makes a mess of the kitchen. If your intention is to transmute poison into medicine, you're going to have poison lying around. The raw instincts of the unconscious will have to come to the surface before they can be transformed into qualities. While this is going on, they will be evident to others as well as yourself. It's embarrassing.**

> *– On Becoming an Alchemist*

But it wasn't just about being embarrassed – I couldn't have gone out even if I wanted to as I didn't have any money. Most of my clothes were also threadbare leaving my self-confidence in tatters (I'd been a bit too ruthless during my last clear out leaving me with fewer clothes than I realised). Throw in the never-ending downpour of rain the UK was also experiencing and the whole thing was a washout of Noah's Ark proportions.

Shortly after my 'refuelled car' dream – by which time my anger had finally subsided and I'd completely given up by impersonating a vegetable – while wondering when this interminable apathy and self-pity would end my friend, Nina, emailed me details of a mythology workshop she'd be attending in Paris the week after my Tantra workshop.

She asked if I'd be interested in attending it along with her and her family. As much as I'd have loved to go I just felt too sorry for myself. Neither did I want to admit that I had no money. I didn't want to burden her sunny disposition with my miserable spotty-arsed self, so I thanked her for letting me know about it and left it at that.

But the strange thing was I'd recently had a hankering to visit Paris again. I'd even watched Woody Allen's *Midnight in Paris* a couple of nights before she'd emailed. Though barely perceptible, it felt like spring was returning to a corner of my psyche. Whatever it was I *really* wanted to go.

After reading the tour itinerary I wondered if Big might be interested in attending and so I forwarded the email to him. This, though, was when I did something most out of character for me. In my email I mentioned it was something I would have liked to do but couldn't afford as my finances were at 'an all-time low.' What you have to understand about me is I'm a very proud person. Even if I'm struggling, I won't let on. My way of dealing with such situations is to withdraw from the world and just keep to myself.

To let this slip, especially to someone like Big, revealed a rare crack of vulnerability on my behalf. So when he emailed straight back asking if I needed any help I was both surprised at his offer and warmed – especially as we'd barely spoken in months (I sensed he was in a place of *being* rather than *doing* so had left him to it). I asked him what he meant by 'help.'

'Financial help,' he came back. 'Need a few quid?' After squirming about the house for half an hour or so I decided to swallow my pride and say yes – especially as my laptop also needed replacing (on account of the key Finn broke and the fact that mum was now regularly hijacking it). Then there was my Tantra workshop to pay for. I was in dire need of some new clothes. And my iPod had died taking several treasured lectures with it. Even my umbrella had been blown inside out. (When I say everything died or broke that summer I mean *everything*.)

When he emailed over the figures he was willing to lend me, I was shocked at his generosity. But it was the reply he wrote after I'd told him his offer had made me squirm which left me in tears:

And absolutely no need to squirm. I used to be a banker, remember? Trained to identify good people worthy of support and help bridge the gap in their finances knowing that, ultimately, you would be paid back and, in the meantime, feel good about your contribution to the creative process!

It was the synchronicity of it all that got me, though. Had Nina not emailed me details of the Paris trip – a friend who reappeared in my life right around the time I was breaking up with Finn – I would never have forwarded it on to Big and, consequently, opened up about my financial woes which led him to offer me a loan. This is what I mean by allies who appear at critical times of the Hero's Journey in order to help them complete their 'mission' (a stage Joseph Campbell calls Rescue from Without). Once you say *yes* to the adventure you're never as alone as you think – even if all other lights seem to have gone out.

The decision I now faced was how much to borrow. I asked him what the terms and conditions were. 'Islamic banking,' he replied (in other words, no interest). 'Pay me as and when you can.'

I took the weekend to think it over and cost up everything which had broken down and worn away. Much to my surprise there was a lot. I'd have to spend a fair bit just to bring me back up to scratch, pay my family the back rent I owed them etc. But I still wasn't entirely sure whether borrowing money was the best idea especially as I had no idea how or when I'd pay him back.

Then I had an epiphany: what if this reflected an opportunity to take a gamble – *on myself*? Whatever amount I borrowed would symbolise a self-investment and also reflect the confidence I felt about my eventual ability to repay him.

If, on the other hand, I refused his offer it would show my resistance in accepting help from the Other (the 'not me,' of which Big is a part). By refusing him I'd be blocking the flow of life. And as I'd recently learnt, it takes great strength to receive and say yes to life, to say yes to the Other. Besides, everyone needs a little help from time to time – there's nothing wrong or shameful about that. Every hero needs the assistance of others to help bring their, by now, bone-weary backside home.

With that realisation I decided to swallow my pride and went for the highest amount he'd offered. Within an hour the money was in my bank and I was straight down the shops buying new, much-needed clothes, a new iPod, a ton of specialist psychology books, and an all-singing, all-dancing custom-made laptop.

It was only on later reflection I realised that whereas Cinderella had a fairy godmother, here I was being bankrolled by an ex banker (remember my dream of a year earlier with the banker who worked at the Cooperative

Bank?): a man who, when he first appeared in my life, I suspected there might be more to than first met the eye – and I was absolutely right.

So after several months of *wintering* and generally feeling sorry for myself; after several months of self-imposed sacrifice and being psychologically dismembered, it was time to don my glad rags and go have a *ball*.

ECSTASIS, CATHARSIS

When an email about Ecstasy appeared in my inbox I dropped what I was doing and flapped about the house like a headless flibbertigibbet. They sure know how to unnerve a woman (in the best possible way).

This is, after all, the big one – the fifth and final workshop marking the culmination of what had been, for me, an eighteen-month long journey. Here's Shakti Tantra online blurb:

> This advanced workshop is available to all women and men who have completed level four of our women's and mixed programmes. During Ecstasy we gain a direct experience and deeper understanding of the mystical union between Shakti and Shiva in their highest potential. We will have the opportunity to explore the subtlety and fineness of both male and female pleasure and meet each other in our divine essence.

Of this mystical union (sacred marriage), Nancy Qualls-Corbett says:

> Psychologically, the sacred marriage symbolises the union of opposites. It is the coming together, in equal status, of the masculine and feminine principles, the conjoining of consciousness and unconsciousness, of spirit and matter. It is the mystical process by which disconnected elements are joined together to form a whole. In the consummation of the hieros gamos, sexuality and spirituality are integral aspects, each drawing vitality from the other ... On the transpersonal level, the sacred marriage extends beyond the boundaries of human understanding. One is united with the divine, the source and the power of love. Through the mystical union a portion of divine love is received and contained within oneself. In the act of sacrifice to a greater authority, earthly values, such as ego desires or identification with power, are

transformed into a capacity to love on a plane which surpasses human reasoning.

– The Sacred Prostitute

By the time this workshop rolled around I'd had several dreams which pointed to this sacred marriage on an inner level: white walls had been painted red; I was given a signet ring to wear by a king as a mark of his authority; there was mention of ruby stones and ruby earrings were firmly fixed in my ears; there had been several weddings and sacred-sexual unions, and my legs had been tattooed with red marks. This increased *reddening* in my psychic interior indicated a *rubedo*, a *coagulatio*, a 'blood-marriage,' as inspiration took up permanent residence in my heart – the seat of the soul.

In Bernini's sculpture of St Theresa reeling in ecstasy, for example, the angel is aiming the spear at her heart, not her sex. This is why I say it takes great strength to receive, to surrender, to open your heart to the penetration of the Other and give your life over to something greater than you in the ego sense, because the vessel that is your soul (your body) has to be strong enough and to have been sufficiently prepared to withstand such an ecstatic union and/or influx of inspiration (the latter of which many artists and creatives speak of when, after years of practising their craft, they suddenly find themselves 'overtaken' by a force that seems to write them, dance them, inspire them far beyond any level they've ever known before).

Having said that, if none of this talk of sacred marriage makes sense, don't worry. Many couldn't care less about mystical unions; they have quite enough on their plates trying to open their hearts and surrender to a human other in a relationship, let alone a divine Other. One step at a time.

Anyway this workshop fast became known as 'The blokes are coming!' (and no, that isn't a euphemism) as experienced Shivas (male Tantrikas) were scheduled to join us halfway through our week-long workshop to help us complete our training. This I couldn't wait for.

I'd been itching to work with men in a sacred setting since the end of Women Behaving Badly. I was ready to be reacquainted with the otherness of men at a more mature level. Throw in the fact I'd been nowhere near a man for seven and a half months and I relished the opportunity for a conscious reconnection in an environment conducive to mutual respect and honouring.

I have a deep affinity for women and the female form. The walls of my parents' home are adorned with countless paintings of women in varying states of undress and nudes by, among many others, Toulouse-

Lautrec and Schiele (unlike mum, my aunt has a great love of women in their varied shapes and sizes). But it wasn't until I'd immersed myself in the realm of the feminine over a prolonged period of time that I realised how much I appreciated the difference between males and females for, as Qualls-Corbett goes on to say:

> **In order for a union to take place, two distinct opposites must exist. The masculine and feminine principles must first be differentiated ... this sacred marriage can only occur after there has been a differentiation of the masculine and the feminine principles.**

> *– The Sacred Prostitute*

When I talk about the 'other' and 'otherness' this is what I mean. It's not something I would have consciously thought about before this women's training programme, but since doing this work I've come to appreciate the otherness of men, how different their bodies are from ours, their whole way of being. They now seem even more magnificent to me.

When Hilly's email arrived I mulled over my intentions for this workshop. One of the first questions I asked myself was: 'How does my sexuality *feel* right now?' I realised it had changed. Since hanging out in the Underworld I'd felt a shift in my sexuality: I was darker now – not in a 'bad' way; neither was I trying to be outrageous, shocking, or sexually overt. As opposed to the lighter Aphroditic, beatific, romantic end of the sexual spectrum, it now felt dark and slippery, seductive, erotic, and wet, red and black, shadowy and slithery, labyrinthine, low-lying, intense – quietly so. Then I nailed the word which summed it up – *scorpionic*.

Whereas I burst out of myself at Women Behaving Badly and exploded across the walls like a Venusian volcano, this felt entirely different. This was the conscious controlled rise of the chthonic; the bitter taste of pomegranates and skin tainted with the netherworld; this was the rise of the initiated Dark Feminine.

While out walking and pondering how I wanted to approach a particular structure, I 'got into character' by listening to a song by Massive Attack called *Danny the Dog*: a dark, brooding piece which, for me, taps into such scorpionic energy. It was a technique I'd employed during my method acting days whenever I was attempting to get closer to the feeling tone of the character I was playing.

I also watched movies such as *Black Swan* and Bertrand Bonello's *House of Tolerance* as part of my pre-workshop 'warm-up.' I was looking for inspiration to help give me the courage necessary to embody my newfound scorpionic sexuality.

262

I also sensed I was 'bigger' now: which was why my other intention for this workshop was to honour my truth by merging my theatricality, sexuality, and intellectuality. I didn't care if anyone got what I was doing or not, or if they thought I was trying to show off or take over. As with Athens I knew that, with this workshop, I had the chance to finally face all my innermost fears and insecurities. In my journal I wrote that I wished 'to align with, and honour, my innermost truth as opposed to attempting to please, pacify, impress, or play a role for another/s.' I also wanted to hold the intention throughout the workshop that 'I *do* deserve.'

With that, I set about preparing and gathering together what I needed to bring my larger-than-life, ritualistic plans to fruition (which, by the way, ended up being an *incredible* if terrifying experience – but I'm *so* glad I was true to myself).

Finally, though I didn't share it in the opening circle I also wrote out one of my favourite passages by Marion Woodman which I referred to throughout the course of the week. I wanted to honour her teachings and influence on my journey by keeping her close by:

In ancient rites
we would have met the mystery
in an underground passage,
an inner surrender
to our deepest eroticism.

Giving up desire,
in aloneness and despair
we would have surrendered
to what we believed was death.
We would have known the coming together
of matter and spirit
of human and divine:
a love marriage with the god.

We cannot go back.
We cannot go back to the ancient mysteries.
Yet we can make the journey
below and back again.
We can know the light in our darkness
can find again, within our body,
the sacred mystery.

– Coming Home to Myself

As usual I'm not going to say what we did or disclose anything which went on. But I will share a few of my own random, curious, and delicious experiences.

The first happened after doing a root chakra (*muladhara*) exercise when my nose suddenly and inexplicably flared up with intense heat – my right nostril, to be precise. I know I'm a fire dragon in Chinese astrology but this took it to whole new levels. For a moment I was convinced I'd start snorting flames.

After the structure, while out walking with my friend Grace I asked her if she could feel my hot nostril. She said it felt a bit warmer but couldn't really tell. With my head held back I tried cooling it down with the breeze blowing in off the Atlantic Ocean. What I didn't discover, until much later, is that the base chakra is connected to the nose. Apparently it's something to do with the sense of smell being connected to our survival instincts which is what the root chakra's associated with. Why it made my nose flare up so intensely with heat I still don't know (for someone who's supposed to be a Reiki teacher I'm a bit rusty on the old chakra front). Still, I thought it was curious.

The next experience happened the following morning in meditation – something I'd hitherto struggled with. Although I've never been interested in chasing transcendent experiences I have, nevertheless, been graced with several eye-opening, mind-shattering moments – this being one of them. Describing it isn't going to come anywhere near what I experienced or how it left me feeling but it'll give you a bit of an idea.

So I'm sat there when, suddenly, these two face outlines (similar to the statue of Janus) appear from out of nowhere and start moving towards one another. There wasn't any great detail to them: all I knew was one was female and the other one male. But as they moved towards one another I grew frightened. In a flash of intuition I knew that, should these two faces merge, something big would happen. But no sooner had I 'voiced' my fear when a non-voice voice replied, 'Stay calm, you can hold this' then – BOOM – the faces merged, my head exploded, and I burst into space.

I say 'burst into space' as, if you can imagine something spontaneously combusting, bursting into flames, that was how my consciousness felt; except there was no 'I' – just... *space*. Boundless, without form, I was space – *all of it*. I don't know how long I was out of it or how long it lasted. All I do know was when I finally got my head together I was wearing a stupid grin and spent the rest of the day floating about. On a scale of one to ten of 'far out man' moments this was definitely a ten.

The other peculiar experience came during one of the ritual structures we did with the men. I've practised different body-oriented exercises over the years during which you're encouraged to reconnect with various body parts, ask them what they want. At first it feels nothing short of ridiculous as you strike up a 'conversation' with whichever body part it is. But I'd never heard my body 'talk back,' not really – that is, until now. Because it was during this ritual that I first heard my yoni 'speak up.'

'Him,' she said, clearly and calmly. 'I like him.'

I thought I was losing the plot as this voice from the depths interrupted my Zen-like calm and offered me its opinion on one of the men. The bursting into space experience I could handle but this body-talk business was unchartered territory. To be clear when I say my yoni spoke up the only way I can describe it was I heard an inner voice and in that split second I knew exactly where it had originated from. It was as though the voice itself had roots which I could feel and, in that same split-second, trace back to their source. *Am I going out of my mind?*

'No,' replied my yoni, 'I like him.'

I wouldn't mind if I was turned on, but I wasn't – not remotely. There was nothing sexual about what we were doing; if anything the atmosphere was quite solemn. Neither had I particularly noticed this chap until this point as we hadn't worked together. For a rational, logical person this sort of stuff freaks me out. I'd heard the idea the mind is located in every cell of the body and that 'your body speaks your mind,' but c'mon – *seriously?*

Step aside The Vagina Monologues this was My Vagina's Monologue and now she wouldn't shut up, firing off a steady stream of comments. For a moment or two I was afraid to look down in case I saw a deviant creation from Jim Henson's Creature Shop staring up at me.

Suffice to say I took no notice. Until, that is, the following morning. Prior to doing the structure I'd made arrangements to travel home with Sarah, the honey-voiced one. But over breakfast she told me she'd changed her travel plans and suggested I ask LL – the guy my yoni had been yakking on about – if I could, perhaps, travel back with him. I nicknamed him 'LL' because all the Ladies *Lurved* him – a fact I later found out.

In light of this turn of events, I found myself inwardly consulting my yoni. (*Should I travel home with him? What made you say that last night?*) Listening to the opinion of body parts is the sort of behaviour that has folks carted off to padded climes, so the fact I was now curious about my vulva's point of view worried me. I was convinced I was going out of my mind – which, in a way, I *was*: out of my mind and deeper into my body.

By the way, I don't expect you to believe any of this. If I'd have read someone saying their vajra or yoni had a mind – and voice – of its own, I'd have immediately dismissed them as a stark, raving nutter and filed them away under Avoid At All Costs. But though I may make light of what happened I would later be humbled by my body's foresight and wisdom.

Anyway, one of the other women who lived near me said she'd also changed her travel plans and would now be travelling straight home and that I was welcome to join her. Being the Artemis-identified woman that I am and, as such, loyal to the sisterhood, had she been travelling alone I'd have gone with her. But as she had company courtesy of another of the women who was staying at her house I decided to travel back with LL who was on his own. So, with some trepidation (as I didn't really know him), I asked him whether he'd like some company to which he said, yes, he'd be most grateful, especially as you tend to leave these workshops in a somewhat altered state. With that it was settled – my yoni had had her way.

Back in ritual space, we were presented with the opportunity to 'let something go.' Thankfully it was a long ritual as it took me an absolute age to think of something I wanted to release. But what I didn't want to do was squander the moment, waste it on something meaningless or superficial. Then, finally, it hit me – Finn. There couldn't have been a better, more reverential atmosphere in which to let go of him and the ghost of our relationship past.

The more I thought about it the more I realised I wanted so dearly to let go of the pain, the insecurities, and all the other barriers, conscious and unconscious which kept me from healing and moving on. I wanted to open my heart again and to love completely, fully, and with absolute and utter abandon.

When I admitted I wanted to open up and love again I immediately felt my heart's vulnerability, its fear, its trepidation, its utter dread about revealing itself, of losing control, and surrendering, not just to the divine Other, but to a human other. Yes, Finn's emotional and physical withdrawal had turned me back on myself and brought me back into a loving relationship with myself and the Self; but I also realised, after a long, dark winter, that I was finally ready to open my heart and love again.

By doing so – by saying yes to love – I knew I'd also be saying yes to sorrow and sadness and disappointment and all the other inevitable heart-breaking disillusionments which accompany it. But I'd also be saying yes to joy and to pleasure and to happiness. By opening my heart to love I'd be opening my heart to life, but I was ready now, so ready, to open my heart fully to love *and* to life so that they might yield their fruits at both a personal and a transpersonal level.

By honouring myself by not diving out of one relationship and straight into another; by not leaping out of one man's bed and straight into another's I'd rekindled a quiet, resolute sense of self-worth, self-belief, and self-love – all of which would stand me in good stead once I eventually met someone else.

So, in heartfelt supplication, I offered up a prayer of thanks and with deep gratitude and love I released Finn and let go of our relationship before finally saying: *I surrender, I'm all yours. Here's my heart, it's all yours – I'm ready to receive.*

Later that day, at the end of the workshop, and after one of the most incredible weeks of my life, Hilly, Sue, Sarah, and the other assistants thanked and honoured each of us for the journey we had taken. We'd done it. We'd finished what we'd started.

'Now, go into the world,' Hilly said, 'hold your heads up high and be the queens that you are. Beggars no more, your cups are full. Never forget that.'

After saying goodbye to everyone, I jumped in the car with LL and we set off on our long drive home. It turned out my yoni was onto something after all as we spent the next several hours engrossed in stimulating conversation spanning a breadth of spiritually and mythically-oriented subjects about which I had no idea he was interested in.

One of my biggest light-bulb moments to come out of the workshop was just how bound up my intellect is with my sexuality. Mental stimulation arouses my attention and, frankly, turns me on. I *so* appreciate a conversation where the sparks are flying and the banter's bouncing back and forth. Doesn't matter what's being discussed just so long as there's an underlying passion to the words being shared. God knows why it's taken me this long to figure this out – better late than never.

So while talking with LL it dawned on me that this conversation was making me tingle and getting me het up – in all the *right* ways. I'd barely noticed this guy in the workshop such was his quiet, unassuming, almost mouse-like nature (compared with my, now, vociferous, leonine manner). I was fast getting a lesson in how I shouldn't judge a book by a cover.

When we stopped at a service station to grab a coffee, halfway through our journey, I laid aside my previous dilly-dallying, dithering tendencies and asked him, outright, if I could stay with him that night. He'd already booked into a hotel at a motorway service station nearby where I lived in order to break up his journey. Smiling, he told me he'd like that very much.

The thing about the men we'd worked with at this workshop was how different they were to those I'd met before. These were mature, humble men committed to honouring both the masculine and feminine within themselves and in the other (females). If the greater culture had been witness to the mutual honouring, respect, and love that was manifested in our workshop, if they could see what men and women are ultimately capable of when they meet one another at their highest, most heart-felt potential, our world would be transformed, and radically so, overnight. I was privy to scenes of hope, beauty, and profound sacrality that will carry me for the rest of my life. This was radical, powerful, transformational work of the highest and most inspiring degree.

It was, for these reasons, and many more, that I wished now to be further acquainted with LL, to 'know' him. So perhaps I shouldn't have been surprised that, when we finally came together, I experienced one of the most nourishing, exquisite, and heartfelt honourings I had ever known. In the words of Emily Dickinson:

> To my small Hearth His fire came –
> And all my House aglow
> Did fan and rock, with sudden light –
> 'Twas Sunrise – 'twas the Sky –

He pored over my body as though a scholar absorbing long-lost, sacred texts. He considered me, my wants, my desires; he soothed me, held me. Like waves on the ocean we rocked, flowing back and forth in a sea of bliss. Entrusting myself to his tender-handed care my body felt replete, open, relaxed, and, for the first time in my life, *vulnerable* – something I had never truly felt before with another. Never.

I surrendered, wholeheartedly surrendered and it was then that, for the very first time, I felt my heart open, expand, and burst back into life in a way that momentarily took my breath away. And to think I'd previously thought intimate unions could amount to little more than a sex-stirring orgasm. Finally, I understood what Anaïs Nin meant when she said, 'Only the united beat of sex and heart together can create *ecstasy*.'

It was the most fulfilling and delicious sexual experience I'd ever had, but it also marked a pivotal turning point in that I remained utterly present and in the moment. I didn't try to drag it out or hope I might see him again for I knew, deep down, what this was – a preview: a reanimating *kiss of life*.

But it wasn't until the following day that it suddenly hit me – we hadn't had penetrative sex. Because we hadn't made orgasm the goal, as had been the case in previous sexual liaisons, I'd relaxed and, in doing so, my heart had expanded and I'd completely surrendered. And as I later said to a friend, 'You expand when the pressure's off.'

As soon as I arrived back home I started preparing and packing for my trip to Paris where I'd be heading out, a couple of days later, to meet my friend, Nina – a trip I could now afford, thanks to the generosity of my cooperative fairy Godbanker. But not before I received a call from my friend Kwasi: he wanted to speak to me as soon as possible as he had some 'important news.'

As I was running to a dental appointment I missed his call. I later texted him to say I'd ring him when I was back from Paris. But what caught my attention was his sense of urgency. This wasn't like Kwasi. He's one of the most laid-back guys I know so I wondered what important news he may have.

Then I remembered an earlier intuition I'd had – namely, that, if I went deep enough into my (Tantra) work, all the way down into my body's roots, I'd eventually end up in the realm of the ancestors: those ancestors being my Ghanaian ancestors. So the fact he rang me the day after our fifth and final workshop had ended alerted me to the fact that something was up. Meantime, I wrote a wee piece about my experience at Ecstasy:

ECSTASY: WORKSHOP REVIEW

'The body is an instrument which only gives off music when it is used as a body. Always an orchestra, and just as music traverses walls, so sensuality traverses the body and reaches up to ecstasy.'

– Anaïs Nin

This training makes a woman out of you.
W. O. M. A. N.
I'll say it again.
This is the level you realise you've been living a half-life, telling yourself half-truths, accepting half-realised, half-conscious relationships; the level where the wheat is absolutely, unapologetically separated from the chaff; the level where you are introduced to your utmost potentiality, the fullness of your being; the level after which there is no going back – which is why not everyone can go the distance. Some drop out after level one; others complete all the workshops up to level four. But Ecstasy is a level all to itself. You cannot begin to imagine the depth, beauty, and sacredness of what we experienced at this level. No wonder it felt like Last Woman Standing.

I was fortunate enough to be graced with several mind-shattering, ecstatic moments. As always, I can't say anything about the structures, rituals, or ceremonies in which we participated. In the spirit of the ancient mystery religions these aren't experiences to be shared with the uninitiated. Even those who have gone as far as level four (Women of Substance) would be surprised at how much the ante is upped at Ecstasy. Which is what makes the group of women with whom I did this workshop all the more magnificent and formidable: these were women who had the courage to stand in the fire of their fears and finish what they started.

This was where 'real' Tantra took centre stage and we stepped into a timeless, sacred, ritual space of embodied wisdom steeped in numinosity and mystery; a space where the Other is consciously, lovingly honoured. Yes, this is the level where Shakti finally meets Shiva – both without and within. And what a heartfelt, conscious meeting it was.

We descended into the depths, plumbed the bowels of our innermost being. You want to ride the lift to the topmost, transcendent floor of Ecstasy? Well, the only way in is at the ground floor. We're talking base chakra, baby.

We revelled in love and acceptance, were honoured and honouring, were overwhelmed by blissful experiences that had us rolling about like sirens while wearing Cheshire cat grins. We travelled across space and time, through eastern and western cultures, sat with the ancestors, evoked the old time religions. We purged deep-rooted, unconscious hurts, worked through headaches, let go of heartache.

We laughed and cried, argued and made up; went stir crazy from sleep deprivation; filled up on porridge and prunes while discussing the previous night's dreams; crammed a sauna in the middle of the night and sang our hearts out; took midnight walks by the ocean and drank in the Milky Way while wishing on shooting stars. At times we were nervous as hell but got on with it anyway and did so with grace, dignity, maturity, and a single-minded determination.

I'm still processing the events of the week. In fact, my memories are so precious to me, I feel any attempt to share even a smidgeon of what I experienced somehow desacralises, dilutes, and dishonours them. I want to draw a protective arm around them (memories) and hold them close to my heart away from the prying eyes and ears of others. I don't feel it's an exaggeration to say I feel grateful to be alive and experience what I did at this level. I'm grateful from the bottom of my being.

But, I do want to say this: if you want to live your life as fully as possible do this work. If you do this work go all the way. Then you will know how it feels to shine from the inside out, to be animated from soul to bone. Then you will know the truth of your Being and you will experience, not just your own magnificence, but the magnificence of the sacred Other. And when you leave the workshop you will walk out the door and know this is just the beginning of a life fully lived.

Then you will know **Ecstasy**.

* * *

The crowning moment of my journey to the Underworld, however, happened while I was in Paris. We'd already visited Chartres Cathedral where I paid my respects to Our Lady of the Pillar – the same one I'd seen a month before I consciously/unconsciously signed up for Shakti Tantra's women's programme. It seemed fitting and poignant, somehow, to bookend either side of my initiation with visits to this Black Madonna – the Dark Mother, Queen of the Underworld.

Though frequently challenging I felt she'd guided me, taken me deep into the folds of her chrysalis-like tomb-womb, before safely delivering me out the other end – *twice born* (much like in the dream where I opened the door at the end of a long, pitch-black passage).

A couple of days later Nina and I were in Le Bon Marché, a fancy, upmarket department store on the Left Bank, checking out clothes, when I noticed one of the sales assistants, a woman, staring at me – *really* staring at me. Embarrassed and somewhat amused I disappeared behind a rack of clothes to escape her prolonged, penetrative gaze while I waited for Nina who was in the changing rooms trying on tops.

So when Nina took her clothes to this woman to pay for them I knew there'd be no escaping her. But it was then that she said something which made me smile all the way down into the soles of my feet.

To my friend, Nina, she said, 'You are very beautiful. But she,' she said, now turning to me in unabashed admiration, 'she is a *queen.*'

And so it was, in a land without a monarchy – which even when it had one only ever had kings – that the announcement rang out to herald the return of spring:

The Kore is dead. Long live the Queen!

SANKOFA

On my return from Paris I went to Kwasi's for dinner to hear about his big news.

As I got ready to go and see him, though, I noticed I was dragging my feet. Something in me felt incredibly resistant for reasons unknown. It was also during the walk over to his place that I felt, for the first time, I was 'with book' in the way a woman might say she's with child. This was new. Normally I have to camp out in front of my laptop and wait for inspiration to strike. But I could already feel the book's form inside of me and that it was very clear about what it wanted to say.

I knew I'd write a follow-up book to *Running into Myself*, but I'd never thought about when I might sit down and write it, when the right time might be. On a subliminal level I think I'd been waiting for a sign of some sort to tell me I'd come full circle on my journey, that it was time to put fingers to keyboard.

When I finally arrived at Kwasi's I felt incredibly nervous about what his news might be. This was the first time I'd ever been to his place. We normally only ever met up in town for drinks so this only added to my anxiety. He'd cooked me traditional Ghanaian fare of rice, lamb, and plantain. I'd rarely eaten any African dishes since childhood when my mum suddenly forgot how to cook them. How anyone could forget a ton of recipes, all-of-a-sudden-one-day I've no idea, but she had. With that, another thread of my Ghanaian ancestry had disappeared. Now, it seemed, it was making a comeback.

It turned out Kwasi was being made a chief in his tribe – a huge honour which explained why he'd been so keen to tell me. I couldn't have been more thrilled for him. He'd been travelling to Ghana for twenty years reconnecting with his father and other family members, gradually piecing his own ancestry together and reconnecting with his heritage (like me, Kwasi is bi-racial – but whereas my grandfather is Ghanaian, his father is).

We'd originally met, years earlier, on social networking site, MySpace. At the time he knew nothing of my background nor I of his. It was only as time went by that our shared heritage gradually transpired. When we eventually met up we traded ancestral stories with him telling me all he'd learnt about the culture and traditions. But it always struck me as curious that this Ghanaian-Mancunian link (we were both born and raised in Manchester) had been established and had been quietly simmering away – until now.

Though I'm passionate about mythology I know little to nothing about any African mythology, let alone Ghanaian. This is probably because it's a society that originally had no written tradition. As such, an enormous emphasis is placed on the spoken word. Throw in the fact that my grandfather ran away and didn't wish for his family to return and it's left me feeling disconnected and somewhat suspicious of it all.

One of the reasons Kwasi was being made chief was due to the significant, ongoing contribution he'd made to his village which included the refurbishment and ongoing maintenance of a library. He shared some of the plans for the library, one of which included talking with the elders and writing down their stories, myths and so on, so they wouldn't be lost as is frequently the case with oral traditions.

As he's telling me all this I sat looking at him thinking someone, somewhere was having a proper good laugh at my expense. *My only Ghanaian descended friend is being made a chief and he's establishing a library which will record the mythology of the local people? And I just happen to be of the same ancestry and am also interested in mythology and encouraging people to reconnect with their life's story? You couldn't make this shit up.* But we weren't done yet. Oh no.

As our conversation wore on I told him about a couple of Aboriginal designs I'd been mulling over for another tattoo I had in mind, but that I'd also had a dream in which it felt excruciatingly painful to have them done – a dream which swiftly put an end to that idea.

'Why Aborigine?' he asked. 'Why not choose from one of the Adinkra symbols? It is your heritage, after all.'

'What are Adinkra symbols?' I asked.

'Ghanaian symbols,' he went on, 'which represent concepts and sayings. Here, let me show you.'

He pulled out a sheet of paper with hundreds of symbols I'd never seen before.

'Pick one,' he said.

Oh no, this is where the trouble starts. I scanned the images and was quickly drawn to an elaborate heart-shaped design. Kwasi started laughing. *Oh God, here it comes.*

'What are you laughing at?' I asked.

'It's the Sankofa symbol,' he said. 'That heart is one of two images which represents the mythical Sankofa bird – a bird which flies forwards with its head turned backwards.'

'It would be mythical, wouldn't it?' I said. 'Why shouldn't I be surprised that, of all the symbols, I go and pick the one with the mythical bloody bird?'

'Sankofa,' he went on, 'literally means, *Go back and get it*. In other words, we must go back, return to our past and reclaim it so that we can move forward. This helps us better understand why and how we came to be who we are today. It's good to look back, reflect, and draw the necessary wisdom so that we might carry that wisdom forward into life and have a better future. That's why, although the bird is flying forwards, its head is facing backwards. It's also said to mean that, no matter how far away we've travelled sometimes we have to go home again and that there's nothing wrong with that.'

In light of my personal interests and my family's history he thought it was funny as hell that I'd picked this symbol. I, on the other hand, couldn't believe it. But there was more.

'Ah, actually, hold on,' he said. 'I have something. Seeing as you've picked this symbol I think you might want to see it.' With that, he disappeared into a back room. Meanwhile, I stood in his living room looking at all the African carvings and sculptures on his walls. Eventually he reappeared with an ornamental wooden stick which looked like a caduceus (herald's staff) – the stick carried by the Greek messenger god, Hermes.

'That's a talking stick!' I squealed.

'A what?' he said.

'A talking stick; you know, the stick you pass around a sacred circle and hand to someone when it's their turn to talk.'

'Oh, you mean a linguist's staff?'

'Sounds like the same thing,' I said.

'Well,' he said, 'this isn't a talking stick – it's a walking stick, a cane with a Sankofa bird on it.'

'No it isn't,' I answered. '*That's* a talking stick. Wow, talk about uncanny timing. I can't believe it. In our final sharing circle of the workshop I've just done, I sat there thinking – as you do – that I'd like one. And now look!'

'Well in that case then you'd better have it,' he said.

'I can't take that from you,' I said. 'It's yours.'

'It's obviously been waiting for you since I brought it back from Ghana. Here, take it. I want you to have it. It's obviously called you.'

A linguist's staff is a rod of office carried by linguists within the courts of the Akan chiefs in an area of West Africa once known as the Gold Coast. These magnificent staffs are carved of wood and are often coated in gold leaf. The top part of the staff usually has a symbol designed to communicate specific messages or proverbs either about the status, experience, and sagacity of the linguist or the message he or she, as a diplomat, is authorised to convey on behalf of the chief.

They're said to be crafted after the cane used by the first court linguist – a woman – who walked with one because of her great age.

Kwasi described these linguists as 'living libraries' who are familiar with all the stories, rules, customs, rituals, and history of their people. Their knowledge, diplomatic skills, and eloquent use of language make them essential as counsellors, confidants, ambassadors, orators. As such, most Akan monarchs and chiefs have several in their service.

As the chief's 'voice on earth' they act as an intermediary between the chief and his people. Anyone wishing to speak with the chief can only do so by going through the linguist. Likewise, the chief never speaks directly to the people but only ever through their linguist. In essence, they act as a 'bridge-builder' in much the same way the Pope does between the deity and humanity which is why they (linguists) play an invaluable role in Akan circles of leadership, occupying the most illustrious positions outside of royalty.

My grandfather was from the Gold Coast. My aunt tells me that my grandma wrote all his correspondence on his behalf as he couldn't read or write. His signature on their marriage certificate was marked by a small cross. Now, here I was, his granddaughter, a writer, storyteller, and lover of myth being handed a Sankofa adorned linguist's staff by my only Ghanaian friend who also happened to be a chief-in-waiting. Overwhelmed doesn't come close to describing how I felt when Kwasi handed me that 'rod of office.'

It was then that I had a flash of intuition: *Go back and get it – I have to go back to Ghana, the land of the original Dark Mother.* Like I said, no sooner have you caught sight of the myth that you're living then you're already onto your next.

'Ah,' I said, 'no wonder I felt so strongly about introducing you to my friend, Grace, at my birthday dinner party. You remember her, don't you? The photographer? That's why I sat you next to one another. We have to come with you.'

'What do you mean?'

'When you're initiated as chief. I have to see it and Grace has to take photos. After all, it's not every day your only Ghanaian friend is initiated as a chief. Look at what you're doing with the library – that has my sticky fingers all over it. The chief and his linguist – all I'll say is the ancestors have one hell of a sense of humour.'

'Yeah, I'd love that,' he laughed.

The rest of the night, Kwasi and I watched documentaries on the Ashanti people: in particular, their medicine men and women. It all felt so alien to me compared to what I'd spent the past several years studying.

I think it may have been this unfamiliarity, together with my family's disassociation from our ancestral roots that caused me to burst into tears as soon as I left Kwasi's. The strange thing was I didn't feel upset; rather, I felt I was being cried *through* – as though by my ancestors. I was just glad it was night-time and pouring with rain so I could blub away, unseen, beneath my umbrella.

But as I carried the stick home it seemed to get heavier and *heavier*; not in a literal sense (it weighed very little), but in a figurative sense; as though it was weighed down with a burden of responsibility I wasn't sure I wanted, let alone felt I could handle.

The following day Kwasi emailed me saying it was great to be able to chill and discuss such things with me. It's a rare occasion, he said, that he brought people to his shrine. He often poured libation for people but rarely together with them at his shrine. The ancestors, he said, must really be calling me. 'Yes,' he went on, 'I'd say the gods, ancestors, and all else are definitely shining on you.'

Meantime, back home, my aunt cornered me. 'Where did you get that talking stick from?'

'See,' I said, now feeling vindicated, 'I knew it was a talking stick!'

'Yeah,' she went on, 'that's a talking stick. My father had one. We used to have one in the house along with other statues and ornaments he regularly brought back. Where did you get it from?'

'Kwasi gave it to me,' I said. 'It's from Ghana.'

'Hmm...' she trailed off, deep in thought. 'It's beautiful. Bit of a shock to see it, though. It's been a long time since we've had any African objects in the house.'

She wasn't the only one ruffled by its presence. The first few nights I wasn't sure how I felt about it either. It felt like a Mexican stand-off with me suspiciously eyeing this staff I'd hung facing my bed. For the first few nights my sleep and dreams were unsettled. I felt like I'd opened Pandora's Box stirring up old, unknown, ancestral issues that I had no right poking about in.

Then I got to thinking about how I'd been waiting for something to show me that I'd finally come full circle on my own Great Round of Transformation. Looking at this Sankofa adorned talking stick now hung up in my room I don't think I could have had a better sign.

In fact, I don't think I've ever come across a symbol which so eloquently sums up the essence of what each of us faces on our own personal Hero's Journey: *It is not wrong to go back for that which you have forgotten.* Or, as George Eliot said: 'It is never too late to be what you might have been.'

As for this particular ten-year cycle of my own Great Round of Transformation? Well, it's not quite over yet. Not only are there still several threads playing out as I write (such is life), but this book marks the beginning of my own rebirth and return after a long season of *wintering*: the fruit of a spiritual pregnancy.

I also have one final threshold left to cross – The Crossing of the Return Threshold – about which Campbell says:

> **This brings us to the final crisis of the round, to which the whole miraculous excursion has been put a prelude – that, namely, of the paradoxical, supremely difficult threshold-crossing of the hero's return from the mystic realm into the land of common day ... He has yet to confront society with his ego-shattering, life-redeeming elixir, and take the return blow of reasonable queries, hard resentment and good people at a loss to comprehend.**

> ### – The Hero with a Thousand Faces

This leaves me in something of a quandary – namely, that I can't come full circle until I've 'returned to the village' with the elixir: the 'elixir,' in this case, being my story. But who knows? Perhaps we're supposed to find out, together, how this particular Great Round comes full circle.

But in case we don't meet again – and before we go our separate ways – I'd like to thank you for joining me on my meandering path and leave you with this parting wish:

> *May you walk in beauty and leave trails of inspiration; may you rise in your magnificence and radiate joy; may you keep a sense of humour when it all turns to shit (because it will – trust me); may you dig deep and find within yourself the golden taproot of self-worth, of abundance: a source of strength and hope. And when you find this golden taproot, I hope you, too, have the courage, the humility, and the generosity of spirit to share – honestly and to the best of your ability – all that you have learned with others. Be kind to yourself, honour your body. Walk tall. Stay curious. But above all else, never, never, never give up.*
> *Go now.*
> *Go forth and be fruitful.*
> *Be fruitful and **throw yourself like seed.***

Epilogue:
The End Where I Begin

Watch this space...

SELECTED BIBLIOGRAPHY

Ávila, Teresa of. *The Life of Saint Teresa of Ávila by Herself*. London: Penguin, 1957.

Bolen, Jean Shinoda. *Goddesses in Everywoman: Powerful Archetypes in Women's Lives*. New York: HarperCollins, 1985.

——————. *Gods in Everyman: Archetypes that Shape Men's Lives*. New York: HarperCollins, 1989.

Campbell, Joseph. *The Hero with a Thousand Faces*. London: Fontana Press, 1993.

Campbell, Joseph with Bill Moyers. *The Power of Myth*. New York: Broadway, 2001.

Carrellas, Barbara. *Urban Tantra: Sacred Sex for the Twenty-First Century*. New York: Celestial Arts, 2007.

Dodson, Betty. *Sex for One: The Joy of Selfloving*. New York: Three Rivers Press, 1996.

Edinger, Edward F. *The Anatomy of the Psyche: Alchemical Symbolism in Psychotherapy*. Illinois: Open Court Publishing Company, 1994.

——————. *Ego and Archetype*. Boston: Shambhala, 1972.

——————. *The Mystery of the Coniunctio: Alchemical Image of Individuation*. Toronto: Inner City, 1994.

Eliade, Mircea. *The Sacred and the Profane: The Nature of Religion*. New York: Harper Torchbooks, 1961.

——————. *Rites and Symbols of Initiation: The Mysteries of Birth and Rebirth*. Connecticut: Spring Publications, 2005.

Gilligan, Carol. *The Birth of Pleasure: A New Map of Love*. London: Vintage, 2003.

Greene, Liz. *Astrology for Lovers*. London: Connections Book Publishing, 2009.

Greene, Liz and Juliet Sharman-Burke. *The Mythic Journey: The Meaning of Myth as a Guide for Life*. New York: Fireside, 2000.

Gould, Joan. *Spinning Straw into Gold: What Fairy Tales Reveal About the Transformations in a Woman's Life*. New York: Random House, 2006.

Gustafson, Fred (ed.). *The Moonlit Path: Reflections on the Dark Feminine*. Berwick: Nicholas-Hays, 2003.

Haddon, Genia Pauli. *Body Metaphors: Releasing the God-Feminine in Us All.* New York: Crossroad, 1988.

Hall, Nor. *The Moon and the Virgin.* New York: Harper & Row, 1980.

Harding, M. Esther. *The Way of All Women.* New York: Harper & Row, 1975.

Hillman, James. *Healing Fiction.* Connecticut: Spring Publications, 2009.

Johnson, Robert A. *The Fisher King and the Handless Maiden: Understanding the Wounded Feeling Function in Masculine and Feminine Psychology.* New York: HarperCollins, 1995.

Jung, Carl Gustav. *The Archetypes and the Collective Unconscious.* Hove: Routledge, 1990.

——————————. *Man and His Symbols.* New York: Doubleday, 1969.

——————————. *Symbols of Transformation.* New Jersey: Princeton University Press, 1990.

Karcher, Stephen. *Total I Ching: Myths for Change.* London: Piatkus, 2009.

Leemings, David Adams. *Mythology: The Voyage of the Hero.* New York: Oxford University Press, 1998.

Lewis, C. S. *Mere Christianity.* London: HarperCollins, 2012.

Lincoln, Bruce. *Emerging From the Chrysalis: Rituals of Women's Initiation.* New York: Oxford University Press, 1991.

MacCoun, Catherine. *On Becoming an Alchemist: A Guide for the Modern Magician.* Boston: Shambhala, 2008.

Mookerjee, Ajit. *Kali: The Feminine Force.* London: Thames and Hudson, 1988.

Moore, Thomas. *Dark Nights of the Soul: A Guide to Finding Your Way through Life's Ordeals.* London: Piatkus, 2004.

Murdock, Maureen. *The Heroine's Journey: Women's Quest for Wholeness.* Boston: Shambhala, 1990.

Neumann, Erich. *Amor and Psyche: The Psychic Development of the Feminine.* New Jersey: Princeton, 1971.

——————————. *The Origins and History of Consciousness.* New Jersey: Princeton, 1995.

Osho. *Intimacy: Trusting Oneself and the Other.* New York: St. Martin's Griffin, 2001.

——————————. *Tantra: The Supreme Understanding.* London: Watkins, 2009.

Paris, Ginette. *Pagan Grace: Dionysos, Hermes, and Goddess Memory in Daily Life.* Connecticut: Spring Publications, 2006.

——————————. *Pagan Meditations: Aphrodite, Hestia, Artemis.* Dallas: Spring Publications, 1986.

Perera, Sylvia Brinton. *Descent to the Goddess: A Guide to Finding Your Way through Life's Ordeals.* Toronto: Inner City, 1981.

Qualls-Corbett, Nancy. *The Sacred Prostitute: Eternal Aspect of the Feminine.* Toronto: Inner City, 1988.

Queen, Carol. *Exhibitionism for the Shy: Show Off, Dress Up, and Talk Hot.* San Francisco: Down There Press, 1995.

Rank, Otto. *The Myth of the Birth of the Hero: A Psychological Interpretation of Mythology.* Hong Kong: Forgotten Books, 2008.

Russell, Stephen. *Barefoot Doctor's Handbook for Modern Lovers.* London: Piatkus, 2000.

Russell, Stephen and Jürgen Kolb. *The Tao of Sexual Massage.* London: Gaia, 1992.

Ulanov, Ann and Barry. *Cinderella and her Sisters: The Envied and the Envying.* Philadelphia: The Westminster Press, 1983.

Vogler, Christopher. *The Writer's Journey: Mythic Structure for Writers.* California: Michael Wiese Productions, 2007.

White, David Gordon. *Tantra in Practice.* New Jersey: Princeton University Press, 2000.

Whitmont, Edward C. *Return of the Goddess: Femininity, Aggression, and the Modern Grail Quest.* London: Routledge & Kegan Paul, 1983.

Wikman, Monika. *Pregnant Darkness: A Process of Psychological Transformation.* Maine: Nicholas-Hays, 2004.

Wolkstein, Diana and Samuel Noah Kramer. *Inanna Queen of Heaven and Earth: Her Stories and Hymns from Sumer.* New York: Harper & Row, 1983.

Woodman, Marion. *Conscious Femininity: Interviews with Marion Woodman.* Toronto: Inner City, 1993.

Woodman, Marion and Jill Mellick. *Coming Home to Myself: Reflections for Nurturing a Woman's Body and Soul.* San Francisco: Conari Press, 2000.

Woodman, Marion and Elinor Dickson. *Dancing in the Flames: The Dark Goddess in the Transformation of Consciousness.* Boston: Shambhala, 1996.

Woolger, Jennifer Barker and Roger J. *The Goddess Within: A Guide to the Eternal Myths That Shape Women's Lives.* London: Rider, 1990.

von Franz, Marie-Louise. *Alchemy: An Introduction to the Symbolism and the Psychology.* Toronto: Inner City, 1980.

Zweig, Connie (ed.). *To Be a Woman: The Birth of the Conscious Feminine.* Los Angeles: Jeremy P. Tarcher, 1990.

GRATITUDE AND RESOURCES

First and foremost I'd like to offer my heartfelt gratitude to the inspiring and courageous teachers and assistants at Shakti Tantra: Hilly Spenceley, Sue Newsome, Sarah Rose Bright (**sarahrosebright.co.uk**), Julie and Pete Baillie, Annabel Newfield (**thenewfieldnest.com**), and Becky Price (**beckyprice.co.uk**). Thank you for making me feel safe, for encouraging me, and for having such a brilliant sense of humour. For more information on Shakti Tantra's women's, couple's, and mixed programmes, visit their website at **shaktitantra.com**.

You can hear the full story of *The Prostitute and the Pearls of Wisdom* on a CD/digital download entitled *Fate and Destiny: Eye of the Pupil, Heart of the Disciple*. The other two talks I recommend for those new to Michael Meade's work are *Fate and Destiny: The Two Agreements of the Soul* and *The Soul of Change*. Visit his website at **mosaicvoices.org**. Mosaic Multicultural Foundation is a non-profit organisation.

For details of Marion Woodman's BodySoul Rhythms® work, visit **mwoodmanfoundation.org**. I also recommend her audio talks *Holding the Tension of Opposites* and *Sitting by the Well* which are available from **soundstrue.com**.

If you wish to further your understanding of archetypes/symbolism, I recommend *The Book of Symbols*. Better still, subscribe to The Archive for Research in Archetypal Symbolism (ARAS). Regular membership is $100 a year for which you will have access to 17,000 images and 20,000 pages of commentary any time you wish. Visit **aras.org** for further details. Whatever you do, though, do *not* buy a mass-market dream dictionary.

I'm fortunate enough to have among my friends a talented dream tender called Renée Coleman. I highly recommend her book, *Icons of a Dreaming Heart: The Art and Practice of Dream-Centered Living* which is available direct from her website at **reneecoleman.net**. She also provides excellent advice on how to tend your dreams.

Visit the Joseph Campbell Foundation website at **jcf.org** for further information and to download his lectures on myth. I particularly recommend the lecture, *The Inward Journey* and his book, *Myths to Live By*.

The movie, *Finding Joe* also provides an excellent introduction to the Hero's Journey. You can buy the DVD from **findingjoethemovie.com**.

Thank you, also, to Juliette Scarfe at Bareskin Beauty for creating an organic breast massage serum for me (which also doubles up as a rather luscious lube). It provided me with many hours of much-needed healing and delicious self-pleasure. If you'd like your own custom-made serum visit her at **bareskin-beauty.co.uk**.

Thank you to the talented Emma Shaw for creating the most magnificent yoni cushion (aka 'Delilah') complete with a rose quartz clitoris and frilly bits. No Aphroditic temple is complete without one.

I also wish to thank Lisbeth for introducing me to Shakti Tantra – now it's your turn to follow your bliss (aka Italia) and share your gifts.

To all of the Shaktis and Shivas I met at the workshops I have nothing but the utmost respect and admiration for you all. Each of you inspired me more than you'll ever know. Thank you for being so brave and generous.

Thank you to Tigger for harbouring me in Peacock Palace during my threshold crossing. I miss our rambling country runs especially as bouncing is what Tiggers do best!

My immense gratitude to Christopher Brown-Colbert for designing the book cover (and Lynda Moyo for the text), Emma Mountford for sub-editing, and Rowena Roberts (**rowwrites.com**) for the synopsis. Thanks also to Big and Bing for proofreading. This book is underpinned by their help and generosity of spirit.

Finally, if you're reading a print version of this book (release date 1 December 2013) it's because the following generous individuals helped make it possible by means of a crowd-funding plea on my Facebook page (thanks for the 'hurry up and get the book to print' nudge, Bela):

Jay Anjali, Paul Arrowsmith, Kwasi Asante, Damon Birch, Sarah Rose Bright, Mike Chipping, Gail Dean, Adele Farnaby, Michele Fergus, Jill Greig, Eric Haar, Pam Hardy, Kelly Harvey, Nina Hatfield, Bruce Hurd, Alison Kinrade, Linda Jayne Lapington, Jo Milne, Steph Magenta, Annabel Newfield, Sue Newsome, Christian Platts, Sarita Premley, Becky Price, Rowena Roberts, Juliette Scarfe, David J Skelly, Hilly Spenceley, Caroline Swan, Chris Walkden, and David Wood.

Thank you so much for believing in me and my work, and for helping make this book available to a wider audience.

For details of my own workshops and events visit my website at **urbandeva.com**.